Financial Mathematics for Cryptocurrencies

Founded in 1807, John Wiley & Sons is the oldest independent publishing company in the United States. With offices in North America, Europe, Australia and Asia, Wiley is globally committed to developing and marketing print and electronic products and services for our customers' professional and personal knowledge and understanding.

The Wiley Finance series contains books written specifically for finance and investment professionals as well as sophisticated individual investors and their financial advisors. Book topics range from portfolio management to e-commerce, risk management, financial engineering, valuation and financial instrument analysis, as well as much more.

For a list of available titles, visit our website at www.WileyFinance.com.

Financial Mathematics for Cryptocurrencies

TOM J. ESPEL

WILEY

This edition first published 2026

Registered Office(s)
John Wiley & Sons, Inc., 111 River Street, Hoboken, NJ 07030, USA
John Wiley & Sons Ltd, New Era House, 8 Oldlands Way, Bognor Regis, West Sussex, PO22 9NQ, UK
John Wiley & Sons Singapore Pte. Ltd, 134 Jurong Gateway Road, #04-307H, Singapore 600134

For details of our global editorial offices, customer services, and more information about Wiley products visit us at www.wiley.com.

The manufacturer's authorized representative according to the EU General Product Safety Regulation is Wiley-VCH GmbH, Boschstr. 12, 69469 Weinheim, Germany, e-mail: Product_Safety@wiley.com.

Wiley also publishes its books in a variety of electronic formats and by print-on-demand. Some content that appears in standard print versions of this book may not be available in other formats.

Library of Congress Cataloging-in-Publication Data

Names: Espel, Tom J. author
Title: Financial mathematics for cryptocurrencies / Tom J. Espel.
Description: Hoboken, New Jersey : John Wiley & Sons, Inc, [2026] | Series: Wiley finance | Includes bibliographical references and index. | Summary: "Cryptocurrencies, and digital assets by extension, are stepping out of the shadowy corners of finance and going mainstream. What began as an ideological revolt against traditional banking institutions has become an instrument, like many others, to express one's view on the market and manage their risk"— Provided by publisher.
Identifiers: LCCN 2026003767 | ISBN 9781394370078 hardback | ISBN 9781394370092 adobe pdf | ISBN 9781394370085 epub
Subjects: LCSH: Cryptocurrencies—Mathematics | Business mathematics | Digital currency
Classification: LCC HG1710.3 .E87 2026
LC record available at https://lccn.loc.gov/2026003767

Cover Design: Wiley
Cover Image: © Alibuss/stock.adobe.com

10/12 Janson Text LT Std by Lumina Datamatics
Printed and bound by CPI Group (UK) Ltd, Croydon, CR0 4YY

C9781394370078_100226

To my father

Contents

List of Figures

Preface

Cryptocurrencies, and digital assets by extension, are stepping out of the shadowy corners of finance and going mainstream. What began as an ideological revolt against traditional banking institutions has become an instrument, like many others, to express one's view on the market and manage their risk.

When I began my career in the City,[1] right after university, my first job offer was for a blockchain start-up. I decided then to go for a role in traditional finance (TradFi) and still have no regret. The decentralized finance (DeFi) industry, which represents digital assets in finance, had then a long way to go to mature and resolve systemic issues of corruption, money laundering, and other abhorrent malpractices. The air of rebellion and anti-establishment that was rife among the so-called "crypto bros" is slowly fading into a more measured, albeit daring, vision of what this new asset class can offer to investors and practitioners.

Digital assets are the promise that there is a new world beyond the digital frontier, one that allows for a comprehensive treatment of risk—without borders and excessive intermediation. This book is a message to fellow practitioners, in and outside DeFi, to continue to study, explore, and research this fascinating field.

As I write this book, I am not interested in settling the argument about the purpose of digital assets. Neither am I interested in promoting one ecosystem versus another. The fact is, cryptocurrencies are here and are mainstream. Another fact is, we, in TradFi, have observed them from afar and without the lenses of scientific curiosity which have propelled our industry in the past 30 years from an old boy's club to one of the most powerful instruments of economic development.

As quantitative analysts and traders, it is our duty to explore these assets without judgment and misconceptions. Only with knowledge can we ensure safe, efficient, and coherent financial systems. Censoring ourselves, withholding our expertise to certain parts of finance, leaves a vacuum that may be filled with misinformation and dangerous practices, which ultimately threaten the stability of the broader financial system. We might not like what we discover, or we might be excited about this brave new world, but we cannot afford to let one of the fastest-growing parts of how people exchange value fade into darkness. I was still a child during the Great Financial Crisis (GFC), but it has taught my generation that a well-functioning financial system is vital to our everyday lives. Healthy, prosperous economies demand reliable banks and payment networks, and digital assets can be instrumental where these are not yet in place.

I wrote the book I wish I had when I began exploring this digital world. We have many books about equities, fewer about derivatives, and less about foreign exchange. We let

[1]The City of London is Europe's historical premier financial center. It comprises leading banking institutions, established in the historical boundaries of the "Square Mile" of the City of London and Canary Wharf. The term is a metonym for large, established financial institutions and the industry as a whole.

cryptocurrencies on the side and then did the same with non-fungible tokens (NFTs). I am excited about bringing you on this journey of scientific curiosity. I hope I get challenged and maybe proven wrong in the theories I gathered in this book. But as long as we have an educated conversation, based on facts instead of beliefs, I am confident we can achieve greater shared prosperity, a financial system that can work for all.

This book would not have been possible without the incredible people I have met in my professional journey thus far. From London to Hong Kong, Dubai, and Singapore, I am proud of being part of a community of open-minded and curious practitioners who are all trying to answer collectively, "What can we do better?"

Tom J. Espel
Hong Kong
28 April 2025

Acknowledgments

Writing my first book was an exciting, albeit daunting, endeavor. I would like to express my sincere gratitude to my family and friends for their support. In Hong Kong, Penn and Bonan, and in Dubai, Mélanie and Salman, have always encouraged me to pursue my passion for frontier assets in finance.

I have had the privilege of receiving guidance from leading practitioners in their respective fields, whose collective expertise has significantly elevated the quality of this work. Alexander Unterrainer clarified several foundational concepts. Théophile Barry enriched the discussion on carry and discounting. James Newbury offered insightful comments on the discounting and staking pricing sections. Aurélien Dworniczek contributed invaluable input on forward rates pricing. Sofiane El Kouarati shared his insights on the section on options. Laurent Lin provided practical feedback on pricing and discounting.

Huan has been a constant support, and I am grateful for the patience and insightful conversations throughout the writing process. This project would not have come to fruition without such support.

It has been an incredible honor to work on this project, and I would like to thank my editors for their trust.

This work represents my views, as the author, and not necessarily those of my current or former affiliations, employers, or any other organization.

Acronyms

ADV	average daily volume
AMH	adaptive markets hypothesis
AMM	automated market maker
ARCH	autoregressive conditional heteroskedasticity
AVS	actively validated service
BIS	Bank for International Settlements
BSM model	Black-Scholes-Merton model
CAPM	capital asset pricing model
CBDC	Central Bank Digital Currency
CDS	credit default swap
CEX	centralized crypto exchange
CFTC	Commodity Futures Trading Commission (US financial regulator)
CIR model	Cox-Ingersoll-Ross model
DACS	Digital Asset Classification Standard
DAO	decentralized autonomous organization
dApp	decentralized application
DCF	discounted cash flow
DDV	dividend discount valuation
DeFi	decentralized finance
DEX	decentralized exchange
DPoS	delegated proof of stake
DvP	delivery versus payment
EMH	Efficient Market Hypothesis
EOM	end-of-month
ERC	Ethereum request for comments
ETF	exchange-traded fund
EVM	Ethereum virtual machine
FFA	forward-forward agreement
FINMA	Financial Market Supervisory Authority (Swiss financial regulator)
FRA	forward rate agreement
FTAP	Fundamental Theorem of Asset Pricing
FX	foreign exchange
GAAP	generally accepted accounting principles
GARCH	generalized autoregressive conditional heteroskedasticity
GBM	geometric Brownian motion
GENIUS Act	Guiding and Establishing National Innovation for US Stablecoins Act
GFC	2008 Great Financial Crisis
GICS	Global Industry Classification Standard

HHR classification	Härdle-Harvey-Reule (HHR) classification
HJM model	Heath-Jarrow-Morton model
HTLC	hashed time lock contract
IFRS	International Financial Reporting Standards
IMF	International Monetary Fund
IMM	international money market
IOU	I owe you
IRS	interest rate swap
ISDA	International Swaps and Derivatives Association
IV	implied volatility
LDE	linear differential equation
LRT	liquid restaking token
LST	liquid staking token
MEV	maximum extractable value
NFT	non-fungible token
OLS	ordinary least squares
OTC	over-the-counter
OUP	Ornstein-Uhlenbeck process
PCA	principal component analysis
PIK	payment-in-kind
PnL	profit and loss
PoA	proof of authority
PoH	proof of history
PoS	proof of stake
PoW	proof of work
PV	present value
RWA	real-world asset
SEC	Securities and Exchange Commission (US financial regulator)
SVJC	stochastic volatility with a correlated jump
TradFi	traditional finance
TVM	time value of money
USSCR	United States Strategic Crypto Reserve
WWS characterization	Wu-Wheatley-Sornette (WWS) characterization
XCS	cross-currency swap
ZBOT law	Zipf-Briscoe-Odlyzko-Tilly (ZBOT) law
ZCB	zero-coupon bond

Notations

Mathematical Sets

- $\mathbb{N}$ is the set of natural numbers;
- $\mathbb{Z}$ is the set of integers;
- $\mathbb{R}$ is the set of real numbers;
- $:=$ means "is defined as";
- $(x)^+ = \max(x, 0)$ denotes the positive part of a given variable x;
- $\mathbb{R}_+ := \{x \in \mathbb{R} \mid x \geq 0\}$;
- $\mathbb{R}_+^* := \{x \in \mathbb{R} \mid x > 0\}$;
- $\propto$ means "is proportional to."

Probability and Statistics

- $X \sim n(\mu, \sigma^2)$ denotes that the random variable X follows a normal distribution with mean μ and variance σ^2;
- Π_M denotes the money market account as numéraire;
- Π_B denotes the validator account on a given blockchain as numéraire;
- $\mathbb{P}$ denotes the real-world probability measure;
- $\mathbb{B}$ denotes the blockchain measure.

Statistical Estimators

Unless otherwise stated, for a given variable x:

- $\bar{x} = \mathbf{E}[x]$ denotes the mean value of x;
- $\mathbf{E}[\cdot]$ denotes expectation (when the measure is clear from context);
- $\mathbf{E}_{\mathbb{P}}[\cdot]$ denotes expectation under measure $\mathbb{P}$;
- $\mathcal{F}_t$ denotes the information (filtration) available at time t;
- $\mid$ in expectations denotes conditioning, in the form of $\mathbf{E}[X \mid \mathcal{F}_t]$.

Time Conventions

- t denotes physical time;
- t_B denotes network time;
- $\Delta t_{B,a}$ denotes activation queue duration in network time;
- $\Delta t_{B,s}$ denotes staking period duration in network time;
- $\Delta t_{B,e}$ denotes exit queue duration in network time.

Pricing and Valuation

- PV denotes present value;
- P_{face} denotes face value or principal amount;
- $\mathcal{D}$ denotes discount factor.

Introduction

This book is written for quantitative finance practitioners seeking to understand digital assets, and graduate students in financial mathematics or computational finance. Traditional finance (TradFi) professionals transitioning to decentralized finance (DeFi) will also benefit from this book. The material is structured to accommodate this diversity of readers.

Scope. The scope of this book is to provide an introduction to financial mathematics for digital assets. We refer to digital assets as all assets traded and recorded on a blockchain, as part of DeFi. This includes cryptocurrencies, coins, and other tokens, such as NFTs.

Throughout most of this book, we discuss cryptocurrencies in more detail. We use the terms cryptocurrencies, tokens, and digital assets interchangeably where their financial-mathematics properties coincide; differences are highlighted when relevant.

We adapt standard methodologies from TradFi with adjustments specific to digital assets. Our core approach is to extend proven mathematical frameworks to accommodate the characteristics of blockchain-based markets.

We use blockchain and network interchangeably, defining a blockchain as a database distributed across a network of nodes. For all tradable assets discussed, the database serves as a record of transactions, which we refer to as the ledger.

Because we focus on financial mathematics, we do not present in-depth the technology of blockchains unless it is relevant for applying financial mathematics to these assets. Practical pricing applications are emphasized over theoretical completeness, acknowledging that the field is still evolving.

Prerequisites. As an introductory book, we divided its content into small chapters, each with sections, that allow for quick navigation. The book does not have to be read linearly. We expect practitioners to skip sections in this book, depending on their current expertise.

A bachelor's degree in mathematics or a related computational field is a solid foundation for the concepts discussed in this book. Readers should be comfortable with the fundamentals of stochastic calculus, and basic probability and statistics. Familiarity with time series analysis and the principles of traditional derivative pricing is a plus.

We provide a glossary of acronyms and notations at the beginning of the book for reference.

Approach and Limitations. We deliberately trade depth for scope: perpetual futures, maximum extractable value (MEV), and complete proofs receive limited treatment. Our objective is to lay foundations, rather than providing definitive coverage; we emphasize usable frameworks over theoretical completeness.

Structure. The progression of this introductory material is from definitions and concepts to more mathematical and technical representations.

The book is organized into six parts, which build progressively from conceptual foundations to rigorous mathematical frameworks. Each part addresses a distinct aspect of financial mathematics applied to cryptocurrencies. At the end of each part, we provide open problems to help ensure one has mastered the key concepts in that part.

The first part of this book discusses the fundamentals of digital assets. It is a nonmathematical introduction to the core concepts essential for model assumptions when building financial models for digital assets. We establish terminology, explore network topology, and examine the characteristics of DeFi assets. The second part continues with network valuation methodologies, adapting traditional business valuation approaches to the network economy, which has applications for pricing specific tokens and for risk management. We then examine market structure in the third part, including liquidity interfaces between TradFi and DeFi, carry and storage considerations for digital assets, and the mathematical modeling of network fees.

The subsequent parts develop the mathematical framework, beginning with price processes and return models adapted for cryptocurrency markets in Part Four. We then present pricing theory in Part Five, extending arbitrage-free pricing to accommodate blockchain-specific features such as staking and stablecoins. The book concludes with an analysis of staking contracts in the sixth and final part.

Each chapter begins with clear objectives. This structure allows readers to navigate directly to topics of interest. Whether approaching from TradFi or the digital asset space, we are confident that readers will find pathways through the material that are suited to their background and goals.

How to use this book

- Practitioners seeking immediate applications can read Parts Two to Three, then Parts Five to Six;
- Students aiming for mathematical depth can proceed through Parts Four to Five before Part Six;
- Each part ends with open problems; selected solutions and code references are listed on `www.tomespel.com/books/mfin25`.

PART One

Fundamentals of Digital Assets

"What is needed is an electronic payment system based on cryptographic proof instead of trust."

Satoshi Nakamoto, Bitcoin Whitepaper

CHAPTER 1

Overview of Digital Assets

This chapter provides a concise introduction to digital assets. While many excellent books cover this topic in depth, a brief overview is essential here due to the lack of consensus on terminology. We establish the foundational language for the mathematical finance treatment that follows.

- Establish key terminology and classification of digital assets, including the distinction among coins, tokens, and cryptocurrencies.
- Trace the evolution of digital assets from early electronic currencies through Bitcoin, Ethereum, and the emergence of NFTs.

Some historical context is critical to understanding the present-day characteristics of digital assets, but we begin with the semantics.

1.1 SEMANTICS

Blockchains are a database technology, where information is securely distributed across a network of nodes. The term blockchain comes from how such databases are constructed, with each block of information recorded sequentially, like a chain of blocks.

1.1.1 Digital Assets

A digital asset is an umbrella term to describe any representation of value stored on a blockchain. Because blockchains are decentralized, the financial ecosystem around digital assets is referred to as decentralized finance (DeFi), as opposed to traditional finance (TradFi).

A common classification of digital assets [1] is as follows.

Digital securities represent financial claims;

Digital commodities do not represent financial claims and are fungible[1];

Digital collectibles do not represent financial claims but are not fungible;

Means of payment such as stablecoins, which we discuss in Section 7.2.

---

[1]An asset is fungible if it can be substituted with any other asset of the same type. Not all digital assets are fungible, such as Non-fungible Tokens (NFTs), but all cryptocurrencies are.

Some digital assets blur the lines between these categories, and we discuss classifications in more detail in Chapter 4.

Remark 1.1 *(Security Versus Commodity)*: The regulatory classification of digital assets, in particular their treatment as securities or commodities, varies significantly across jurisdictions. We restrict our attention to considerations relevant within the scope of mathematical finance, without engaging in legal or regulatory analysis.

1.1.2 Blockchain

Blockchains are cryptographically secured, distributed databases. While blockchains are a technology, a blockchain tends to refer to the underlying network that it supports. Each implementation of the technology is unique and is referred to as the protocol. Anything recorded on a blockchain is said to be on-chain.

Most blockchains designed for digital assets support a native cryptocurrency, which is referred to as a coin. Other applications can be built on top of this blockchain, and some of these applications are called tokens. Some tokens are cryptocurrencies, but not all are. This is covered in more detail in Chapter 3. Readers can refer to Figure 1.1 for a visual representation of the semantics of digital assets.

1.1.3 Cryptocurrencies and Tokens

The term cryptocurrency encompasses some types of tokens and all the coins. Coins are the native asset on a blockchain, and their name is often used interchangeably with that of the underlying blockchain.

Altcoins are coins on altchains, which are any blockchain other than Bitcoin and Ethereum.

1.1.3.1 Coins Coins are the native asset on a given blockchain. They are used to reward the participants of the network that support its operations, which are usually called miners or validators. All coins are cryptocurrencies. The first of such coins is Bitcoin.

Historically, all other coins were called altcoins. However, Ether for the Ethereum network has grown in popularity, and the term altcoin tends to refer to all coins except Bitcoin or Ether. Altcoins are associated with their native altchain.

1.1.3.2 Tokens Tokens are more versatile than coins. This is because they are a more recent technology and can, therefore, include more functionalities. A more accurate description of tokens would be of fragments of code executed on the blockchain.

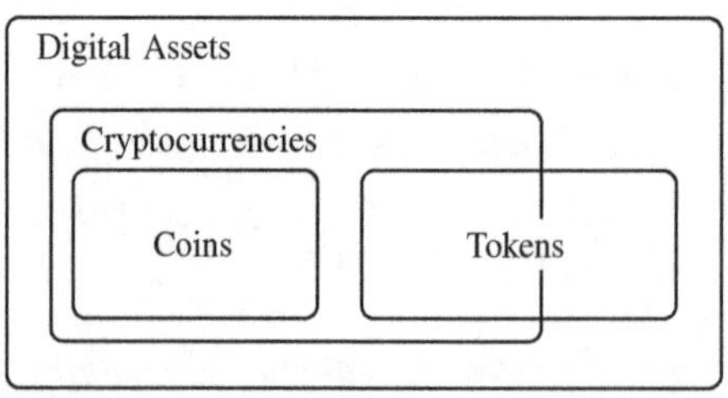

FIGURE 1.1 Semantics of Digital Assets that we will use.

The purpose of tokens is, therefore, broader. Some are used for payment, but they can also be used to distribute rights in an organization. Another common application of tokens is to create an on-chain representation of an off-chain asset, which can be digital or physical.

1.2 BRIEF HISTORY

The history of digital assets is fascinating. This section aims to provide some pointers to key facts, alongside other elements that impact the market structure and other properties in the financial mathematics of digital assets.

1.2.1 Background

There were several attempts at creating electronic currencies in the 1990s. These currencies still required a centralized, trusted bookkeeper to ensure that there was no double spending of digital money. The main application was to provide an alternative to cash with the same level of convenience and privacy. Among these are two early pioneers [2]:

- In 1983, Chaum introduced the concept of digital cash [3]. The focus was on the privacy of transactions;
- B-money was introduced by Dai [4] in 1998. His focus was on decentralization.[2]

Fiat money, by definition, has no intrinsic value. Its value is derived from its utility, which, for most market participants, means that it is a stable store of value. The perception of stability is a result of the trust in the central bank, and the broader financial system. Most currencies, such as the US dollar or the euro, are fiat.[3]

Legal tender is the main utility of money, which means that it must be accepted by everyone within a given jurisdiction, and taxes must be paid in that currency. Practice has shown that even with legal tender, once the trust in the stability of the value of the currency collapses, transactions start to be settled in another, more trusted, currency.

Legal tender is bound by the geography of where the relevant laws apply. The same currency may have legal tender in several jurisdictions, and the same jurisdiction may recognize several currencies as legal tender. However, cryptocurrencies usually have no legal tender.[4]

The Great Financial Crisis (GFC) in 2008 was an inflection point in the public perception of the stability of the financial system and the stability of banking institutions [2, 7]. It is in that context that Bitcoin was introduced.

Like cash, cryptocurrencies are a bearer asset. This means that the ownership of the asset is determined by who has the asset in their possession.[5] Most other financial assets, such as stocks or electronic money, instead have a centralized record of ownership.

[2]Dai is explicitly credited by Nakamoto in his Bitcoin paper [5].

[3]This has not always been the case [6], with the latest major change in 1971 when Nixon suspended the convertibility of the US dollar into gold.

[4]Bitcoin is a notable exception. In 2021, the Central American state of El Salvador made that cryptocurrency legal tender [8].

[5]Technically, in Decentralized Finance (DeFi), this is who has access to the private key of the wallet holding the asset, which allows them to authorize spending the cryptocurrency assigned to that wallet.

Another distinctive feature of cryptocurrencies is that there is no formal concept of issuer. Fiat money, bonds, or shares are issued by a designated counterparty. For cryptocurrencies, the issuer is the network itself, although it might be run by a defined group of individuals or a company. This is an attribute also shared by commodities: gold or oil are not issued by the miners or producers. As we will see in Sections 1.2.2 and 2.1.1.1, this is in part why the entities that run the Bitcoin network are called miners.

1.2.2 Bitcoin

Bitcoin was the first modern cryptocurrency.[6] It was released as a white paper on October 31, 2008, by Nakamoto [5]. Nakamoto is a pseudonym, and who is actually behind the first paper is still unknown.[7] The first block of the Bitcoin blockchain, called the genesis block, was mined on January 3, 2009.

Bitcoin was born out of an ideology, reflected in the title of the white paper: *Bitcoin: A Peer-to-peer Electronic Cash System* [5]. It was designed as a new form of cash without centralized government involvement. In many ways, it was a reaction to the GFC and its aftermath. To paraphrase Harari,[8] if money is a medium of trust, Bitcoin is "a currency of distrust" [9]. This interpretation of the circumstances of the creation of Bitcoin is further reinforced by the fact that the first block of the Bitcoin blockchain contains the following message.

The Times 03/Jan/2009 Chancellor on brink of second bailout for banks

The first Bitcoin market maker was New Liberty Standard [10, 11], which offered two-way quotes of Bitcoins against US dollars with PayPal payments in 2009. This established the very first exchange rate, although other transactions earlier in 2009 had established a value for Bitcoin.[9] In those early days, Bitcoin was priced well below 0.01 USD per BTC.

In 2010, the two first exchanges, BitcoinMarket and Mt.Gox, were launched. Mt.Gox[10] [12] would become the largest cryptocurrency exchange in the world before it was hacked in 2014.

The first transaction involving Bitcoin was the purchase of a pizza in Florida on May 22, 2010, for 10,000 BTC [13, 14]. This transaction is now celebrated as Bitcoin Pizza Day.

Nakamoto withdrew from public engagement in 2011 [13]. That same year, the first Bitcoin Conference took place in Prague, Czech Republic [15].

---

[6]The word cryptocurrency was only introduced at a later stage. In its original definition, Bitcoin is simply referred to as a "coin."

[7]This mystery has undeniably fueled great enthusiasm and speculation about Bitcoin, in particular in its early days. This anonymity has contributed to significant interest in Bitcoin's origins.

[8]Harari provided a broader and more nuanced approach to electronic currencies during his intervention at the 2024 Bank for International Settlements (BIS) Innovation Summit [9], although these have been overshadowed in the media by his statement on Bitcoin.

[9]Most acknowledge the first individual acting as market maker was Martti Malmi, also known as Sirius, who sold 5,050 Bitcoin for $5.02 in 2009 [13].

[10]Mt.Gox was based in Japan, highlighting that by that point, the Bitcoin community was already global.

1.2.3 Ethereum

Subsequently, as Bitcoin gained popularity, several other cryptocurrencies also emerged. These coins became known as altcoins.

Ripple was created in 2012 and has remained a prominent cryptocurrency since then. It was an early attempt to improve on the energy inefficiency of Bitcoin.

In 2014, Buterin[11] published the white paper for Ethereum [16]. The key innovation of Ethereum was the introduction of smart contracts, which greatly augment the functionalities of blockchains.[12] An important property of the Ethereum blockchain is that it is Turing-complete, which in practice means that it can run algorithms like any other computer.[13] The part of the protocol on Ethereum in charge of these computations is called the Ethereum Virtual Machine (EVM).[14]

The first Ethereum block was generated in July 2015 [7], and Ethereum has remained one of the most popular blockchains since.

1.2.4 Tokens and Layer 2

As the Ethereum blockchain grew, an increasing number of smart contracts were released. They allowed off-chain events to be recorded on the Ethereum blockchain, and this new layer became known as layer 2. Ethereum Request for Comments (ERCs), which are standardized smart contracts, were introduced, in particular ERC-20 in 2015, which established modern-day tokens.

Other prominent blockchains enabling smart contracts emerged in the ensuing period, most notably Cardano, launched in 2017 by entrepreneur Charles Hoskinson, whose company IOHK was based in Hong Kong at the time. Prior to that, Hoskinson had also been involved in the creation of Ethereum. Cardano was one of the first blockchains to introduce a consensus mechanism called Proof of Stake (PoS),[15] which was eventually also adopted by Ethereum.

Tokens gained widespread adoption and offered faster transaction times and reduced fees compared with native coins.

1.2.5 dApps and Layer 3

Following the introduction of smart contracts, the concept of decentralized autonomous organization (DAO) emerged. The idea was that by combining smart contracts to run the decision-making process, larger organizations could be organized and managed securely and without a central authority.

[11]An interesting aspect of Buterin's life is that he was awarded a $100,000 grant to drop out of university and pursue Ethereum development full time. The grant originated from the foundation of Peter Thiel, a prominent venture capitalist associated with PayPal, Facebook, and Palantir.

[12]The idea of smart contract predates blockchains and is attributed to Szabo in 1997 [17].

[13]The technical definition of Turing-completeness is that such a system can perform any computation that can be performed by a Turing machine, a theoretical representation of the modern computer. Turing machines can find solutions to any problems that can be resolved computationally, which means they can run all forms of algorithms.

[14]Ethereum is even at times referred to as a decentralized computing platform, as opposed to a conventional blockchain.

[15]We discuss consensus mechanisms in more detail in Section 2.3.2.

These DAOs would be generalized as decentralized applications (dApps), which are applications that run autonomously on a blockchain and have no central governing entity. This was a new layer in blockchains technology and is now referred to as layer 3.

The most famous dApp is Uniswap, an open-source decentralized exchange (DEX) launched in 2018 that allows users to trade tokens without a centralized intermediary [18, 19].

1.2.6 Meme Coins

Meme coins are a type of token, often built upon the ERC-20 standard, that are created primarily for entertainment. They often leverage internet popular culture to gain attention. Many such tokens were created during the COVID-19 pandemic. While the vast majority remain illiquid and speculative, a few have gained significant traction and market capitalization, most notably Dogecoin and Shiba Inu.

1.2.7 NFTs

Non-fungible tokens (NFTs) are a type of token that are indivisible and unique. They gained popularity with the introduction of a technical standard[16] on the Ethereum blockchain in 2018. This blockchain remains one of the most popular for such digital assets. NFTs can be conceptualized as transferable certificates of ownership. What is stored on the blockchain itself might be a link to the digital asset but is usually not the item itself.[17]

From the beginning, NFTs were used to represent digital art. Most recognize McCoy's *Quantum*, a digital artwork minted in 2014 [20], as the first NFT.[18] Around 2021, several art projects gained popularity, mainly on the OpenSea marketplace, which drew significant speculative interest to NFTs. One such project was the Bored Ape Yacht Club, which comprises 10,000 cartoon monkeys, all computer-generated images with combinations of 160 different traits [21]. We present an example of such artistic NFT in Figure 1.2.

NFTs were also used to represent ownership of virtual assets beyond art. These include virtual plots of land in the metaverse, in particular under the project Decentraland [22]. Several video games also used NFTs to represent ownership of in-game assets, typically character modifications. Some brands have also used NFTs to represent ownership of their products or to engage more with their customers, such as Gucci's *Supergucci* project [23].

The same NFT technology can be used to represent ownership of physical assets, such as real estate deeds. These are called real-world asset (RWA) tokens. However, this introduces a custodian risk since the NFT is just the representation of ownership of the asset on the blockchain instead of the asset itself.

We will not discuss the valuation of art NFTs, as it is outside the scope of traditional quantitative finance applications. For NFTs that represent the ownership of physical assets, Chapter 6 and Section 15.1 are relevant.

Following the explosive growth in the early 2020s of NFTs and DeFi applications, the 2022 "crypto winter" saw major corrections in asset prices and the collapse of prominent exchanges, most notably FTX.

---

[16]The name of this standard is ERC-721 [24], which we discuss in more detail in Section 2.3.1.2.

[17]It is also worth noting that not all projects grant all rights, such as IP or commercial rights, to the token-holder.

[18]It has since been preserved as an ERC-721 contract in 2021 on the Ethereum blockchain [20].

FIGURE 1.2 *Mars Cat in Spacesuit #237* is an **Example of NFT.** It was developed as part of the Mars Cat Voyage Project [25] and is a typical ERC-721 token on the Ethereum blockchain. The smart contract of this asset points to this picture.
Source: NFT reproduced with the consent of the smart contract owner. The original is a 700 × 700 px PNG color file.

1.2.8 ETFs

An exchange-traded fund (ETF) is a TradFi instrument commonly used by investors as a diversified investment vehicle. As its name suggests, an ETF is traded on an exchange and has a market price. There is a broad range of such products on the market, allowing investors to gain portfolio exposure to various assets, including real assets.[19] ETFs have grown in popularity in the 2010s, and several markets introduced such products for cryptocurrencies.[20]

The main benefit of ETFs for investors compared with directly investing in digital assets is that ETFs are standardized products that have regulatory approval and can be easily added to existing TradFi portfolios. They do not require domain-specific knowledge in the field of digital assets, in particular managing wallets and asset self-custody.

The launch of the spot Bitcoin ETF in the United States in 2024 was a significant milestone for the cryptocurrency industry [27, 28]. While other products were launched in other markets before [29], this was a landmark decision that increased the adoption of digital assets within the broader financial industry. The ETF regulatory approval in

[19]These include real estate, commodities like gold and even wine.
[20]The first ETFs for cryptocurrencies focused on Bitcoin and tended to track the futures contracts instead of the spot. In the United States, such a Bitcoin futures ETF was launched in October 2021 [26].

the United States continued and accelerated an existing trend of institutional investors[21] becoming more comfortable with digital assets [30, 31]. The introduction of new ETFs tend to draw significant volumes to the underlying asset upon introduction [26, 27].

1.3 MAJOR COINS

We present in Table 1.1 the major coins and stablecoins that are presently regarded as the most important in the digital asset ecosystem. They acquired their prominence either by age, by technology, or by market capitalization.

Some of the coins in Table 1.1 were announced to be part of the United States Strategic Crypto Reserve (USSCR), whose announcement in 2025 [32, 33] was regarded as a milestone for digital assets.

TABLE 1.1 Major Coins and Tokens in the Digital Asset Ecosystem, as of 2025

Blockchain	Coin (Ticker)	First Block/Launch	Characteristics
Bitcoin	BTC	2009	First cryptocurrency
Ethereum	ETH	2015	Smart contract
Solana	SOL	2020	High-speed Altchain
Ripple	XRP	2012	Enterprise-focused
Dogecoin	DOGE	2013	Initially meme coin
Cardano	ADA	2017	Altchain, with roots in academia
Avalanche	AVAX	2020	Altchain with subnet architecture
Tether	USDT	2014	First major Stablecoin, token
USD Coin	USDC	2018	Regulated Stablecoin, token

[21] Institutional investors include pension funds, which manage considerable funds. They are usually perceived as the bellwether for the breadth of adoption of a financial product.

CHAPTER 2

Topology of Networks

Blockchain networks form the technical foundation for all digital assets, with their architectural choices directly impacting asset pricing and behavior. This chapter examines how each blockchain balances the competing demands of security, scalability, and speed through specific consensus mechanisms and layered structures.

- Classify blockchain networks by their technical characteristics and consensus mechanisms.
- Discuss network topology.
- Introduce network indicators for valuation models.

We progress from foundational network concepts to specific technical implementations, beginning with core blockchain components, then exploring network extensions through sidechains and layers, before concluding with network indicators and staking mechanisms.

2.1 BLOCKCHAIN NETWORKS

Blockchain networks are the foundation of digital assets. As discussed in Section 1.1.2, they are distributed databases that are shared across a network of nodes. The main network of a blockchain is called the mainnet.

We usually refer interchangeably to the blockchain network and the digital asset that is supported by the network natively. Namely, Bitcoin is the name of the blockchain network and the digital asset that is supported by the network. The same convention applies to Ethereum in practice, despite the coin being actually called Ether.

2.1.1 Ledger

Most blockchains are databases where transactions or account balances are stored. The ledger refers to the record of the transactions and is distributed across nodes in the network.

Consequently, if one were to falsify the transaction records, one would need to convince the majority of participants in the network that their version of the ledger is the correct one.

The initial intuition introduced by Bitcoin [5] was that by making the process of adding transactions mathematically difficult using cryptographic techniques, it would be virtually impossible for one individual node to recreate a believable alternative ledger. Ledgers are believed to have the following characteristics:

- **Immutable:** Once a transaction is added to the ledger, it cannot be removed.
- **Transparent:** All participants in the network can see the transactions that are added to the ledger.[1]
- **Distributed:** The ledger is replicated in full across all nodes on the network.[2]

2.1.1.1 Mining and Validation Mining is the process where on some blockchains, a new block of transactions is verified by participants in the network. The nodes involved in that process are called miners when they perform a set of computationally intensive mathematical operations, which will result in the validation of the new block. The difficulty of these operations is quantified as the hash rate. Mining was introduced by Bitcoin in its original paper [5] and is the foundation of the Proof of Work (PoW) consensus mechanism.

Remark 2.1 *(Why Mining?)*: As discussed in Section 1.2.1, Bitcoins are issued by the network itself. As is the case for commodities, the miners are not issuing the cryptocurrency; they are rewarded for "extracting" it from the network, thus their name.

In blockchains with a different consensus mechanism, the process of validating a new block of transactions is called validation. The participants in the network that will validate the new block are called validators.

Almost all blockchains will compensate miners or validators for their work. This compensation is usually the issuance of new coins, called the block reward, and the transaction fees. The block reward is the main monetary supply of the network.[3] Some blockchains, like Ethereum, will burn the transaction fees, which reduces the inflationary pressure of the block reward.

2.1.2 Three Pillars of Blockchains

One can view blockchains as a compromise between three main pillars, which we illustrate in Figure 2.1. These pillars are balanced by the consensus mechanism, itself discussed in Section 2.3.2.

Scalability is one of the main differentiators between blockchains and other databases. This is also referred to as decentralization.

Security often includes immutability of the records.

Speed is the main benefit of blockchains versus conventional methods of access-controlled database replication.

---

[1] All blockchains will enable participants to see a record of the transactions. However, how detailed the record is varies. Some are totally transparent showing the notional and the participants in the transaction, while others will just show a footprint and conceal the rest of the information.

[2] Some blockchains accept that only a handful of nodes replicate the entire ledger, but these are uncommon and still rely on having some nodes holding the full copy of the ledger.

[3] Some blockchains like Bitcoin cap the total number of coins ever issued to prevent excessive inflation.

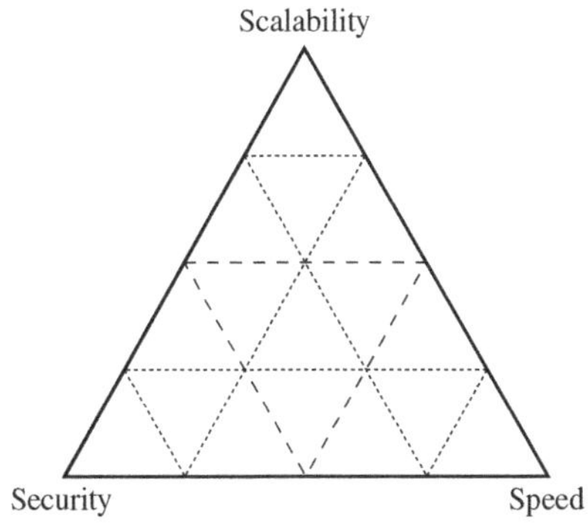

FIGURE 2.1 The Three Pillars of Blockchains are scalability, security, and speed. These are balanced by the consensus mechanism of the network. This forms a ternary diagram to represent different blockchains, where they can be represented within the triangle based on the pillars prioritized in their protocol construction.

There are other characterizations, many that also include transparency as a pillar of blockchains. However, the degree of transparency, either of the records or of participants, has varied and is more of a property of the network consensus mechanism than a design choice.

Remark 2.2 *(Speed and Scalability)*: Speed and scalability can be achieved with full transparency, and there is no trade-off required, which is why we did not include it as a pillar in our representation.

One can view all blockchain networks as a trade-off between these three axes. As a case in point, a fully decentralized and fast network might have to make sacrifices in terms of security to allow efficient changes to the database records.

2.1.3 Forks

Forks are common occurrences in blockchains.

Definition 2.1 *(Fork)*: A fork is the permanent divergence of two versions of the ledger on a blockchain network.

Forks are the result of failed consensus between different versions of the ledger on a blockchain network. Two of the most common reasons for the loss of consensus are

- software changes that are not adopted by all the participants in the network; or
- a disagreement on the transaction history on the ledger.

Forks can be intentional, in which case they are called hard forks, or unintentional, in which case they are called soft forks.

One of the most notable hard forks was the split of Bitcoin into Bitcoin and Bitcoin Cash in 2017. Most miners of the Bitcoin network decided to adopt a software change, called BIP 141 [34], while a smaller group did not and forked into Bitcoin Cash [35].

When the divergence persists, it leads to the creation of two separate blockchains and the fork point is the last block that is shared.

2.2 SIDECHAINS

While blockchains networks provide the foundation for digital assets, the ecosystem extends through various supplementary networks that enhance functionality and performance.

Definition 2.2 ***(Sidechain)*****:** Sidechains are blockchains that are connected to a parent blockchain, called the mainnet.

Sidechains have their own consensus mechanism and their own native coin.

One of the main benefits of a sidechain is that it extends the functionalities of the mainnet, typically to provide shorter transaction times. They are part of the broader concept of layer 2 solutions. A prominent sidechain is Polygon. It is a sidechain of Ethereum, compared with which it offers faster and cheaper transactions [36, 37]. It is also an example of a sidechain that is interoperable with several mainnets [37].

Sidechains are designed to be interoperable with the mainnet, through a bridge that typically enforces a two-way peg[4] [38, 39] that allows the transfer of assets between both chains. This means that the assets on the sidechain are backed by the assets on the mainnet, which are locked up or released accordingly. The entity, which can be a code or a group of validators, that ensures that the total value of the sidechain matches the value of the locked-up assets on the mainnet is called the federation [40, 41].

Definition 2.3 ***(Federation)*****:** A federation is the entity that manages a bridge between a sidechain and a mainnet.

Potential issues with sidechains are forks, which can lead to the loss of assets on the sidechain [38]. Under that scenario, the majority of the validators on the mainnet may decide to isolate the sidechain from the mainnet.

Miners or validators on the sidechain are rewarded with transaction fees which are paid in the native coin of the sidechain. The sidechain can also have its own block reward, which is also usually paid in the native coin of the sidechain. Merged mining [38] and merged staking [39] allow the miners or validators to earn block rewards on both the mainnet and the sidechain.

For pricing purposes, sidechains are usually considered as separate networks. While their assets are securely backed on the mainnet, they are not directly tradable on the mainnet and rely on the confidence in the peg and have counterparty custodian risk with the federation.

[4]Some sidechains opt for deterministic pegs instead.

2.3 TECHNICAL CHARACTERISTICS

Having established the basic network structures, we now examine the key technical decisions that differentiate blockchain implementations. These characteristics directly impact network performance and economic properties.

In this section, we discuss some of the main network characteristics that enable a broad classification of blockchain networks. Some of these features are relevant for the more comprehensive classifications of digital assets discussed in Chapter 4.

2.3.1 Protocol Layer

A blockchain network can be divided into four layers, as shown in Figure 2.2. This is the most common representation of the different parts in a blockchain architecture.

Remark 2.3 *(Alternative Layer Names)*: Schär [42] proposed alternative labels to layers in DeFi. These alternative names, and division of layers, have not been adopted broadly. However, we introduce this framework in Section 4.4.1 as a form of classification of digital assets.

2.3.1.1 Layer 1 Layer 1s are the original form of blockchains. They typically tend to prioritize security over speed and scalability. They are also associated with a native coin that is used to compensate for the processing of transactions.

To compensate for the lack of speed, and the high cost of transactions, additional layers were developed to extend the functionalities of layer 1s.

2.3.1.2 Layer 2 Layer 2s are applications built on top of layer 1 protocols. In practice, this means that they operate off the main blockchain on layer 0 and will post a summary[5] of their operations on layer 1. This allows layer 2s to be faster and more flexible than layer 1 protocols.

It is important to understand that layer 2 protocols are not independent networks. They rely on layer 1 for distributivity and security.

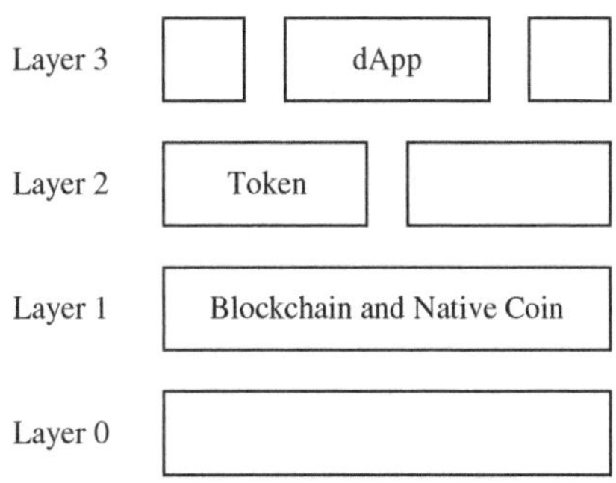

FIGURE 2.2 **Layers of Blockchains.** There are four conventional layers that are built on top of each other. Layer 1 corresponds to the oldest blockchains. Layer 0 may or may not be shared across different layer 1s if these are designed for interoperability.

[5]This is sometimes called a rollup, in reference to Ethereum Rollups which popularized that process.

Ethereum, which was first described in 2013 and released in 2015, is the most prominent blockchain that was developed with layer 2 protocol applications in mind, from its inception. In particular, it introduced smart contracts, which are on-chain, self-executing, coded instructions. The collection of these smart contracts is referred to as the EVM.

Bitcoin's Lightning Network, launched in 2018, is a layer 2 payment protocol that addressed some of Bitcoin's original scalability limitations, reducing fees and increasing transaction speed.

Definition 2.4 ***(Smart Contract)*****:** A smart contract is a self-executing code that is stored on a blockchain.

Some of these smart contracts can be used to define tokens. There exist standards for how these smart contracts are implemented, which are called Ethereum Request for Comments (ERCs), or implementation patterns. We discuss the two most prominent ones for tokens on Ethereum.

ERC-20 is the Ethereum token standard. It is the most popular implementation pattern [43].

ERC-721 is the standard for NFTs on Ethereum. The main difference with ERC-20 is that each token is unique, and cannot be divided [24].

Both these standards are used as foundations for other ERCs that improve on their functionalities. One of the most notable of such improvements is ERC-1155 [44], which allows grouping under one contract multiple ERC-20 and ERC-721 tokens. Another recent ERC that has grown in popularity follows.

ERC-4626 is the Tokenized Vault Standard, which introduces yield-bearing vaults. It allows for the automated creation of ERC-20 token vaults that generate a separate ERC-20 token as a yield. One important caveat is that the token that represents the yield is not of the same type as the original token inside the vault.

Some popular layer 2 tokens include stablecoins, which we discuss in Section 7.2.

2.3.1.3 dApps and Layer 3 Smart contracts allowed for the development of dApps, which can rely on one or multiple smart contracts.

Definition 2.5 ***(dApp)*****:** A dApp is a decentralized application that runs on a blockchain network using smart contracts.

Common applications on layer 3 include DEXs, such as Uniswap. Uniswap was launched in 2018 [18, 19] and provides liquidity automatically as an Automated Market Maker (AMM) [45, 46]. The growth in popularity of Uniswap has had a substantial impact on the broader liquidity of digital assets [45], and more DEXs have been launched since.

Another notable group of projects on layer 3 are related to the metaverse, the collection of virtual environments that were historically built as video games.[6] Two popular examples are Decentraland (created in 2017) [22, 47] and the Sandbox (2018) [48, 49]. In such

[6]Not all worlds in the metaverse are built on blockchains.

projects, different underlying layer 2 solutions are used, such as NFTs to track ownership of parcels of digital land or tokens as currency for in-game transactions [50–52].

Tokenization has also been used to represent Real-world Assets (RWAs). These also use NFTs to make use of the non-fungible nature of these assets. RWAs rely on an off-chain custodian, and these assets are hybrids between DeFi and TradFi.

2.3.1.4 Layer 0 Given the lack of interoperability between layer 1s, new solutions were introduced, which we now refer[7] to as layer 0.

These are essentially platforms that allow for easier development of blockchains by sharing code and features. Having interoperability built in the code allows for a higher level of security. We briefly discuss two of the most popular of such platforms.

Polkadot was introduced in 2016 by Wood[8] [53] as a "scalable heterogeneous multi-chain." It can be viewed as a set of blockchains that share their security features and become interoperable.

Cosmos was developed in 2016 [54] and allows independent blockchains to communicate with one another. It is associated with the Interchain Foundation, which runs several projects linked to blockchain interoperability.

Remark 2.4 ***(Other Interoperability Solutions)*:** There are other solutions developed to allow for interoperability, such as bridges for sidechains. However, these are not layer 0 solutions.

2.3.2 Consensus Mechanism

Definition 2.6 ***(Consensus Mechanism)*:** The consensus mechanism is the protocol that allows the nodes on the mainnet of the blockchain to agree on the state of the blockchain.

The choice of consensus mechanism must balance security, scalability, and speed. It is essential that it guarantees the integrity of the ledger, ensuring immutability and preventing double-spending.

Every consensus mechanism must meet three properties, dubbed the blockchain trilemma by Abadi and Brunnermeier [55]:

- Fault-tolerant, in particular as a protection against double-spending
- Fully transferable, in the sense that any type of transaction should be processed
- Resource-efficient, for which we provide possible indicators in Section 2.4

2.3.2.1 Proof of Work and Proof of Stake There are two dominant types of consensus mechanism, one is called Proof of Work (PoW) and the other is called Proof of Stake (PoS). The former relies on computational power held by miners to process a new block of transactions, while the latter relies on the amount of tokens held by a validator instead.

---

[7]Some dispute this terminology, claiming these belong to layer 1 and that interoperable blockchains on these solutions are layer 2s.

[8]Wood was one of the cofounders of Ethereum, which we discuss in Section 1.2.3, alongside Buterin.

TABLE 2.1 Key Terminology for PoS and PoW Block Times

Feature	Proof of Work (PoW)	Proof of Stake (PoS)
Network Node	Miner	Validator
Consensus Mechanism	Computational Power	Staked Tokens
Energy Requirement	High	Low
Speed	Low	High
Blockchain	Bitcoin	Ethereum

Proof of Work (PoW) is the consensus mechanism used by Bitcoin, and is the oldest form of consensus for blockchains. It was initially introduced by Back as Hashcash in 1997 [56] and adapted to Bitcoin by Nakamoto when Bitcoin was created [5]. PoW is relatively slow and is energy-intensive by modern standards. However, it is also highly secure, with the computational power needed to add new blocks called the hash rate.

Proof of Stake (PoS) is a consensus mechanism introduced in 2012, but it was made popular when Ethereum transitioned to it in 2022. Validators stake assets as collateral, which may be slashed if they approve illegitimate transactions. PoS is faster and more energy-efficient than PoW [57], but it is sometimes seen as less secure than PoW, if we go back to the three pillars in Figure 2.1.

We summarize the main ideas discussed to this point in Table 2.1.

2.3.2.2 Other Consensus Mechanisms While there are many other consensus mechanisms, the following are worth mentioning.

Delegated Proof of Stake (DPoS) is a consensus mechanism where token-holders vote for which validator nodes will process a new block of transactions. It is used by Sui.

Proof of Authority (PoA) is a consensus mechanism that relies on the reputation of validators to process a new block of transactions.

Proof of History (PoH) is a consensus mechanism that relies on the timestamp of transactions to process a new block of transactions. The timestamp is generated with the Verifiable Delay Function (VDF), which is a cryptographic function that takes a long time to compute but is easy to verify. PoH was developed for Solana, which has become widely used thanks to its network speed.

Remark 2.5 ***(Classification for Pricing)*:** While consensus mechanisms are important to understand how digital assets behave, they are inadequate for a classification geared toward financial mathematics.

- Networks can migrate to different consensus mechanisms over time, while not altering the market dynamics and core features of the network. For instance, Ethereum has transitioned from PoW to PoS in 2022 [58].
- New consensus mechanisms emerge over time, and a comprehensive categorization is difficult to achieve.

2.3.3 Anonymity

A common misconception is that cryptocurrencies are anonymous networks. This is incorrect, given that to ensure the integrity of the network, all transactions are recorded on the ledger and are visible to all participants.

However, not all networks will record all the information from transactions on the ledger. The identity of the participants can also be concealed for increased anonymity.

The level of anonymity on the Bitcoin network is referred to as pseudoanonymous, since for a given transaction only the transaction addresses[9] and the notional are recorded on the blockchain.

Higher levels of anonymity can be achieved even in pseudoanonymous protocols, using mixers. Mixers will mix transactions from different participants to make them harder to trace on the network.

Some protocols were designed with anonymity in mind, most notably Zcash [59]. Those protocols will typically use cryptographic protocols that do not reveal transaction information or participants, while maintaining security, most notably using Zero-knowledge Proofs (ZKPs) [59–61].

2.4 NETWORK INDICATORS

These technical characteristics translate into measurable network properties that inform valuation models, as we discuss in Chapter 5.

Several parameters can be used to characterize a blockchain network. These allow for easy comparison and can be used as inputs to valuation models, which we discuss in Chapter 5.

Block Time is measured in seconds and is the average time T_B that it takes for a new block to be added to the blockchain. This directly reflects transaction throughput and network capacity.

Market Capitalization K is the total value of the blockchain network, expressed in a fiat currency. It can also be expressed as $K = X \cdot N_C$, where X is the price per coin, or exchange rate, and N_C is the total number of coins in circulation.

Transaction Activity is usually measured in number of transactions per day. It is preferred to Average Daily Volume (ADV) used in TradFi given that many networks conceal the volume of transactions.

Number of Participants is the number of either validator or miner nodes, or the number of users on a blockchain. There is however some issue with being able to count the number of active users. Another potential issue is that the same end user may control multiple nodes or wallets on the network.

We reuse the classification of blockchain attributes introduced by Casino et al. [62].

Consensus Mechanism is an essential property that influences the speed, security, and scalability of the blockchain. We introduced it in more detail in Section 2.3.2.

[9]Those are cryptographic addresses that do not correspond to an off-chain identity. However, all the transactions to and from such address are public.

Anonymity is the quality of the degree of confidentiality of the participants in the network. It is discussed in Section 2.3.3.

Protocol Efficiency and Consumption is a measure of the energy cost of the blockchain network. It is usually measured in terms of energy consumption per transaction.

Immutability describes potential attacks that can occur on the blockchain to alter the ledger. This is a qualitative measure.[10]

Ownership and Management describes the degree of centralization and if nodes need permission to join the network.

Transaction Approval Time is the time it takes for a transaction to be recorded on the ledger. It is usually measured in seconds. It is usually a multiple of block time T_B.[11]

We present several classification systems for digital assets in Chapter 3.

2.5 STAKING

The consensus mechanisms discussed earlier, particularly PoS and DPoS, rely fundamentally on the staking process to secure networks and validate transactions.

Staking is associated with PoS and DPoS consensus mechanisms.

Definition 2.7 ***(Staking)*****:** Staking is the process of committing digital assets to support the validation of new blocks on a blockchain network.

While we will treat staking in general terms, we will discuss many concepts in reference to Ethereum, since for historical reasons it has led many of the innovations in the process. Staking contracts are widely adopted in DeFi.

We discuss mathematical representations of staking in Chapter 12 and present a formal definition of staking contracts in Definition 17.2. The dynamics of staking over the total coin supply are still an active field of research [63–65].

2.5.1 Direct Staking

During the process of staking, a minimum[12] amount of native coins must be locked in a wallet to participate. The locked coins are collateral in case the validator approves fraudulent transactions, thus the name of the process [66]. There are generally speaking three main risks associated with staking.

- **Validator risk**, which includes slashing[13] or other penalties depending on the behavior of the validator: this includes approval of fraudulent transactions, downtime, etc.
- **Market risk** since the staking reward is paid in the native coin

[10]Casino et al. [62] mention more specifically collusion attacks.

[11]There exist different conventions to recognize a transaction as approved, although the most common is to count a set number of blocks after the block that contains the transaction.

[12]This minimum is defined by the protocol and can vary significantly between different networks. On Ethereum, for example, the minimum is 32 ETH, while on Solana there is no theoretical minimum.

[13]The loss of all funds staked.

- **Liquidity risk** since the coins staked are not accessible during the staking period and most blockchains demand a sizeable minimum commitment per validator

The reward for a new block creation is usually fixed, but the number of validators is not at any given point in time, leading to a variable reward. There are different ways to stake directly [66].

Self-staking is when the user runs a validation node on the blockchain directly. All profits are kept, but the risks are higher, and they must commit the full amount of coins.

Pooled staking is when several users pool their coins together to run a validation node and share the risks and rewards. The risks are lower, but the rewards are also lower.

Staking-as-a-service providers will run the validation node on behalf of the user in exchange for a fee. This introduces a counterparty risk to the end user.

The prime purpose of staking is to stabilize the network, and in the earliest versions it was not possible to withdraw staked tokens. These were locked up indefinitely. In practice, staking directly is not an easy process, and the incentive remains to leave the tokens staked indefinitely.

Remark 2.6 ***(Staking and TradFi)*****:** One can argue there are strong similarities between direct staking in DeFi and how central banks operate in TradFi.

- In both cases, only a limited pool of participants can stake. In DeFi this is because of the high minimum staking amount on some chains, and the existence of entry and exit queues. In TradFi, this is because only licensed banks can deposit funds and earn interest from the central bank.
- This illiquidity has created new products available to users, such as liquidity pools and synthetic assets.

2.5.2 Liquid Staking

Liquid staking is a recent solution developed to allow users to still trade funds which are staked. This is done by issuing a token that represents the staked funds, called Liquid Staking Tokens (LSTs). These can be traded and used as collateral.

Definition 2.8 ***(Liquid Staking Token)*****:** An LST is a tradable token, which represents a claim on tokens staked on a blockchain network.

Remark 2.7 ***(Liquid Staking Token Peg)*****:** Liquid staking tokens are typically pegged to the underlying staked asset.

To collect their reward, investors can either sell the LSTs on the secondary market, or they can initiate the withdrawal[14] process. That process requires significant time and is less common.[15] We discuss pricing of LSTs in more detail in Section 18.1.

[14] This is also called the unstaking process.

[15] These are often subject to cool-down periods in the context of LSTs.

An extension of LSTs are Liquid Restaking Tokens (LRTs), which have been growing in popularity.

Definition 2.9 ***(Liquid Restaking Token)*****:** A Liquid Restaking Token (LRT) is a tradable token that represents a claim on staked assets that secure multiple applications.

By allowing investors to stake their underlying across multiple services, LRTs typically offer higher expected returns. An LRT will usually represent a stake on a mainnet and be staked on multiple additional microservices.

These microservices are called Actively Validated Services (AVSs) and are commonly used by new DeFi projects to provide applications while leveraging the security of an existing mainnet. One of the first and most popular restaking platforms is EigenLayer on Ethereum [64, 67], with Babylon a popular Bitcoin-based counterpart [68]. LRTs are a fast-growing and quickly evolving sector in DeFi.

Definition 2.10 ***(Rehypothecation)*****:** Rehypothecation is when the LSTs are used as collateral to borrow assets, which are then re-lent to obtain more LSTs.

Rehypothecation, as per Definition 2.10, is a form of collateralized lending in DeFi.

2.5.3 Yield Farming

Definition 2.11 ***(Yield Farming)*****:** Yield farming is a strategy where investors provide liquidity to a DEX in exchange for rewards.

The reward for yield farming is typically the fees arising from the provision of liquidity on a Decentralized Exchange (DEX). It is functionally analogous to liquid staking, except that it does not support the operations of the network but supports an individual dApp instead. Another difference with liquid staking is that there is no lockout period. In essence, it is the closest to a time deposit at a retail bank.

While some argue that yield farming is akin to liquid staking, we argue this is incorrect for two reasons.

- The rewards are specific to a protocol, not to a blockchain. Participating in yield farming carries a greater degree of risk relative to the native staking behavior.
- The rewards are not paid in the native coin, but in the token of the protocol. Not all these tokens are liquid; this adds a liquidity risk to the reward.

We summarize the different staking concepts presented thus far in Table 2.2.

TABLE 2.2 Comparison of Staking and Yield Farming Methods

Feature	Token	Counterparty	Collateral
Direct Staking	No	No	Native coins
LST	Yes	No	Staked tokens
LRT	Yes	AVS applications	Staked tokens securing multiple applications
Yield Farming	Yes	DEX	Liquidity provided to DEX

CHAPTER 3

Asset Characteristics

Digital assets possess unique features around fungibility, storage, and transferability that distinguish them from TradFi. This chapter examines these distinctive characteristics and their implications for valuation and classification.

- Establish the distinction between networks and assets, examining how blockchain infrastructure shapes the characteristics and valuation of digital assets.
- Discuss asset classes in TradFi and relate them to DeFi.
- Provide a brief introduction to derivatives.

We begin by clarifying the distinction between the underlying blockchain and the assets it supports.

3.1 NETWORK VERSUS ASSET

There is often confusion between the network and the asset in the context of cryptocurrencies, and digital assets by extension. The network is the infrastructure that allows the asset to exist. The asset is one of the potential digital representations of value that is exchanged on the network. As opposed to financial assets where the network to transact is not relevant, digital assets only exist within a network. It is for that reason that the concepts of network and asset are intertwined.

One singular attribute of digital assets is that there is no clear concept of storage. The assets are recorded and located on the blockchain itself. On the network, the link of ownership is to a wallet. The wallet is a software concept that manages access to the digital assets on the blockchain.

Definition 3.1 ***(Wallet)*****:** A wallet is a software or hardware interface that stores the cryptographic keys to authorize transactions on a blockchain.

The ownership of the wallet is linked to a cryptographic key,[1] which is necessary to authorize transactions from that wallet.

[1]This is in essence like a password, usually 12–24 words from a standardized list in English.

The cryptographic key is not an account number. Wallets are accessed via network addresses, and there can be many addresses generated from the same cryptographic key, all pointing to the same wallet. This is a security feature, as it makes it harder to track the wallet. We discuss this in more detail in Section 2.3.3. On the other hand, this also means that the sole knowledge of the key gives control to the digital assets, which has implications for storage and carry costs, that we discuss in Chapter 6.

However, we argue this still does not mean that digital assets must be valued solely by their blockchain. The asset price is more broadly influenced by the balance of supply and demand.

Remark 3.1: An analogy is to look at gold, where one values, on the one hand, the extraction, supply, and distribution channels and, on the other, observes the price of gold itself. The latter is undeniably influenced by the former, but it is incorrect to value gold solely by looking at its trading network.

3.2 CONVENTIONAL ASSET CLASSIFICATION

Classification of assets in TradFi is usually done by asset class, and then either as cash instruments or derivative instruments. These broad classifications are shared with digital assets in DeFi.

Cryptocurrencies are spot assets and, therefore, are cash products. However, they can be used as underlying for derivatives, such as futures and options, which we discuss in Section 3.2.4.1. For mathematical finance applications, the methodology to derive the price of non-cash products in DeFi is similar to TradFi, which is why we will not cover that topic in too much detail.

3.2.1 Financial Instruments and Assets

Definition 3.2 ***(Financial Instrument)*****:** A financial instrument is a tradable contract that represents claims on cash flows or on an underlying financial asset.

Remark 3.2: Many financial practitioners will take a broader definition of financial instrument, as any asset that is tradable in financial markets. Instruments in that context refer to the contracts that are traded, as opposed to the underlying.

We note that financial instruments may be a financial asset themselves.

Definition 3.3 ***(Financial Asset)*****:** Financial assets are intangible assets that are tradable in financial markets.

Definition 3.3 is a broad definition of financial assets. Other definitions, in particular in the context of accounting,[2] are restrictive to assets that represent claims[3] on future cash flows or on ownership.

[2]Under International Financial Reporting Standards (IFRS), the relevant standard is the IFRS 9 [69].
[3]We discuss claims in more detail in Section 3.2.7.

Remark 3.3: Accounting definitions do not aim to meet the same purpose as financial definitions. In the context of accounting, valuation and recognition of variations in value are a key consideration. In mathematical finance, we focus on the practice of market participants with the aim of quantifying market parameters and constructing models.

While for accounting purposes, cryptocurrencies are often not classified as financial assets,[4] they are treated as such by market participants. This is because one can argue that most market participants for digital assets and cryptocurrencies in particular do not use these assets as a means of payment, but rather as an investment or as a speculative vehicle.

3.2.2 Asset Classes

While there are slight nuances between categorizations, practitioners usually recognize two types of instruments.

Traditional investments also called financial assets include equities, government bonds, and sometimes also include precious metals such as gold and silver.

Alternative investments include all remaining instruments, including digital assets.

The difference between traditional and alternative investments has historically been whether institutional asset managers[5] included these investments in their portfolio. Another commonly used definition is to consider which assets are commonly accepted as collateral.

This dichotomy is becoming obsolete, not only because new products, such as ETFs, blur the line between the two categories, but also because some alternative investments, such as funds or real estate, have become mainstream investment vehicles.

Practitioners will most commonly refer to asset classes. One categorization includes three main families.

Securities comprise all equity instruments, and most closely overlap with the traditional investments in historical classifications.

FICC stands for fixed income, currencies, and commodities. Each of these is a distinct asset class. Fixed income in this context usually comprises all forms of debt obligations, from government bonds to corporate credit. Currencies are more commonly referred to as foreign exchange (FX). Commodities are sometimes split into subcategories, with precious metals being often categorized as a standalone asset class.

Alternatives include everything else, including digital assets, as per Figure 3.1.

[4]The IFRS regards digital assets [70] as intangible assets, but not as financial assets. Digital assets do not qualify as cash. They are recorded as inventories. Under Generally Accepted Accounting Principles (GAAP), they are recorded as intangible assets [71].

[5]Those are often called in the context of TradFi the "real money." We refer to Footnote 21 in Chapter 1.

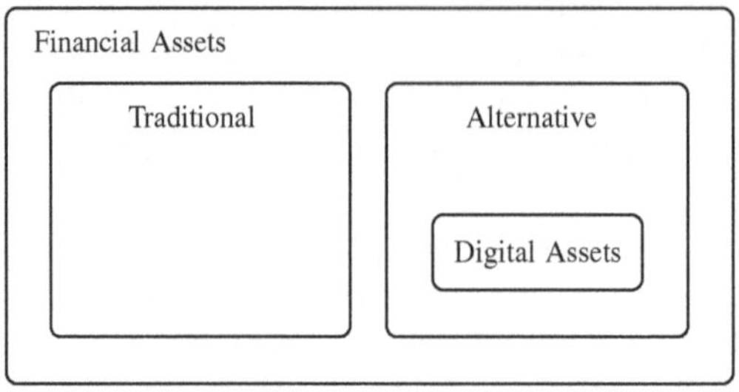

FIGURE 3.1 Categories of Financial Assets: Traditional, alternative, and digital assets as a subset of alternative.

Remark 3.4: With respect to digital assets specifically, they have sometimes been categorized as part of FX, or part of commodities. As the asset class has grown in size and developed coherent, distinctive characteristics, it is reasonable to expect growing consensus to see it as a standalone asset class.

3.2.3 Cash Products

Cash products are financial instruments that have the following characteristics:

- A direct representation of the underlying asset, including potential physical ownership
- An immediate settlement, subject to market conventions[6]

The market where cash products are traded is called the spot market. There exists a spot market in every asset class.

While for most asset classes in TradFi, most of the liquidity is on the spot market. This is not the case for DeFi. Like for FX and commodities, the liquidity is predominantly on the derivatives market.

3.2.4 Derivatives

Derivatives typically address more complex financial needs and are traded by professional investors.

3.2.4.1 Definition

Definition 3.4 ***(Derivative)*****:** Any product that is not a cash product is called a derivative. These can be either or both of

- a contract that derives its value from an underlying asset, or
- a contract that is settled at a later date.

Derivatives involve future performance obligations, requiring contract holders to execute certain actions at a specified time. Two of the most common of these contracts are

[6]Conventions differ between markets with regard to the settlement timeline, but it is usually within two business days.

futures and forwards, which we discuss in Sections 3.2.4.3 and 3.2.4.2. Some derivatives have an optionality component, which means that the holder of the contract has the right, but not the obligation, to exercise the contract. This is usually referred to as an option, which we discuss in Section 3.2.5.

Historically, derivatives were probably among the first traded financial instruments. There are records of Mesopotamian cuneiform tokens used to keep track of goods, mostly agricultural, as early as 3,000 BC [72]. Their modern form is attributed to financial innovations in the United States in Chicago from the second half of the nineteenth century. The Chicago Board of Trade (CBOT) listed the first modern standardized forward contract, a precursor to the modern futures (see Section 3.2.4.3). These contracts were mainly grain contracts and expanded to financial products, such as currencies, from the 1970s onward, by the Chicago Mercantile Exchange (CME).[7]

During the second half of the twentieth century, securitization has accelerated the introduction of derivative products.

Remark 3.5: Derivatives are often seen as a sign of maturity for an asset class, with their introduction signaling depth of liquidity and sophisticated investors being active within this asset class. Most, but not all, asset classes have an established derivatives market.

In most jurisdictions, the rules that apply to investors differ between spot and derivative products.

Remark 3.6 ***(SEC and CFTC)*****:** In the United States, the regulator for derivatives markets is the Commodity Futures Trading Commission (CFTC), while the Securities and Exchange Commission (SEC) oversees securities.

In the context of digital assets, almost all derivatives have liquid cryptocurrencies as underlying. This is because these assets have greater depth of liquidity and are the most mature in DeFi. Derivatives are popular instruments for cryptocurrencies, in particular given they allow investors to leverage their positions.

Most cryptocurrency exchanges will offer derivative accounts on margin. This means the following:

- Key levels for options have important implications at microstructure level, and can be linked to liquidations.[8]
- Futures, in particular the perpetual futures, are the most liquid products in the cryptocurrency space. We present this instrument in more detail in Section 3.2.4.4, given its importance in the cryptocurrency ecosystem.

International Swaps and Derivatives Association (ISDA) introduced a standardized definition of digital asset derivatives in 2023 [73]. This definition, called the ISDA master agreement,[9] is a standardized contract that can be used by market participants. This was a significant milestone, given ISDA is the main trade organization for

[7]The International Money Market (IMM), a division of the CME, introduced contract dates that are still standard settlement dates for contracts to this day.

[8]We discuss liquidations in Section 6.1.

[9]Such master agreement typically includes standardized settlement terms and other provisions.

over-the-counter (OTC) derivatives, and its master agreement is the most widely used contract in TradFi. It is not yet broadly adopted in DeFi, where for on-chain derivatives smart contracts can be used.

3.2.4.2 Forwards

Definition 3.5 *(Forward Contract)*: A forward contract is an agreement between two parties to buy or sell an asset at a specified future date for an agreed price. That date is called the maturity of the contract.

The price of a forward contract is called the forward price, and the plot of the forward prices as a function of the time to maturity is called the forward curve.

Definition 3.6 *(Forward Curve)*: Let $F(t; M)$ denote the price of a forward contract of maturity M at time t. We call the forward curve at time t fixed the function $F : M \mapsto F(t; M)$.

By convention, we will state that $S(t) := F(t; 0)$ is the price of spot at time t.

Remark 3.7: In most cases, $F \in \mathcal{C}^0(\mathbb{R})$, but $F \in \mathcal{C}^\infty(\mathbb{R})$ is often assumed.

This curve in Definition 3.6 can have different shapes, as per Definition 3.7. We illustrate Definition 3.7 in Figure 3.2.

Definition 3.7 *(Forward Curve Shape)*: There are two main types of shape for the forward curve.

Contango is when the price of a forward contract at a long-dated maturity is higher than the spot price.

Backwardation[10] is when the price of a forward contract at a long-dated maturity is lower than the spot price.

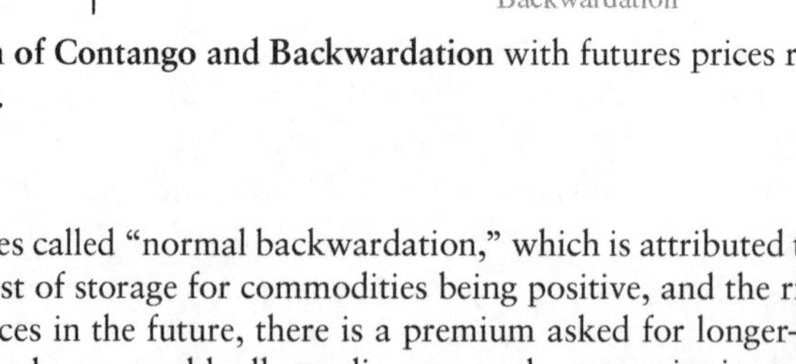

FIGURE 3.2 **Illustration of Contango and Backwardation** with futures prices relative to spot price as a function of maturity.

[10]This is also sometimes called "normal backwardation," which is attributed to Keynes [74, 76, 77]. The idea is that the cost of storage for commodities being positive, and the risk being greater given the fluctuation for prices in the future, there is a premium asked for longer-dated maturities. This means commodities producers would sell at a discount to the spot price in exchange for future price protection [75].

Remark 3.8: Contango is regarded as the normal state of most markets. That is because there is usually a cost associated with holding an asset, which is called the cost of carry, which we discuss in Section 6.2. That cost results in a premium for the forward price, for there not to be any arbitrage opportunities.

When a forward contract nears its expiry date, investors can decide either to go to settlement[11] and execute the contract, or they can buy another forward to keep the position open. This process is called a roll.

The divergence in price between a forward contract and its underlying is called the basis, as defined in Definition 3.8.

Definition 3.8 ***(Basis)*:** The basis δ in the context of forward contracts is the difference between the price of the forward F of maturity M and its underlying spot S at time t.

$$\delta(t; M) = S(t) - F(t; M)$$

Remark 3.9: Sometimes the terms in Definition 3.8 are flipped around, such that

$$\delta(t; M) = F(t; M) - S(t),$$

and the latter is more common in the context of financial assets as underlying. Definition 3.8 is closer to the intuitive interpretation of the basis in the context of commodities and currencies.

When quoting a forward contract, the forward price F is called the outright price. It is however not common to use this price in practice, and forward points are used instead, as per Definition 3.9.

Definition 3.9 ***(Forward Points)*:** Let $F(t; M)$ be the price of a forward of maturity M and its underlying spot S at time t. Forward points $f_p(t; M)$ are defined such that the following holds:

$$F(t; M) = S(t) + f_p(t; M)$$

For several markets, the convention is to quote forward points in basis points instead of the outright price.

Remark 3.10: This convention is not used for perpetual futures, which we discuss in Section 3.2.4.4, as they are designed to track the spot price.

We will use Definition 3.8 for the basis, which is the most widely adopted. This leads to the forward points from Definition 3.9 being defined as follows:

$$\forall (t, M) \in (\mathbb{R}_+)^2 \quad f_p(t; M) = -\delta(t; M)$$

[11]This is also referred to as delivery in the context of physical products, such as commodities.

In this context, we can re-express Definition 3.7 as follows:

Proposition 3.1 ***(Basis and Curve Shape)*:** Let $\delta(t; M)$ denote the basis of a forward instrument with maturity up to M, at time t. We look at the quantity Δ.

$$\Delta(t; M) := \int_0^M \delta(u; t) du$$

- contango refers to when $\Delta(t; M) < 0$.
- backwardation refers to when $\Delta(t; M) > 0$.

We can extend Proposition 3.1 in the case of monotonic forward curves.

Proposition 3.2 ***(Basis and Monotonous Curve Shape)*:** Let $F \in \mathcal{C}^1(\mathbb{R})$ be the forward price curve of an instrument, function of maturity M, at fixed time t. $\delta(t; M)$ is the basis. If F is monotonic up until maturity M_+, then for any $M \leq M_+$, the curve is in

- contango if $F(t; M) > S(t) \Longleftrightarrow \delta(t; M) < 0$;
- backwardation if $F(t; M) < S(t) \Longleftrightarrow \delta(t; M) > 0$.

Proof. We use the notations of Proposition 3.1, and know that $\forall t\ F(0; t) = S(t)$ such that $\delta(0; t) = 0$.

Given $F \in \mathcal{C}^1(\mathbb{R})$ is monotonic in M up until M_+, $\delta \in \mathcal{C}^1(\mathbb{R})$ and is also monotonic in M up until M_+.

We apply the property of monotonicity of the integral with t fixed and $M \leq M_+$.

$$\begin{aligned} 0 &\leq \delta(t; M) \\ \int_0^{M_+} 0 du &\leq \int_0^{M_+} \delta(u; t) du \end{aligned}$$

■

It is because forward curves are often assumed monotonic[12] that, as a result of Proposition 3.2, the curve shape and either sign of any basis are used interchangeably.

In all the definitions and propositions to this point, we have made the assumption, which results directly from Definition 3.8, that $\delta(0; t) = 0$, which means that the price of the forward converges toward the spot price for short-dated maturities.

$$\begin{aligned} & \lim_{t \to M} \delta(t; M) = 0, \ \forall t \\ \Leftrightarrow \ & \lim_{t \to M} F(t; M) = S(t), \ \forall t \end{aligned} \tag{3.1}$$

Equation 3.1 is not always verified in practice and corresponds to market inefficiencies. This potentiality leads to what is called the basis risk, as per Definition 3.10.

[12]This is not strictly correct, but it is often observed for short-term maturities of a forward curve.

Definition 3.10 *(Basis Risk)*: Basis risk is the risk that the price of a forward instrument does not converge to the spot price of its underlying as the contract approaches its maturity:

$$\exists t, \lim_{t \to M} \quad \delta(t; M) \neq 0$$

The existence of basis risk is a source of potential arbitrage, and the corresponding basis trade has become pervasive in the cryptocurrency space [78, 79].

3.2.4.3 Futures

Definition 3.11 *(Futures Contract)*: A futures contract is a standardized forward contract that is traded on an exchange.

Most futures will have standardized dates:

- Fixed financial dates, typically End-of-month (EOM) or an IMM date
- Fixed maturity, adjusted for holiday calendars such as one month (1M)

The main difference, from a practical perspective, between a forward contract and a futures contract with the same underlying and maturity is that the futures contract has daily settlements, while the forward contract does not. These settlements adjust for the daily gains and losses of the position. We will see in Proposition 6.1 that their prices are theoretically equivalent when interest rates are constant.

Remark 3.11: In practice, there might be a small difference between the two prices, but these are more attributed to differences in liquidity and credit risk and are negligible in most cases.

An interesting feature of futures is that they allow investors to easily speculate on fluctuations of the spot price without actually holding the underlying spot. This is done in practice by posting a margin, which is collateral to cover potential losses. Periodic adjustments are made as the price of the underlying asset changes, such as to maintain adequate margin levels. We discuss the mechanics of margin lending in more detail in Section 6.1. Additionally, investors can benefit from leverage to increase their position. This is called leveraging and is more common for derivatives because only the margin needs to be maintained. This practice is called margin trading.

Maturities which are close in the future are called near-dated or short-dated maturities. Maturities further in the future are called far-dated or long-dated maturities. While there is no clear standard boundary between short- and long-dated maturities, market conventions usually place this boundary between one and two years.[13]

3.2.4.4 Perpetual Futures

Definition 3.12 *(Perpetual Futures)*: Perpetual futures are futures contracts that never settle.

---

[13]US Treasury bills are issued for maturities up to one year, while US Treasury notes, the reference medium-term fixed income securities, are issued for a duration of 2–10 years.

The only way to close the position is to buy or sell the contract. They are a liquid alternative to the spot market [80].

Remark 3.12: Perpetual futures are also simply called perpetuals. An alternative name that describes more precisely their behavior is perpetual swaps [80].

Perpetual futures are the dominant type of futures contract for cryptocurrencies [81, 82]. They exist for other asset classes, but they are nowhere else as popular and as prevalent as for digital assets. Their prevalence has significant implications for the intraday trading patterns and market microstructure of cryptocurrencies. One potential explanation for their popularity is that they are an ideal speculative vehicle, given their ability to leverage.

A distinctive feature of perpetual futures is the funding rate r_f, a mechanism that allows for the price of perpetuals to stay in line with the underlying.[14] Long and short position holders will exchange payments periodically [81], and the rate is continuously adjusted during the life of the contract.[15]

The funding rate is said to be positive when the perpetual future exceeds the spot price, and long position holders pay short position holders. This makes the short position more attractive and pushes the market down. Negative funding rates describe the opposite mechanism, such that they bring a low perpetual future contract price back up to the spot price.

Definition 3.13 ***(Funding Payment)*****:** Let P be the notional principal of a perpetual futures position, r_f the funding rate applied over the interval Δt, and $F_{\text{perpetual}}$ the mark price of the perpetual contract. Then, the funding payment over the period Δt is given by the following.

$$\text{Funding Payment} = P \cdot F_{\text{perpetual}} \cdot r_f \cdot \Delta t$$

Their origin is attributed to precious metals contracts in Hong Kong [81, 83], at the Chinese Gold and Silver Exchange (CGSE),[16] to reduce the basis risk, as per Definition 3.10, for gold miners. In the context of cryptocurrencies, the BitMEX exchange was among the first to popularize perpetual instruments [84], starting in 2016.

The idea was to enable contract holders, at the end of each trading day, to either roll the contract or take delivery. Because the contracts could be rolled indefinitely, and there was therefore no need for any other maturity to be traded, this created a deeper market. While these undated futures actually took the form of auto-rolling one-day futures, they are widely regarded as the precursor to the modern perpetual future.

Remark 3.13 ***(Perpetual Futures and High-frequency Arbitrage)*****:** In theory, the price of perpetual futures should match closely the spot price of the underlying [80, 81], but high-frequency arbitrage is possible because of temporary imbalances.

---

[14] Which is, for instance, the spot for cryptocurrencies.

[15] Most exchanges will recompute the funding requirements between two and four times per day.

[16] The exchange is now known as the Hong Kong Gold Exchange (HKGX). It was established in 1910 by the Chinese Gold and Silver Exchange Society and remains the only exchange for physical gold to this day in Hong Kong, as per Figure 3.3.

FIGURE 3.3 Photograph of the **Hong Kong Gold Exchange** on Mercer Street in Sheung Wan, Hong Kong, in 2025. The first perpetual futures contracts were traded here in the 1980s.

For pricing applications, we will assume that the price of perpetual futures $F_{\text{perpetual}}$ is equal to the spot price S of the underlying asset, as per Equation 3.2, most times t.

$$F_{\text{perpetual}}(t) \approx S(t), \forall t \tag{3.2}$$

Perpetual futures are referred to as zero-cost contracts because there is no basis risk, as per Definition 3.10.

Remark 3.14 ***(Perpetual Futures Versus Spot Equivalence)*****:** While Equation 3.2 holds for pricing theory, meaning perpetual futures prices converge to spot through the funding mechanism [81, 84, 85], perpetuals are not perfect spot substitutes [82]. During extreme market conditions, funding rates can increase significantly and basis can persist through liquidation cascades [86]. We omit detailed perpetual futures analysis to maintain focus on foundational theory in this material.

We summarize the main differences between forwards, futures, and perpetual futures in Table 3.1.

3.2.5 Options

Option contracts play a vital role in TradFi and are rapidly developing in DeFi, in particular on major coins.

Definition 3.14 ***(Option)*****:** An option is a type of derivative that gives the buyer the right, but not the obligation, to buy or sell an underlying asset at an agreed price at a future time.

TABLE 3.1 Comparison of Forward, Futures, and Perpetual Futures

Feature	Forward	Futures	Perpetual Futures
Type	OTC	Exchange	Exchange
Maturity	Fixed	Fixed	N/A
Settlement	At maturity	Daily mark-to-market	Periodic funding payments
Clearing	Bilateral	Clearing house	Clearing house
Margin	Bilateral or none	Yes	Yes
Funding	N/A	N/A	Funding rate paid between long/short positions

Options are commonly used derivatives, both to hedge risk and to speculate on price movements.

There are two main forms of option contracts:

- The call option gives the holder the right to buy the underlying.
- The put option gives the holder the right to sell the underlying.

When exercised, the price at which a holder buys or sells the underlying is called the strike price K, and an option contract will expire at its maturity T.

Note that the actual price of the option contract itself is the option premium. It is not the same as K. At initiation of the option, the buyer pays that premium to the seller of the option, which is the actual price of the contract.

3.2.5.1 Moneyness The concept of moneyness in the context of options describes how favorable the price of the underlying is compared to the strike price. We define it in Definition 3.15.

Definition 3.15 ***(Moneyness)*:** Moneyness characterizes the value of the option relative to the current spot price of the underlying.

In-the-money (ITM) The option holder would make a profit if the current spot price for the underlying is observed when the option is exercised.

At-the-money (ATM) The spot price is the same as the strike price.

Out-of-the-money (OTM) The option holder would realize a loss, limited to the premium paid, if the current spot price for the underlying is observed when the option is exercised.

Remark 3.15: In practice, because of the premium paid or received, even an ATM option as per Definition 3.15 would carry a small loss or gain.

The payoff of the option is the difference between the strike price and the spot price of the underlying at maturity $S(T)$, which is the payoff of the holder, as per Equation 3.3.

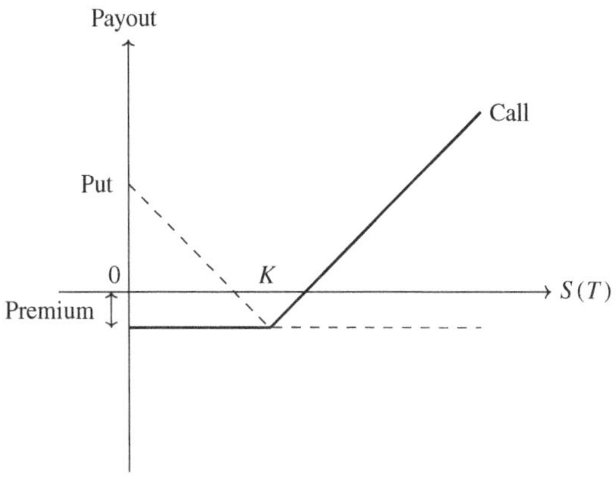

FIGURE 3.4 **Payout Chart of European Call and Put Options** as a function of the underlying price at maturity $S(T)$, with strike price K. In most payout charts, the PnL is represented and is a translation of the payout corresponding to the option premium, visible at strike price K.

The payout, a terminology commonly used in the context of options, is the PnL of the contract, so the sum of the payoff and the premium, which is positive or negative depending on whether the contract is bought or sold.

Options can be settled either with exchange of underlying S, or by settling the payout. The latter is called cash-settled and is the most common in DeFi.

$$\text{Payoff}(S(T), K) = \begin{cases} \max\left(0, S(T) - K\right) & \text{for a call option} \\ \max\left(0, K - S(T)\right) & \text{for a put option} \end{cases} \tag{3.3}$$

A common representation of Equation 3.3 as a function of the price of the underlying at maturity $S(T)$ is the payout chart,[17] as represented in Figure 3.4.

3.2.5.2 Option Types The way optionality is exercised will depend on the type of option. This will determine when the option can be exercised and what the option payoff is. There are several types of options, with some of the most common ones listed next, also called vanilla options.

European options can only be exercised at maturity, and the strike price is set at initiation.

American options can be exercised at any time before maturity, and the strike price is set at initiation.

The most common type of option on cryptocurrencies available on exchanges is European options [87–89]. American options are less common, are usually only available on OTC markets, but are growing in popularity.

[17] The payout chart is sometimes called hockey stick graph, although it is not related to the homonymous graph in private equity. It is a payout graph when the option premium is represented, as in Figure 3.4; otherwise, it is the payoff chart.

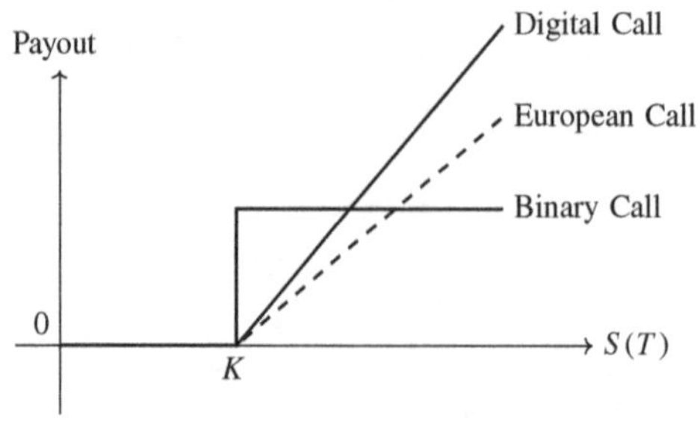

FIGURE 3.5 **Payout Chart of Binary and Digital Call Options** as a function of the underlying price at maturity $S(T)$, with strike price K. Note that we do not represent the premiums on this payout chart, as these would be different, in particular between the European and the digital call options. The binary call pays a fixed amount if $S(T) > K$, while the digital call pays a variable amount above K.

Usually, any option contract that is neither European nor American is called an exotic option. A number of these have gained widespread adoption.

Asian options have a payoff that is based on the average price of the underlying asset over a certain period. They are used to smooth volatility risk for the payoff, since an average is used instead.

Barrier options are options that only trigger if the underlying asset spot price hits a specified barrier level.

There are two types of exotic options that are commonly used in DeFi. These exotics are typically used for very short maturities, in the range of minutes or hours. We present their payoff structures in Figure 3.5.

Binary options are options that have a fixed payoff if the underlying asset spot price is above or below a certain level at maturity. They are a bet on the direction of the underlying price.[18]

Digital options are options that have a variable payoff[19] if the underlying asset spot price is above or below a certain level at maturity.

A distinctive feature that has helped with their popularity with retail investors in DeFi is that neither of these has the underlying exercised; they only provide a cash settlement.

3.2.5.3 European Option

For the most common type of option, called the European option, the prices of both puts and calls are linked by the put-call parity, as per Definition 3.16. We represent this relationship in Figure 3.6.

Definition 3.16 ***(Put-call Parity)*:** At any set time t fixed, let C be the price of a European call option, P the price of a European put option with the same strike K and maturity T,

[18]Binary options have a sulfurous reputation with many scam schemes having run with this type of option [90].

[19]Typically, a broker will offer a proportion of the difference between the spot price at maturity and the strike price. This is different from the standard call option when the payout is linear to the underlying price.

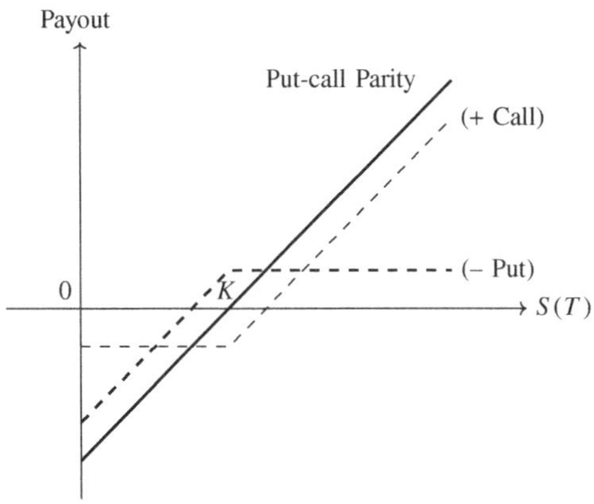

FIGURE 3.6 **Payout Chart of European Options, with Put-call Parity Line** as a function of the underlying price at maturity $S(T)$, with strike price K. The thick line represents the put-call parity: $C - P = S(T) - K$. In this theoretical example, the premiums cancel out.

and the same underlying asset with spot price S. The following relationship exists and is called put-call parity:

$$C(t) - P(t) = S(t) - \mathrm{PV}\,(K, T - t)$$

with PV the Present Value (PV)[20] of the strike K.

Proof. We construct two portfolios:

- One is long the call and short the put, with same strike K and expiry T.
- The other is long the underlying S and borrowed K until time T.

At maturity T, the first portfolio has a payoff of $S(T) - K$ if the call option is exercised, same if the put is exercised. Both cases are mutually exclusive. The second portfolio has a payoff of $S(T) - K$ in all cases.

Given both portfolios have the same payoffs, they have the same price.[21] ∎

Modern option pricing theory was developed in the late 1970s. The most notable works are Black and Scholes' [91], and concurrently and independently Merton's [92]. This led to the introduction of the reference pricing model for options, the Black-Scholes-Merton (BSM) model [92], which has a closed-form solution for the price of European options.

Theorem 3.1 ***(BSM Model Pricing Equation [Call]):*** *Let C be the price of a European call option with strike K, maturity T, underlying asset spot price S, risk-free interest rate R_f, and volatility σ. The BSM model pricing equation is as follows:*

$$C = S\Phi(d_1) - Ke^{-R_f T}\Phi(d_2)$$

[20] We present a more rigorous introduction to the concept of PV in Section 12.2.5.

[21] This argument, called no-arbitrage, is discussed more formally in Section 12.2.1.1.

with

$$d_1 = \frac{\ln\left(\frac{S}{K}\right) + \left(R_f + \frac{\sigma^2}{2}\right)T}{\sigma\sqrt{T}}$$
$$d_2 = d_1 - \sigma\sqrt{T}$$

where Φ *is the cumulative distribution function of the standard normal distribution* $n(0, 1)$.

Proof. The proof is out of scope for this introduction. It is, however, a classic result of options pricing that can be easily found online, and we direct the interested reader to Hull's comprehensive treatment of the proof in his book [93]. ■

The BSM model equation from Theorem 3.1 assumes no cash flows[22] arising from the underlying and constant volatility. While the no cash flow assumption can be problematic for TradFi stocks, it is actually appropriate for cryptocurrencies; the constant volatility assumption remains a significant limitation. Nevertheless, the BSM model remains widely used in practice, thanks to its simplicity and closed-form solution.

Remark 3.16 ***(Interpretation of the BSM Model):*** We note that there are two terms with normal distribution in the BSM model:

$\Phi(d_1)$ corresponds to the risk-adjusted probability of the option being ITM at maturity.

$\Phi(d_2)$ corresponds to the risk-adjusted probability of the option being exercised.

Corollary 3.1 ***(BSM Model Pricing Equation [Put]):*** *Let P be the price of a European put option with strike K, maturity T, underlying asset spot price S, risk-free interest rate* R_f*, and volatility* σ*. The BSM model pricing equation is as follows.*

$$P = Ke^{-R_f T}\Phi(-d_2) - S\Phi(-d_1)$$

Proof. We apply the put-call parity, which we defined in Definition 3.16, to the BSM model pricing equation of Theorem 3.1.

We introduce the PV, which we present in more detail in Section 12.2.5, of the strike K at maturity T as follows:

$$\mathrm{PV}(K) = Ke^{-R_f T}$$

with the same notations as the Corollary, and now apply the parity:

$$\begin{aligned} P + S &= C + \mathrm{PV}(K) \\ P &= C + \mathrm{PV}(K) - S \\ &= S\Phi(d_1) - Ke^{-R_f T}\Phi(d_2) + Ke^{-R_f T} - S \end{aligned}$$

[22]In TradFi, if such underlying is a stock or a bond, it assumes no dividend or coupon payment.

And we note that $\Phi(x) - 1 = -\Phi(-x)$, as it is the cumulative distribution function:

$$\begin{aligned} P &= S\left(\Phi(d_1) - 1\right) - Ke^{-R_f T}\left(1 - \Phi(d_2)\right) \\ &= -S\Phi(-d_1) + Ke^{-R_f T}\Phi(-d_2) \end{aligned}$$

■

A notable feature of the BSM model is that it assumes that the price of the underlying asset follows a Geometric Brownian Motion (GBM), which we discuss in Section 11.2.1. Under the GBM, asset returns are normally distributed,[23] and the BSM model closed-form pricing equation uses the standard normal distribution for the risk-adjusted probabilities of the model.

3.2.5.4 Greeks Option prices are sensitive to several market factors. These sensitivities are formalized by practitioners as coefficients called the Greeks.[24] The most common Greek is called delta (see Definition 3.17), which is the sensitivity of the option price to the spot price of the underlying.

Definition 3.17 *(Option Delta)***:** Let C be the price of an option and S the spot price of its underlying. We define the Greek delta Δ of such an option as follows:

$$\Delta = \frac{\partial C}{\partial S}$$

Remark 3.17: The Δ in Definition 3.17 has no association with the integrated basis in Proposition 3.1.

The concept of delta in Definition 3.17 relates to two important ideas.

- The hedge ratio is the amount of underlying needed to cover the position. This is also referred to as delta-hedging, and is used in the proof of the BSM model.
- The concept of moneyness was introduced in Definition 3.15. A call option will have $\Delta_C \in [0; 1]$, while a put option will have $\Delta_P \in [-1; 0]$. The deeper OTM, the closer $\Delta \to 0$; the deeper ITM, the closer $|\Delta| \to 1$. An ATM option is expected to have $|\Delta| \approx 0.5$, given roughly equal chances of having the underlying spot price at the same level as now at maturity.

While Greeks are defined for all options, we have some interesting results specific to the European option, such as the delta parity in Proposition 3.3.

Proposition 3.3 *(Put-call Parity of Deltas)***:** Let C be the price of a European call option and P the price of a European put option with the same strike price K and maturity T:

$$\Delta_P = \Delta_C - 1$$

[23]This translates in the Geometric Brownian Motion (GBM) to a log-normal distribution of resulting asset prices.

[24]The name Greek refers to the fact that these standardized measures are denominated using Greek alphabet letters.

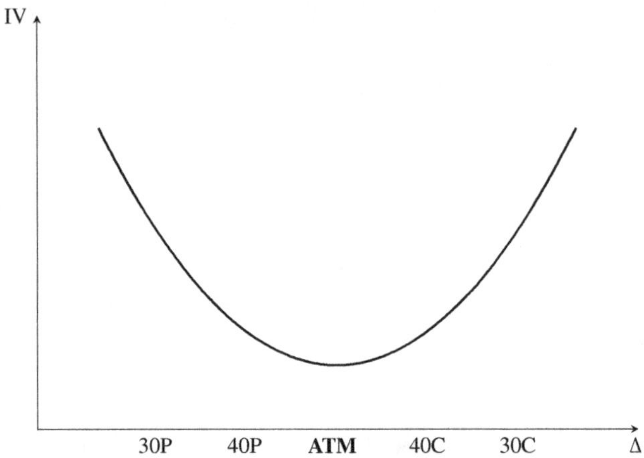

FIGURE 3.7 **Illustration of the Volatility Smile.** The Implied Volatility (IV) is plotted as a function of the distance to money Δ, showing the typical parabolic smile shape observed in some options markets. The Δs on such smile plots are often represented without premium adjustment.

Proof. Direct application of Definition 3.16. ■

Deltas are commonly quoted as whole numbers or as percentages. To illustrate, a call option with a delta of 30% is quoted as "30C" which is the same as the delta for a put option with a delta of –70%. One can expect, given Proposition 3.3, that buying 30C or selling 70P is equivalent for delta exposure, as is shown in Figure 3.7.

Another commonly used Greek is called vega, which is the sensitivity of the option price to the volatility of the underlying.

Definition 3.18 ***(Option Vega)*:** Let C be the price of an option and σ the volatility of its underlying. We define the Greek vega ν of such an option as follows:

$$\nu = \frac{\partial C}{\partial \sigma}$$

There also exist Greeks for other explanatory variables and for higher orders of derivation.

3.2.5.5 Implied Volatility One of the main applications of the BSM model is to derive the Implied Volatility (IV) of options. The idea is to use observed market prices and compute what volatility would be needed in the BSM model to match such price, thus the name Implied Volatility (IV).

A shortcoming of the BSM model is the assumption of constant volatility for all strike prices. In practice, when practitioners use the BSM model to back out IV, for the same underlying but different strike prices, they observe increased IV the further away the strike is from the current stock price. This phenomenon is called the volatility smile, since that phenomenon resembles a smile when plotted, as per Figure 3.7.

One explanation of the volatility smile is that while the BSM model assumes a normal distribution, investors are aware of the fact that price return distributions are fat-tailed,[25]

[25]We discuss this point in greater detail in Section 10.3.1, in particular as Stylized Fact SF2.

meaning large price variations are more likely than the normal distribution would predict. When implied through a constant, normal distribution, this corresponds to higher IV [94, 95].

For equity options in TradFi, a volatility skew, instead of a volatility smile,[26] is observed. In that context, the IV plot is no longer symmetrical around the ATM strike and resembles more of a slope. This can be explained by an imbalanced perception of risk [94].

Volatility smiles and smirks are observed in DeFi for cryptocurrency options [96–98]. This means that IV behaves more like FX options, with a more symmetrical IV around the ATM strike. However, smirks were observed at times when there was a strong price trend for the underlying cryptocurrency spot price, which we discuss in Remark 10.5.

Remark 3.18 ***(Leverage Effect)*****:** Smirks are closely linked to the market's perception that lower underlying prices correspond to increased leverage for open long positions, and in turn translate to higher risk, and thus higher IV. This is not always true for cryptocurrencies, and we discuss this point specifically in Section 10.3.1 with the leverage effect, which we refer to as Stylized Fact SF5.

In practice, supply and demand imbalances also account for smile and smirk effects. A known example in TradFi equity options is the increased demand on the downside of the smile due to market participants hedging their long positions in the underlying.

The volatility skew can also be represented as a function of the time to maturity of the option,[27] resulting in the so-called IV surface. In general, the smile tends to be more pronounced as we get closer to the maturity of the option.

Remark 3.19 ***(Observing the Smile)*****:** Most major DeFi exchanges provide free, real-time options data for the leading coins and token pairs. We encourage readers to explore these resources to observe the volatility smile firsthand.

3.2.6 Hybrids

While the introduction of layer 2 has enabled smart contracts, most derivatives with cryptocurrencies as underlying rely on the performance of actions off-chain. This is for mainly two reasons:

- TradFi already has well-established protocols and conventions for derivatives.
- Smart contracts have associated execution costs, to be paid in the coin of the underlying blockchain. This introduces settlement risk, and security risks are also associated with more complex smart contracts.

As a result, these products are often referred to as hybrids,[28] as they are a mix of on-chain and off-chain asset claims, performance obligations, and cash flows. These derivatives are not settled with a smart contract on-chain, but rather by a designated counterparty, such as an exchange or a broker. The cash flows linked to the settlement are not

[26] The term smirk is also used to describe smiles with still significant skew.
[27] The set of different maturities for the same underlying is commonly called the term structure.
[28] The term hybrid is quite broadly used in the context of DeFi to refer to products that are a mix of DeFi and TradFi.

always recorded on-chain. Most forwards and options contracts on cryptocurrencies are in this category. The classification frameworks we discuss in Chapter 4 help distinguish between purely on-chain assets and these hybrid structures.

Remark 3.20: By nature, spot transactions between a digital asset on-chain and a fiat currency are also hybrids, as they involve a transfer of ownership of the digital asset on-chain, but the fiat currency is not recorded on-chain.

Another example of hybrid product, which arises from performance obligations and cash flows of an off-chain custodian, is stablecoins. We discuss stablecoins in greater detail in Section 7.2.

3.2.7 Claims and Cash Flows

A simple classification system, analogous to the one in TradFi, is to break down assets by the cash flows they generate.

3.2.7.1 Fabozzi Classification One such classification is Fabozzi's [99], who characterizes instruments by claims.

Debt instruments have claims on a fixed dollar amount and include bonds, loans, and mortgages. Cash flows are usually fixed and known in advance, or the cash flows are linked to a benchmark rate.

Equity instruments have claims on a variable dollar amount and include stocks. Cash flows are usually variable and depend on the performance of the underlying asset. Cash flows on such instruments cannot be known in advance, and payments are usually made at the discretion of the issuer. Furthermore, such instruments have lower priority in the capital structure than debt instruments, which means that their holders are only paid after the debt holders have been paid.

Combination instruments are instruments with characteristics of both categories. They include convertible bonds and preferred stocks.

Under the above classification, assets that do not generate cash flows are not considered financial instruments. An additional category is often added, to represent these assets such as foreign exchange and commodities.[29]

3.2.7.2 Girón Classification Girón suggested a broader classification using only cash flows [100].

General financial claims represent one initial payment and then subsequent payments that are predetermined at initiation.

[29]Note that derivatives of these assets are financial instruments by all definitions because they represent claims on underlying assets and lead to contractual cash flows.

Dual payments is similar to the previous category, but only two payments are made, one at the beginning and one at the end. Both payments are predetermined at initiation.

Equity has one initial payment and then stochastic payments.

Forwards have no initial payment, and then stochastic payments throughout the life of the contract.

Options have one initial payment, and then only one other stochastic payment at the end of the contract.

Cash only has one single certain payment at the end of the contract.

The Girón characterization by cash flows is more generic and can be easily applied to digital assets.

3.2.7.3 IMF Classification The International Monetary Fund (IMF)[30] issued in 2022 a guidance note [101] on the classification of digital assets for statistical purposes, focusing on fungible digital assets.

General medium of exchange is a digital asset that is used as a medium of exchange. These include stablecoins and Bitcoin.

Medium of exchange within a platform include payment tokens. These assets are limited to their platform only.

Security tokens have counterparty liability.

One feature of this classification is that it does not include any hybrid category. The IMF classification does not include non-fungible assets, such as NFTs.

3.2.7.4 Challenges and Limitations A classification of assets based on cash flows, analogous to TradFi, serves as a solid foundation, but has limitations due to the on and off-chain nature of digital assets. One of the challenges lies in hybrids, where only some of the cash flows are represented on-chain, while others are not. We discuss further, in Chapter 7, the concept of liquidity interface and how it can be used to classify digital assets.

[30] Girón was one of the coauthors of that classification, which precedes his broader classification based on cash flows.

Open Problems

These thought experiments are guided explorations into the concepts discussed in this part of the book.
Hints are available at www.tomespel.com/books/mfin25.

Problem I.1: Assume a coin is bridged to a sidechain and the federation stops providing support for the bridge. What are the potential risks and implications for the value of the coin on the mainnet?

Problem I.2: Describe the implications of mainnet congestion for a pegged sidechain with a federation using smart contracts.

Problem I.3: Assume a mainnet and two sidechains, where the same mainnet coin is bridged to both sidechains. What are the implications of the mainnet moving to PoS while one of the sidechains remain on PoW?

Problem I.4: Assume two options, one with the cryptocurrency spot and the other with the perpetual future as underlying. Both options have the same strike and maturity. Which one would you expect to be more expensive and why?

PART Two

Network Valuation

"Investing is a popularity contest, and the most dangerous thing is to buy at the peak of its popularity."

Howard Marks, The Most Important Thing

CHAPTER 4

Digital Asset Classification

Multiple classification systems have emerged for digital assets, yet none have achieved widespread acceptance. This chapter examines the key taxonomies and their practical implications, as classification directly impacts the pricing models and risk frameworks we can apply.

- Analyze prudential and sectoral classification systems, including regulatory frameworks and industry taxonomies.
- Examine quantitative classification methodologies based on market dynamics.
- Discuss functional classification frameworks that capture properties unique to digital assets.

The challenge lies in balancing generality with specificity; overly broad classifications lack practical applicability, while overly narrow ones become complex. The choice of classification system directly impacts the pricing models we develop in subsequent chapters, as assets within the same class tend to share similar risk characteristics and pricing methodologies.

This chapter progresses from regulatory and industry classifications to quantitative methodologies that capture market dynamics, concluding with functional frameworks that leverage the unique technical properties discussed in the previous chapter. Table 4.1 summarizes the main classification approaches covered in this chapter, their primary purposes, and connections to valuation methods discussed in Chapter 5.

TABLE 4.1 Overview of Digital Asset Classification Systems

Classification	Purpose and Key Features	Metrics	Valuation Links
Prudential (BIS)	Regulatory capital requirements; risk-based grouping	Groups 1 and 2	Risk management
Sector (HHR, DACS)	Industry categorization; use-case based	Seven classes (HHR); hierarchical (DACS)	Peer comparison methods in Section 5.2.1

(Continued)

TABLE 4.1 (*Continued*)

Classification	Purpose and Key Features	Metrics	Valuation Links
WWS Market Cap	Quantitative growth dynamics	Growth rate r, variance σ^2	Factor analysis in Section 5.6
Ecosystem (Schär)	DeFi stack positioning	Layers, Schär numbers & range	Network valuations in Section 5.3
Functional	Operational characteristics	Issuance, reward, fungibility, peg	Determines applicability of valuation methods

4.1 PRUDENTIAL CLASSIFICATION

The Bank for International Settlements (BIS) [102] has proposed a classification system for digital assets, which is based on their prudential treatment within the Basel framework. The classification, introduced in 2022, is based on the type of asset and the type of risk it represents. A simplified version of the classification is presented next.

Group 1 Assets that are linked to traditional financial assets. To qualify for Group 1, the digital asset must also satisfy tests that cover redemption risk and infrastructure risk.

- **Group 1a** Digital assets that represent a TradFi asset.
- **Group 1b** Stabilized assets, such as stablecoins.

Group 2 Other digital assets that are deemed more risky.

- **Group 2a** Liquid assets.[1]
- **Group 2b** Other nonliquid assets.

This type of broad classification is appropriate to understand the risks associated with these assets, but it lacks sufficient granularity.

4.2 SECTOR CLASSIFICATION

While prudential classifications serve regulatory purposes, sector classifications aim to group assets by their intended use cases and market positioning. This is similar to industry classifications used for stocks in TradFi.

4.2.1 HHR's Classification

A notable classification was proposed by Härdle et al. [104] in 2019.

[1]The formal definition is set out in Basel SCO60.55, also called the hedging recognition criteria [102]. ISDA suggested a hedging framework for derivatives in 2022 [103] for this subgroup.

Definition 4.1 ***(HHR Classification)*****:** The Härdle-Harvey-Reule (HHR) classification of a digital asset is the set of the HHR classes to which it belongs.

The HHR classification categorizes digital assets into seven classes:

Transaction mechanisms such as Bitcoin
Distributed computation tokens such as Ethereum
Utility tokens that are blockchain assets
Security tokens that represent financial securities
Fungible tokens
Non-fungible tokens (NFTs)
Stablecoins which has its own subcategories

The HHR classification blends network and asset characteristics and is broad enough to capture all digital assets. While some categories do overlap, it is an excellent starting point.

4.2.2 Other Sectoral Classifications

Sectoral classification systems have been developed by private companies, most notably the Digital Asset Classification Standard (DACS) in 2021 [105]. Other similar classifications exist, such as the CF DACS [106], but have achieved limited adoption.

The fundamental principle underlying this classification methodology is to assign each digital asset to a sector (broadest), an industry group, and an industry (most specific). It is similar to classifications used for stocks in the context of indices in TradFi, in particular the Global Industry Classification Standard (GICS) or the Industry Classification Benchmark (ICB).

Sectoral classifications are ideally suited for exchange-traded coins and tokens. However, one of the limitations of such methodology is that some digital assets, such as wrapped tokens, or tokens solely used for transaction fees, cannot be classified easily.

4.2.3 Limitations

One of the challenges of a sectoral classification is that most coins or tokens will change sector over time. Notable examples include meme coins. While some may argue it is also the case for stocks, such changes tend to occur faster within digital assets, given the infancy of the industry. Another challenge lies in constructing sectors that balance exhaustiveness with breadth.

One of the main benefits of sector classification in TradFi is that for pricing purposes, it creates groups, often called baskets,[2] of assets that tend to follow the same price dynamics and conventions. This is not as relevant for digital assets at this stage.

We therefore suggest using classifications that rely on technical and functional characteristics, instead of social and environmental characteristics, for applications in financial mathematics.

[2]Those same groups are often picked to curate TradFi thematic ETFs.

4.3 WWS MARKET CAP CHARACTERIZATION

We now examine quantitative methodologies that characterize digital assets based on their market behavior and dynamics.

Wu, Wheatley, and Sornette (WWS) introduced in 2018 a classification methodology for cryptocurrencies [107] based on their market capitalization. This classification is suitable for all fungible digital assets but can also be easily extended to collections of NFTs.

The authors extend frameworks by Malevergne et al.[3] and Gibrat[4] [108, 109] and compute stochastic proportional growth model parameters for a group of coins and a group of tokens [107]. This allowed the authors to classify these groups of assets by the dynamics of their market capitalization.

Definition 4.2 ***(Malevergne et al.'s Rule of Proportional Growth)*****:** For each digital asset, the market capitalization K_i follows

$$dK_i(t) = K_i(t)\left(rdt + \sigma dW_i(t)\right)$$

with $r \in \mathbb{R}$, $\sigma \in \mathbb{R}_+$ common to all digital assets in the same group and W_i a Wiener process unique to that digital asset.

We propose extending Definition 4.2 by computing the parameter values for each individual digital asset:[5]

- The growth rate of market capitalization r
- The growth standard deviation σ

We can compute the values using Definition 4.2 with the small time interval operator Δt:

$$\mathrm{E}\left(\frac{dK_i}{K_i}\right) = rdt$$

$$r \approx \frac{\mathrm{E}\left(\frac{\Delta K_i}{K_i}\right)}{\Delta t} \tag{4.1}$$

$$\mathbf{Var}\left(\frac{dK_i}{K_i}\right) = \sigma^2 dt$$

$$\sigma^2 \approx \frac{\mathbf{Var}\left(\frac{\Delta K_i}{K_i}\right)}{\Delta t} \tag{4.2}$$

Definition 4.3 ***(WWS Characterization)*****:** Each digital asset is characterized over an interval of time ΔT by its WWS rate of growth r and variance σ^2.

[3]This framework [108] is an extension of Zipf's Law, which we discuss in Section 5.3.4.

[4]Gibrat's Law of Proportional Growth [109] is an empirical law that has found applications across multiple economic time series.

[5]Wu et al.'s model [107] is more subtle as it introduces birth and death parameters and discusses tail exponent of the distribution of the market capitalization of different assets within one group.

Because these parameters can be computed individually, we will refer to this methodology as the WWS Characterization. The individual parameters can be assigned to category ranges to derive a classification.

The parameters in Definition 4.3 are computed according to Equations 4.1 and 4.2.

Remark 4.1: We chose to characterize assets by their variance instead of the standard deviation used in Wu et al.'s [107] original paper to follow the parametrization conventions found in probabilities, such as for the normal distribution.

The WWS Characterization is an intuitive characterization system that allows quantification of an essential economic parameter of a digital asset. It also ties up well with Gibrat's Law, which has been observed in multiple fields. Because the WWS Characterization provides quantified values, it allows for easy comparison, ranking, and categorization of digital assets at a similar stage of growth.

Its main downside is that the WWS numbers are very sensitive to the measured economic data, and by extension, the time interval Δt over which they are computed.

4.4 ECOSYSTEM CLASSIFICATION

The quantitative approaches just discussed capture market dynamics but may not reflect the technical dependencies and network relationships in Decentralized Finance (DeFi). We now discuss classification systems that consider assets' relative position in the broader digital asset ecosystem.

4.4.1 Schär's Classification

In 2021, Schär [42] introduced a conceptual framework for the DeFi ecosystem. This framework introduced labels and layers that do not fully align with the technical protocol classifications in Section 2.3.1. Table 4.2 presents our interpretative mapping between Schär's functional layers and conventional technical layer terminology, though these frameworks serve different purposes and should not be considered directly equivalent.

We extend Schär's framework to classify digital assets based on their position in the DeFi stack. Assets can therefore be categorized in one of five layers:

1. **Settlement layer** corresponds to native coins.
2. **Asset layer** corresponds to tokens and other assets issued on the mainnet.
3. **Protocol layer** corresponds to specialized applications, such as DEXs or derivatives contracts. We suggest categorizing all derivatives for settlement and asset layer tokens, and tokens used specifically to govern these protocols, in the protocol layer.
4. **Application layers** are user-friendly interfaces to smart contracts. We propose to extend it to all applications that relate to facilitating interactions on-chain and off-chain. We can categorize here all assets that relate to interaction with these smart contracts. These include utility tokens used to pay for these services and tokens that represent off-chain assets.
5. **Aggregation layer** combines different applications and protocols together. All assets that relate to the governance or paying for the services of these aggregators can be categorized here.

TABLE 4.2 Interpretative Mapping of Schär and Conventional Layer Classifications

Schär Layer	Description	Conventional Layer
Settlement Layer	Native coins	Often layer 0 or layer 1
Asset Layer	Tokens and assets issued on the mainnet	Typically layer 1
Protocol Layer	Specialized smart contract-based protocols	Often layer 2, or on-chain layer 1 implementations
Application Layer	On-off-chain interactions	Often layer 3
Aggregation Layer	Meta-applications	Layer 3 (or Meta-layer)

Where Schär's classification was inadequate from a technology standpoint, we believe it can be extended to make use of its intuitive and spatial quality, which is difficult to capture otherwise. The fact that digital assets tend to be built on top of others and share the limitations and interoperability constraints of the underlying protocol is a key characteristic of the DeFi ecosystem.

Another advantage of such classification is that while a given asset might sit within multiple layers, these layers are always contiguous. We call these the Schär numbers, which we define in Definition 4.4.

Definition 4.4 *(Schär Numbers)***:** We define as Schär numbers of a given digital asset the lower and higher layer number to which it belongs in Schär's classification.

Any asset will therefore have a lower Schär number that corresponds to its importance in a given blockchain ecosystem and an upper Schär number that corresponds to its relative exposure to outside the blockchain ecosystem.

The range, in Definition 4.5, is a measure of asset versatility.

Definition 4.5 *(Schär Range)***:** We define the Schär range of a digital asset as the difference between its lower and higher layer number in Schär's classification.

Remark 4.2: For the simplest assets, the Schär range will be zero. Bitcoin being a native coin, its Schär numbers would be 1:1 and its range would be 0.

4.4.2 Linnaean Classification

The Linnaean classification system is used in biology to classify living organisms. It was introduced in 1735 by Linnaeus in his *Systema Naturae* and is the predecessor to contemporary taxonomic systems. Significant revisions were made to reflect evolutionary theory and recent developments. This system is based on hierarchical order, which gives it a distinctive tree representation, where each item only belongs to one branch.

One unique feature of DeFi is that blockchain protocols follow an iterative development cycle, analogous to the evolution of a given species. The protocol forks are also easily represented in a Linnaean classification. This makes such a system well-suited for digital

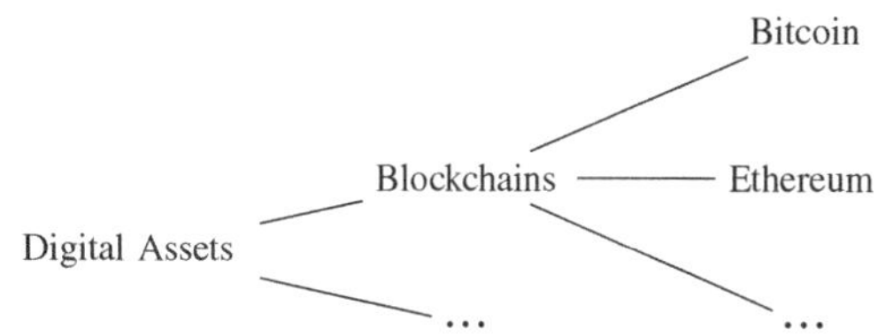

FIGURE 4.1 **Root Nodes of the Linnaean Classification** of digital assets. The root node is *Digital Assets*. The first level is the split between blockchain and other digital assets.

assets. Another advantage of a Linnaean system is that the taxonomy is descriptive and does not rank or quantify features, such as security or speed.

We propose a similar system to classify and describe digital assets. This classification is not intended for day-to-day usage, but helps to represent the dependency between digital assets and risk factors for pricing. We represent the root of the tree in Figure 4.1.

Definition 4.6 ***(Linnaean Classification of Digital Assets)*:** We define a Linnaean-style classification of digital assets as a tree structure representing shared similarities between underlying networks and protocols. We suggest the following rules:

1. The taxonomic root node is *Digital Assets*.
2. The first level is the split between blockchains and other digital assets.
3. Beyond the first level, the parent group name is chosen after the oldest surviving branch on the tree.
4. Hard and soft forks lead to the creation of new blockchain stems on the tree.
5. We represent soft forks and protocol upgrades as extinct blockchains.

Using Definition 4.6, we can represent an example of such a tree for Bitcoin in particular in Figure 4.2.

4.5 FUNCTIONAL CLASSIFICATION

While ecosystem classifications capture network dependencies, functional classifications focus on the operational characteristics. These consider the characteristics of both the asset itself, and the network it operates within, building on Chapter 2.

4.5.1 FINMA Classification

The Swiss Financial Market Supervisory Authority (FINMA) classification, introduced in 2018 [110], is notable for its simplicity. It classified coins and tokens in three categories:

Payment Tokens are digital assets that are used as a means of payment. FINMA stresses that they must not be linked to specific projects.

Utility Tokens are digital assets that are used to access a specific service.

Asset Tokens are digital assets that represent a claim on assets or cash flows, and are alike to equities and bonds in TradFi.

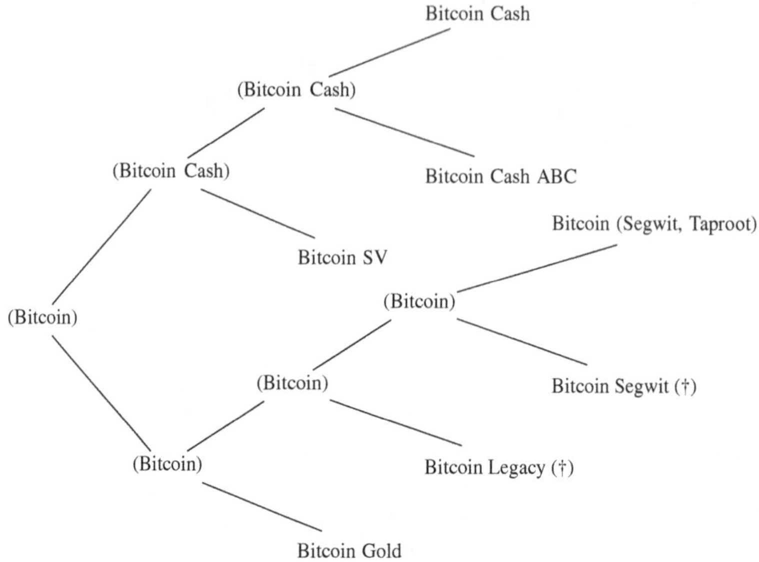

FIGURE 4.2 Example of the **Bitcoin Tree in the Linnaean Classification** of digital assets. We note the soft forks are also labeled on the tree, with unused older protocol versions labeled with a dagger (†). The tree is not exhaustive but represents the main branches of the Bitcoin tree.

Aside from stablecoins, payment tokens are generally subject to lighter regulatory oversight than other types of coins or tokens. The threshold to qualify as an instrument of payment varies by regulator.

4.5.2 Enhanced Functional Classification

In Section 2.3, we presented properties that were exclusive to blockchain networks. We suggest in this section a classification of digital assets that includes some of the properties of their underlying network.

Definition 4.7 *(Functional Classification)*: We categorize digital assets based on their issuance rules, the components of the reward of network operators, the fungibility of the asset, and the existence of a peg.

For each attribute of the classification in Definition 4.7, we suggest the following possible options.

Issuance describes if there is a cap to the number of assets created and who makes that decision

- **Open-ended protocol** with no option for third-party intervention
- **Open-ended entity,** which can be an individual node or a collective of network participants
- **Close-ended** with a cap, with origination process decided by either the protocol or an entity, with no option for third-party intervention to remove the cap

Genesis-only with all assets existing at the time the first block was created

Reward of the network nodes

Origination-only when the entire reward paid to network nodes is newly issued assets

Network fees only when the entire reward paid to network nodes is paid by network participants as transaction fees

Mixed when the reward is a combination of origination and network fees

Fungibility of the asset

Fungible assets interchangeable

Non-fungible assets unique

Peg of the value of the asset

Pegged to any other instrument or asset

Free-floating with market-determined value

In this functional classification system, we attribute to each feature a value, and the collection of the features makes up the categorization of a digital asset. Such methodology makes it easy to compare two assets' shared features. Readers may notice that we do not differentiate native coins versus other tokens on the mainnet.

We want to discuss how two special cases would be treated within the classification system.

- When the reward mechanism changes over time, it is assessed over the entire history of the asset. This means that if the reward, say, was initially pure origination and eventually became pure fees, the rating would be classified as mixed.
- When all coins are created at the genesis of the network, but one entity holds a proportion of this coin in a reserve, the coin issuance is still classified as genesis-only. This indicator relates to monetary creation rules, not asset distribution.

Remark 4.3: We can write two examples to illustrate such classification:

- **Bitcoin** would be classified as closed-ended issuance, mixed reward, fungible, free-floating.
- **Typical stablecoins** would be classified as open-ended entity issuance, no network reward as it is a token, fungible, and pegged.

CHAPTER 5

Network Valuation

Traditional valuation models from corporate finance, developed for industrial corporations with clear ownership structures and financial statements, face fundamental challenges when applied to blockchain networks. This chapter develops valuation frameworks suited to the decentralized, network-based nature of digital asset ecosystems.

- Examine traditional business valuation methodologies from corporate finance and assess their applicability to blockchain networks.
- Develop network-specific valuation frameworks based on user adoption patterns.
- Introduce relative valuation techniques through interchain basis analysis, using wrapped tokens as instruments to assess network risk differentials.

We argue that adequate valuation of blockchains requires distinguishing the network from its assets. However, network valuation proves critical in DeFi for pricing governance tokens and adjusting for network risk when pricing wrapped tokens. We present in Table 5.1 a summary of the main network valuation methodologies covered in this chapter, their core principles, and practical applications.

TABLE 5.1 Overview of Network Valuation Methods

Method	Core Principle	Data Requirements	Best For
Market Cap Multiple	$V = \rho K$	Asset prices, circulation	Governance tokens
Network Laws	Value from user connections		
Sarnoff	$V \propto N$	Active users	Small networks
Metcalfe	$V \propto N^2$	Active users	Broad networks
Reed	$V \propto 2^N$	Active users	Subgroup interactions
ZBOT	$V \propto N \log N$	Active users	Mature networks
DCF/DDV	Discounted cash flows	Fee projections, growth rate	Fee-generating protocols
Volume Multiple	$V \propto \Phi$	Transaction volume	Payment networks

(*Continued*)

TABLE 5.1 (*Continued*)

Method	Core Principle	Data Requirements	Best For
Cost Accounting	Energy/operational costs	Hash rate, electricity cost	PoW networks
Factor Analysis	Multi-factor regression	Historical prices, risk factors	Comprehensive
Interchain Basis	Relative network risk	Wrapped token price spreads	Cross-chain risk analysis

5.1 MARKET CAPITALIZATION MULTIPLE

The market capitalization K of all the assets on a network is easy to observe. Assume there is only one coin in circulation N_C with individual price P_C. We can express market capitalization as follows:

$$K = N_C P_C$$

In practice, there are many assets in circulation, and we generalize the concept to a network with Definition 5.1.

Definition 5.1 *(Market Capitalization)*: Let M be the total number of assets in circulation on a network, and let P_i be the price of asset i with N_i being the quantity of asset i in circulation. Then the market capitalization K of the network is defined as follows:

$$K = \sum_{i=1}^{M} N_i P_i$$

As previously discussed, valuing a network is different from valuing the collection of assets using that network.[1] If we were to agree on the value V of a network, we could derive a multiple ρ such that the value is obtained as follows:

$$V = \rho K \tag{5.1}$$

where V represents the network value and K the market capitalization of assets on that network. Throughout this chapter, we will denote K as market capitalization, and V as network value.

This model is the most basic and also the least likely to work. While the intuition is that a network is more valuable if more expensive assets use it, it lacks consideration for the actual drivers of such valuation. This model exhibits susceptibility to high fluctuations of P_i, which can lead to large variations in K and therefore V. There are also significant differences between blockchains, and there is no assurance that ρ would be consistent across them, which is something we will also discuss in similar methodologies such as in Section 5.5.1.

Remark 5.1 *(Governance Tokens)*: In most cases, this methodology is not comparable to the market capitalization of companies in equities. Stocks are floating claims on a company's future cash flows, while most coins are not.

[1] A trivial example is that the value of a supply chain is not the sum of the value of all the goods in it.

The only case where this comparison could be made is for governance tokens. In that case, these tokens can present a close analogy to stocks, where owning all the governance tokens would equate to control over the protocol. However, we argue that in most circumstances, such governance tokens serve dual purposes, including payments.

We do not recommend using this model for valuation, apart from governance tokens as per Remark 5.1.

5.2 BUSINESS VALUATIONS

This section explores valuation methodologies from TradFi. The underlying principle is to view each blockchain as a conventional business and apply known valuation methodologies. This section presents a curated selection rather than an exhaustive catalog of methodologies that could be applied to DeFi networks.

5.2.1 Peer Comparison

Peer comparison methodologies are often referred to as market valuation methodologies. These methodologies are the golden standard in the financial industry, as the best guess for the value of an asset is a recently dealt price for an identical, or at least resembling, asset.

5.2.1.1 Precedent Transaction Analysis Precedent transaction analysis (PTA) is a valuation methodology that assesses a business by examining recent transactions involving similar businesses. The primary limitation is that network acquisitions remain rare in the digital asset space.

However, this would arguably be the most reliable method once more of such transactions are observed and made public. The underlying principle is that a network is worth what a potential buyer would pay to acquire it in its entirety. That potential buyer would probably pay a price similar to the one paid for an identical business in the past.

5.2.1.2 Comparable Company Analysis Comparable company analysis (CCA) is a valuation methodology that looks at financial indicators[2] and compares them to peers with a known or established valuation. This method is widespread but also relies on existing transactions, or at least on another network with a commonly accepted valuation.

We argue that this methodology can be used by looking at blockchain-native indicators, such as the ones discussed in Section 2.4.

While an absolute valuation is not possible until a reference point is established, this method can inform comparisons between networks.

5.2.1.3 Limitations of Peer Comparisons Issues with market valuations include the absence of consideration for broader market sentiment. Most ratios are also lagging and do not account for future growth. In the context of digital asset networks, this is a severe limitation, which leads us to not recommend using these methodologies.

[2]Some of these indicators include price-to-earnings ratio, earnings per share, etc.

5.2.2 Book Valuation

The book value of a business is derived from its balance sheet, which includes assets and liabilities.

This methodology is challenging to apply to networks in general because there are several participants involved, each with their own balance sheet. Because blockchains are decentralized by construction, it is not relevant with respect to the structure of the network.

Furthermore, most assets on the network are intangible and are marked at market value, which fluctuates through time.[3]

5.2.3 Dividend Valuation

The dividend discount valuation (DDV) is a method to value a business by discounting future dividend payments to their present value (PV). The main intuition is that the value of a business corresponds to the total of all future dividend payments received by a shareholder.

Under the assumption of constant business growth over time, this approach is also referred to in the literature as the Gordon growth model. Due to its simplicity, it is commonly used to value high-growth companies and has also been applied to value singular assets such as cryptocurrencies [111].

Definition 5.2 *(Dividend Discount Valuation)***:** Let V be the value of the network, D_t the dividend at time t with all $t \geq 1$ in the future, R the investor's required return, and $\bar{g}$ the perpetual growth rate of the dividend. The value of a network is the sum of all future dividend payments, discounted to the present value:

$$V = \sum_{t \geq 1} \frac{D_t}{(1 + R)^t}$$

The perpetual growth rate is often linked to the expected growth rate of other business parameters, such as sales. The Gordon growth model simplified equation makes the assumption that $g < R$ if both g and R are positive.

Proposition 5.1 *(DDV with Constant Growth)***:** Under the assumption of constant growth, the value of the network is

$$V = \frac{D_1}{R - \bar{g}}$$

with V the value of the network, D_t the dividend at time t, R the investor's required return, and $\bar{g}$ the perpetual growth rate of the dividend.

Proof. The proof is straightforward, knowing that the geometric series with a common ratio strictly less than 1 converges. We define

$$\bar{g} := \frac{D_t}{D_{t-1}} - 1$$

---

[3]US GAAP is actually more conservative and encourages cost accounting as opposed to marking to market for most assets on balance sheets.

the perpetual growth rate of the dividend. We also assume $D_0 = 0$ for simplicity, and we know $D_1 = D_0(1 + \bar{g})$.

$$\begin{aligned} V &= \sum_{t\geq 1} \frac{D_t}{(1+R)^t} \\ &= \sum_{t\geq 0} \frac{D_1(1+g)^t}{(1+R)^t} \\ &= D_1 \frac{1}{R-\bar{g}} \end{aligned}$$

given the common ratio

$$\left| \frac{1+g}{1+R} \right| < 1$$

as per our assumption $g < R$. ■

One of the main limitations with applying this methodology to digital assets is that the concept of dividend is not easy to transpose. One possible interpretation is to look at network fees earned by validators, which we believe is relevant for most layer 1 protocols.

Remark 5.2 ***(Growth Rate Assumptions)*****:** The necessary assumption for the convergence of the Gordon growth model caps the growth rate of the network. This is unrealistic for networks with so-called "explosive" growth in their earliest stage, as observed in early stages of most major altcoins, and for some meme coins.

However, the perpetual growth assumption in the Gordon growth model is problematic as blockchain technologies eventually mature. At that stage, the growth rate $\bar{g}$ can no longer be expected to remain stable and should decrease.

5.2.4 Cash Flow Valuation

The discounted cash flow (DCF) is a method to value a business based on future cash flows. The main intuition is that the value of a business corresponds to the total of all future cash flows. For digital assets, one interpretation would be to look at validator or miner fees. It is arguably one of the most popular valuation methodologies in TradFi, and it is used by most financial analysts.

Definition 5.3 ***(Discounted Cash Flow Valuation)*****:** The value of a network V is the sum of all future cash flows $(CF_t)_{t\geq 1}$, discounted to the present value with the discounting rate R:

$$V = \sum_{t\geq 1} \frac{CF_t}{(1+R)^t}$$

One of the main benefits of the DCF is that it is extremely flexible and can account for different growth regimes. It, however, also relies on precise and accurate forecasting, which we argue is too difficult under conditions of pronounced volatility.

5.3 USER-BASED NETWORK VALUATIONS

In this section, we denote V as the value of the network, N the number of users, and k a constant of proportionality. By construction, $N \in \mathbb{N}_+$ and $k \in \mathbb{R}_+^*$.

5.3.1 Sarnoff's Law

Sarnoff (1891–1971) was an American executive, famous for forming the National Broadcasting Company (NBC) in 1926 in the United States. The linear law that describes the value of a network as a function of the number of users is referred to as Sarnoff's Law in the literature in homage to him.

Definition 5.4 ***(Sarnoff's Law)*****:** The value V of a network is proportional to the number of users[4] N it reaches:

$$V = kN$$

with $k \in \mathbb{R}_+^*$ a constant of proportionality.

5.3.2 Metcalfe's Law

Metcalfe (1946–) is an American engineer and entrepreneur, known for his contributions to the internet[5] in the 1970s. Metcalfe's Law is a step-up from Sarnoff's Law, introducing a square law dependency in the number of users. It is the most commonly used method to value networks.

Definition 5.5 ***(Metcalfe's Law)*****:** The value V of a network is proportional to the square of the number N of users:

$$V = kN^2$$

with $k \in \mathbb{R}_+^*$ a constant of proportionality.

The intuition behind Metcalfe's Law is that the value of a network arises from the number of connections between its participants, as shown in Figure 5.1. The number of unique connections between N users can be expressed as

$$\binom{N}{2} = \frac{N!}{2!(N-2)!} = \frac{N(N-1)}{2}$$

which is close to N^2 for N very large, hence the square law dependency.

Metcalfe's Law is still the industry standard for valuing networks today because of its simplicity and intuition. It remains an essential part of most curriculums in financial analysis and continues to be used as a baseline valuation methodology. It has been actively used in the context of social networks [112–114] and blockchains too [115–118].

[4] This was the number of viewers in the context of the original Sarnoff Law.

[5] Most notably, he is credited for co-inventing Ethernet, a networking technology still in use today.

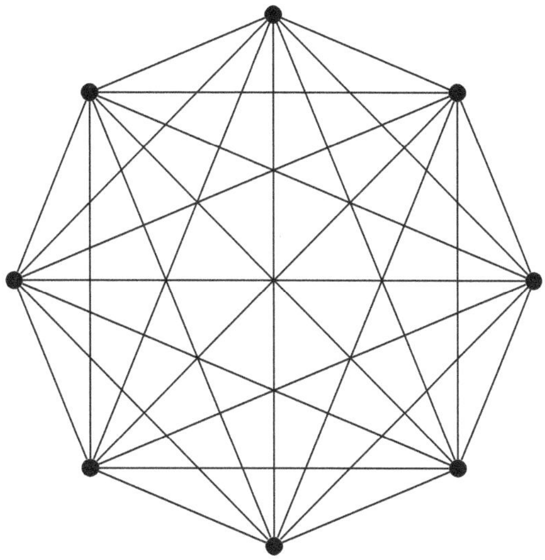

FIGURE 5.1 **Intuition for Metcalfe's Law.** A connected network with eight users, with each user having an individual connection with all others.

5.3.3 Reed's Law

Reed (1952–) is an American computer scientist who worked on networking technologies. He developed an alternative valuation method to Metcalfe's by arguing that the value of a network is linked to the number of potential subnetworks within a larger network.

In group theory, the number of possible subsets of a finite set of size N is given by 2^N. We need to exclude the subsets with zero or one element, which we refer to as the null set and the singletons. This leads to Reed's Law, illustrated in Figure 5.2.

Definition 5.6 ***(Reed's Law)*:** The value V of a network grows with the number of potential subgroups that can be formed, such that

$$V = k(2^N - N - 1)$$

with N the number of users and $k \in \mathbb{R}_+^*$ a constant of proportionality.

Reed's Law is an exponential law and is therefore more aggressive than Metcalfe's Law in terms of valuations.

5.3.4 ZBOT Law

Metcalfe's Law seems accurate in the first stages of a network's growth, where exponential scaling is credible. However, the value of networks to users seems to plateau after a certain point, when the new connections do not bring substantial additional marginal value to users.

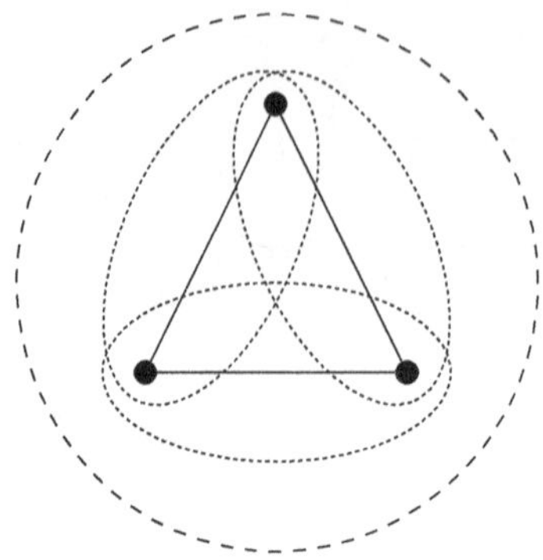

FIGURE 5.2 **Intuition for Reed's Law.** A connected network with three users, with each possible subset accounted for in Reed's Law represented.

Zipf's Law has been proposed as a potential replacement for Metcalfe's Law in the context of network valuations by Briscoe, Odlyzko, and Tilly in 2006 [119]. The Zipf's Law is empirical and was coined by Zipf (1902–1950), a linguist who observed the frequency of words in languages. His observation is that the k-th most frequent word in a language appears with a frequency proportional to $1/k$.

Definition 5.7 ***(Zipf-Briscoe-Odlyzko-Tilly [ZBOT] Law)*:** The value V of a network is proportional to the sum of the logarithm of the number of users N:

$$V = kN \log N$$

with $k \in \mathbb{R}_+^*$ a constant of proportionality.

The intuition is that for any given user of a network, we can rank others by the value they bring to that user. By applying Zipf's Law, we can estimate the value of each user as the frequency of interactions with them. In the original paper [119], the authors use the analogy of an email inbox, but this framework readily extends to payments in a financial system.

In a network with N users, this means there are $N - 1$ other users who will each contribute $1/j$ depending on their rank $j \in [1, N - 1]$. The total value of the network for any given user V_{user} is therefore as follows, by using the harmonic sum:

$$\begin{aligned} V_{\text{user}} &= \sum_{j=1}^{N-1} \frac{1}{j} \\ &= \log(N-1) + \gamma + \mathcal{O}\left(\frac{1}{N-1}\right) \end{aligned}$$

with γ as the Euler-Mascheroni constant. Because the value to all users is computed as the sum of the value to individual users, we obtain for N very large number of users, with N being the number of users:

$$V = NV_{\text{users}} \approx N \log(N)$$

5.4 DISCUSSION ON NETWORK VALUATIONS

5.4.1 Comparison of Network Valuations

If a single valuation function must be selected for networks, we would argue that the ZBOT Law provides an optimal balance and is an elegant generalization of Metcalfe's Law, as shown in Figure 5.3. There are many positive attributes to the ZBOT Law:

- For N small, we know $\log N \approx N$ and therefore, we recover Metcalfe's Law and remain close to Reed's Law.
- For N large, the value of the network grows slower, which is more realistic while not being as conservative as Sarnoff's Law.

However, even the ZBOT Law has limitations in the context of financial networks, which we discuss in the next section.

5.4.2 Limitations

One of the most common criticisms of network valuation is that the quality of each connection in the network, which is the economic value in the context of financial assets, can be very unequal.

It is often argued that there is a ceiling number of connections that any given user can actually value. We can draw the analogy with social sciences, in particular the Dunbar number. Dunbar (1947–) is a British anthropologist who proposed in 1992 that there is a cognitive ceiling to the number of social relationships humans[6] can maintain [120]. Beyond that number, the social connections are of lower quality and are not meaningful. It may therefore be posited that there could be a number of connections in a network beyond which there is no additional value to the user. If that were the case, it would place a limit on the value of every network!

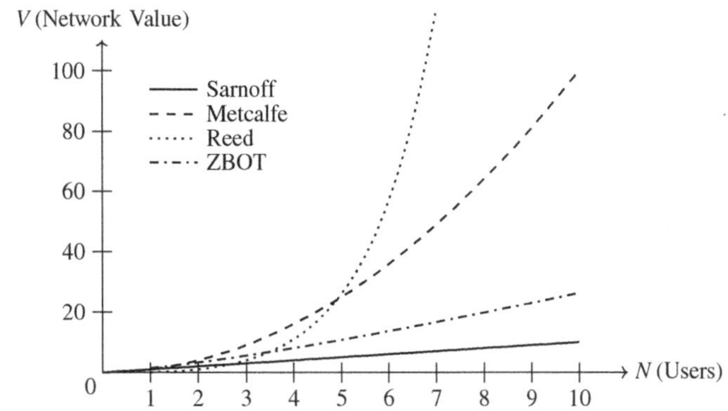

FIGURE 5.3 Comparison of Network Valuations. We can see that Reed's Law is extremely optimistic in terms of valuation compared with the other laws.

[6]The Dunbar number is estimated close to $N_{max} \simeq 150$.

In mathematical terms, it would mean that we would have to calibrate every network valuation to this theoretical maximum value V_{max}, which would be reflected in the constant k.

We note that this is actually captured by the ZBOT Law, although the Dunbar number is more of a hard cap. We shall question if such a hard cap is reasonable because we place value on the option of connecting[7] with people outside our usual network. One should also observe that even accepting that there is a fixed number of users N_{max}, the users that comprise this maximum value subset will change over time.

5.4.3 Beyond User-based Network Valuations

While the ZBOT Law represents a meaningful enhancement of Metcalfe's Law, it is still not clear how accurate it is in the context of digital assets.

There is some ambiguity with what the number N represents. It can be the number of wallets, the mining nodes, or the users of the network. One could also argue, in particular for layer 2 protocols, that N could be the number of applications. This confusion over the definition of N is a limitation of the network valuation theory for digital assets.

5.5 TRANSACTION VOLUME PRICING

The intuition of this valuation method is that the value of a network is proportional to the number of transactions that are processed. This approach addresses several limitations of user-based valuations, most notably the definition of network nodes and the quality of connections. It can also be linked directly to the block time T_b, which is publicly available.

In this section, we will refer to V the value of the network, N the number of transactions processed, and k a constant of proportionality. We also introduce Φ the volume of transactions processed.

5.5.1 Volume Multiple Valuation

The most direct method is to assume that there is a multiplier $k \in \mathbb{R}_+^*$ that links the value of the network to the volume of transactions processed. It is somewhat more refined than the market capitalization multiple, which we discussed in Section 5.1. This is arguably similar to how some investors value payment processing companies.

Definition 5.8 ***(Volume Multiple Valuation)*****:** The value V of a network is proportional to the volume of transactions processed Φ:

$$V = k\Phi$$

with $k \in \mathbb{R}_+^*$ a constant of proportionality.

The main limitation is that the calibration of k is not straightforward. These valuation multiples for stocks are calibrated by looking at peers, which means that this methodology is not absolute but relative. It also means that such valuations are highly sensitive to wash trade for smaller networks.

We recommend against using this methodology.

[7]In the case of financial networks, this means having the option of engaging in a financial transaction.

5.5.2 Block Time Valuations

Sometimes, the volumes processed are either not easy to retrieve or are hidden, typically via encryption. As security concerns have grown in recent years, it is a fair assumption that an increasing number of blockchains will be developed with such privacy features. In that case, looking at the block time T_b is more relevant.

On the Bitcoin blockchain[8] for example, the block time T_b can be linked to the number of transactions processed. That is because each block has a maximum size, which caps the number of transactions that can be recorded per block. This feature is shared by several blockchains, which means that it serves as an upper boundary $N_{\max}$ to the number of transactions processed.

5.5.3 Cost Accounting

An intuitive method of valuing a network is to look at the cost of running it. These cost accounting valuations correspond to a break-even point where nodes that operate the network are compensated for their costs. This method is not interested in the details of the compensation structure of the node operators but looks at the overall inputs and outputs of the network as a whole.

Most of these methodologies are referred to as energy-based valuations in the context of blockchains. Early models focused on PoW networks, but the ideas can easily be extended to other consensus mechanisms where validators are needed.

5.5.3.1 Historical Cost-based Pricing The most direct application of cost accounting to digital asset valuation emerged with Bitcoin's earliest pricing mechanism. Historically, the very first Bitcoin listed price was derived out of the cost of electricity [11]. Daily rate updates characterized this earliest methodology to price a digital asset. Another way to represent this methodology is how much it would cost a lone operator to run the exact same network on their own. The New Liberty Standard Rate was defined as follows:

> Our exchange rate is calculated by dividing \$1.00 by the average amount of electricity required to run a computer with high CPU for a year, 1331.5 kWh, multiplied by the average residential cost of electricity in the United States for the previous year, \$0.1136, divided by 12 months divided by the number of bitcoins generated by my computer over the past 30 days.

We note that a small spread, in the order of magnitude of one-tenth of a basis point, was charged on top of the PayPal transaction fee [11]. Additionally noteworthy is that the methodology uses the retail electricity rate, which is expected given the temporal context and user demographics and operators of the network at that time.

Definition 5.9 ***(New Liberty Standard Rate)*:** The exchange rate $X_{\text{USD/BTC}}$ is a function of the cost per unit of electricity C_E, the computing power of the node P_E, and the number of transactions N_T with a normalization constant k:

$$X_{\text{USD/BTC}} = k\frac{P_E C_E}{N_T}$$

[8] A distinctive feature of Bitcoin is that volumes are public.

The conventional units are *USD/kWh* for C_E, *kWh* for P_E, and *BTC* for N_T. k is dimensionless and adjusts the different horizons to average the values.

5.5.3.2 Network Valuation from Cost Accounting We can immediately infer from Definition 5.9 a network valuation methodology that extends beyond individual exchange rates to total network value.

Definition 5.10 ***(New Liberty Standard Network Valuation)*:** The value of the network V is a function of the cost per unit of electricity C_E, the computing power of the node P_E, the number of transactions N_T, the number of coins N_C, and a normalization constant k:

$$V = N_C \cdot k \frac{P_E C_E}{N_T}$$

The original New Liberty Standard can be refined to reflect actual network conditions. An enhanced version would adjust electricity costs to reflect the actual cost of energy where most mining nodes are located, and update computing power requirements to reflect modern hardware.

We introduce $\bar{C}_E$, the average cost of electricity, weighted by the local electricity costs in countries with miners or validators. P_E is adjusted to the computing power of more recent mining hardware, or validator where appropriate.

Definition 5.11 ***(Global New Liberty Standard Rate)*:** The value of the network V is a function of the average cost per unit of electricity $\bar{C}_E$, the computing power of the node P_E, the velocity of money ν, and a normalization constant $k \in \mathbb{R}^*$:

$$V = k \frac{P_E \bar{C}_E}{\nu}$$

There are other cost accounting models based on factor analysis that are being researched to determine the value of a network and individual assets on the network. Hayes' work on a cost of production model for Bitcoin is a notable contribution [121–123] in the field. These models typically incorporate additional factors such as mining difficulty adjustments, hardware depreciation, and operational costs beyond electricity.

This method is relevant to Bitcoin, for which it was developed, given that the mining process for the PoW is computationally very intensive. Because all inputs are parameters intrinsic to how the network functions, it can be used as a network valuation methodology.

5.5.3.3 Connection to Monetary Theory The ratio N_C/N_T in Definition 5.10 reveals an important connection to macroeconomic concepts. This measure is actually close to the velocity of money used in macroeconomics, which is most commonly defined as

$$\nu = \frac{GNP}{M}$$

with GNP the Gross National Product[9] and M the money supply. $M \simeq M_2$ is often used as a broad measure[10] of the amount of money in circulation, which includes cash and deposit accounts.

We offer analogous definitions in the context of cryptocurrencies.

Definition 5.12 ***(Monetary Supply)*:** The monetary supply is the number of coins or tokens in circulation N_C.

In this context, N_C is the total number of assets created, minus the ones destroyed. Assets which are lost, locked,[11] or in a strategic reserve are not considered destroyed.

Remark 5.3: With respect to dimensional analysis, N_C has actually a unit in Definition 5.12. It is the coin or token unit itself.

The velocity of money ν is often associated to Fisher's equation of exchange [124]:

$$M\nu = PT$$

with M the money supply, P a reference price level, and T the value of transactions. We introduce Definition 5.13 for cryptocurrencies.

Definition 5.13 ***(Velocity of Money)*:** The velocity of money ν is the ratio of the number of coins or tokens in circulation N_C to the number of transactions N_T.

$$\nu = \frac{N_T}{N_C}$$

Remark 5.4: One can argue that Definition 5.13 is closer to coin utilization than Fisher's equation of exchange [124]. However, we make the approximation that $M_2 \approx N_C$ and $PT \approx N_T$.

We want to highlight works on more refined definitions of the velocity of money in the context of cryptocurrencies [127, 128] and, in particular, Campajola et al.'s MicroVelocity [129], which is tailored to digital assets.

We can now rewrite Definition 5.10 using the velocity of money concept.

Corollary 5.1: *Using the same notations as Definitions 5.10 and 5.13:*

$$V = k\frac{P_E C_E}{\nu}$$

This theoretical framework demonstrates how cost accounting approaches to network valuation connect to fundamental monetary economics, providing a bridge between the practical energy-based models and broader economic theory.

---

[9]Sometimes the gross domestic product (GDP) is used instead.

[10]Conventional measures of monetary supply are numbered M_0 to M_4, with M_0 the strictest definition and M_4 the broadest. Not all countries publish all statistics, and the methodologies differ slightly from country to country. M_2 has become the standard as it is continuously published by the US Federal Reserve and includes bank reserves [125, 126].

[11]This could be in smart contracts or for staking.

5.6 FACTOR ANALYSIS

Factor analysis, or factor models, are a class of valuation models that aim to identify variables, called factors, that drive the value of an asset. In the context of network valuations, these are a generalization of several of the previously discussed methodologies.

The Capital Asset Pricing Model (CAPM) is one of the first and most commonly used factor models in finance. It is a linear model that relates the expected return of an asset to the broader market risk [130–133].

5.6.1 Fundamental Factor Analysis

One approach is to select a set of factors believed to have an impact on the value of an asset, for instance a network. These factors are typically picked based on economic parameters and expert knowledge. This methodology can also be extended to use the value of the coins and become a "smarter" market capitalization approach, as described in Section 5.1, that finds the optimal combination of factors for valuation.

These are commonly designated as risk factors or style factors, depending on their source [133].

The most common approach is to use price returns R_c, local variations of the asset price, which we discuss in more detail in Section 10.2, and introduce corresponding factors $(f_i)_i$. Such a model would usually be linear and assign weights $(\omega_i)_i$, such that

$$\forall t, \quad R_c(t) = \sum_i \omega_i f_i(t) + \varepsilon(t)$$

with ε the error term, which we expect under proper calibration of the model to be identically independently distributed.

Synthetic factors might be created at this stage of the process. These are akin to engineered features in machine learning, with the aim of creating more accurate or better quantified factors than original ones. When some inputs are using unquantified data, such a step is necessary to include the corresponding information in the final model. We commonly remove the original features when introducing a synthetic factor to avoid redundancy of information. The weights assigned to the factors are often called loadings, and the stability of the loadings for different training sets is a proxy for factor stability.[12]

We can then average out over longer horizons T the value of these factors and, using the number of coins N_C in circulation, derive an estimate of the network value V. We use the same corrective term as introduced in Equation 5.1 in Section 5.1:

$$V(t) = \frac{\rho N_C}{T} \int_{t-T}^{t} R_c(u)\, du$$

Averaging helps to smooth short-term fluctuations, which corresponds to canceling out the error term ε:

$$V(t) = \frac{\rho N_C}{T} \sum_i \omega_i \int_{t-T}^{t} f_i(u)\, du \tag{5.2}$$

[12]A popular methodology to create robust synthetic factors, with stable loadings, is Cross-validation (CV). It consists in splitting the training and testing dataset into different subsets, called folds, and iterating through training and testing on these folds—instead of having only one training subset and one testing subset.

This allows us to compute $V(t)$ as a function of the factors $f_i(u)$ and their corresponding weights ω_i derived by calibration.

Liu et al.'s 2019 work [134] is one of the most cited[13] factor models for cryptocurrency returns. They explored several common factors, such as volatility and liquidity, and showed good fit on an excess return model with three factors: market, size, and momentum. Factor structure was highlighted not only on cryptocurrency returns, but also on volatility [135, 136], in particular for Bitcoin.

Once several factors are selected, they are typically combined by regression to derive a valuation model. Linear regressions are most common, with coefficients estimated numerically using historical data. Such factors are often constructed as a standalone portfolio, with its performance regressed and compared to that of the digital asset. This methodology is called the factor mimicking portfolio and is credited to Fama[14] and MacBeth [137].

Remark 5.5: Fundamental factor analysis is closely linked to the quantamental style of investing. This approach combines elements of quantitative analysis, such as factor analysis, with fundamental analysis, which is the study of the value of an asset based on economic factors.

5.6.2 Regressions

A simple and commonly used regression method is Ordinary Least Squares (OLS). Under OLS, we aim to find the best-fitting linear relationship between the factors and the target variable. For a dataset with observations at times $t_1, t_2, \ldots, t_n$, the matrix representation is commonly used, with

$$\mathbf{v} = \rho N_C \cdot \mathbf{F}\boldsymbol{\omega}$$

where $\mathbf{v}$ is the vector of normalized valuations $\left[\frac{V(t_1)}{\rho N_C}, \frac{V(t_2)}{\rho N_C}, \ldots, \frac{V(t_n)}{\rho N_C}\right]^T$, $\mathbf{F}$ is the $n \times k$ matrix with factors $f_i(t_j)$, and $\boldsymbol{\omega}$ is the vector of weights $[\omega_1, \omega_2, \ldots, \omega_k]^T$.

This matrix formulation is equivalent to the time-dependent representation:

$$V(t) = \rho N_C \sum_i \omega_i f_i(t)$$

It is simple to implement,[15] and its coefficients are easy to interpret. However, OLS tends to perform poorly when there is strong correlation between the factors. In the context of regression, we call multicollinearity the situation when two inputs are highly correlated.

Because OLS will tend to assign a weight to each factor, when the number of factors is large, other methods such as LASSO[16] [139] and Ridge regression [140] are used instead. These methods are referred to as shrinkage methods, as they shrink the

[13] We strongly encourage the reader interested in factor analysis to get familiar with that paper [134], which was one of the first rigorous applications to cryptocurrencies.

[14] That same methodology would become the basis of the Fama-French model [138], which expanded the CAPM.

[15] The simplest form of OLS does not even need any code, and conventional spreadsheet software suffices.

[16] LASSO stands for Least Absolute Shrinkage and Selection Operator.

coefficients assigned to input factors that are less significant. While these methodologies are better at handling multicollinearity, they generate parsimonious models which can be less robust in operational contexts.[17] LASSO in particular has been used for multiple applications in cryptocurrencies, both in return prediction [136, 141, 142] and for risk management [143].

5.6.3 Principal Component Analysis

Sometimes, it is difficult to identify factors, even with regression methodologies that can select among different features. An alternative approach involves constructing new features as a combination of original ones, with the aim of reducing the number of inputs into the final model. This process is referred to as dimensionality reduction.

We introduce principal component analysis (PCA) [144, 145], one of the most popular algorithmic methods to derive such factors. PCA is a statistical method that reduces the dimensionality of a dataset. It takes a set of vectors, which for instance are potential factors, and finds a new set of orthogonal vectors that are linear combinations of the original ones. The new vectors are called principal components. It is sometimes called spectral decomposition, in reference to the algebraic method used to derive the principal components.

The covariance matrix of the original factors is computed, and by eigendecomposition, the principal components are derived as the eigenvectors, and the corresponding eigenvalues are the variance explained by each component. By convention, the principal components are ordered by decreasing eigenvalues, which means decreasing explainability of the initial dataset. It follows that only the first few, if not only the first, principal components are used in practice. The first principal component is the one that explains the most variance and, therefore, is the most significant [146, 147].

PCA has been used in the context of cryptocurrencies to derive factors that explain both price returns [148–150] and volatility [136]. It is also used to construct PCA-based indices [150].

While PCA is very robust, its main downside is that the principal components may not be interpretable financially. Furthermore, because in practice only the first few principal components are used, there is some loss of information, as for all dimensionality reduction techniques.

5.6.4 Limitations

By construction, factor analysis is dependent on the quality of factors. Some factors may have high explainability but might be difficult to quantify or might be excessively lagging. Synthetic factors might be created to address this issue, but they can be difficult to interpret. These limitations apply to all factor analysis and are not specific to digital assets.

In the context of digital assets, most factor analysis approaches were applied to derive a fundamental value for the price of a coin or token. As we explained in Section 5.1, we believe this is erroneous in most cases. However, by regressing the returns of the coin, several technical factors that drive the price are identified [151], which can inform other valuation methodologies. Such technical factors include network parameters and transaction costs.

---

[17] Having multiple factors related to one another in a model can create some operational redundancy.

5.7 RELATIVE VALUE PRICING AND INTERCHAIN BASIS

In this section, we develop the idea of the valuation of the network as a network failure risk premium. The concept of risk premium is also often tied to factor analysis [152–154]. In particular, we explore how wrapped tokens can serve as a lens for understanding relative network risks across different blockchains.

An essential property of digital assets is that they only bear value as long as the underlying blockchain is active. If the network permanently fails, then the asset becomes worthless. This is a key difference with traditional assets, where the value is not inherently linked to a network infrastructure.

We argue that this property is important to price wrapped tokens, which are tokens that are issued on one blockchain to represent an asset on another blockchain. The value of the wrapped token is linked to the value of the underlying asset, but it may also reflect the network over which it is issued. The analogy with conventional finance is the credit default swap (CDS), which is a derivative that is essentially an insurance against the default of another counterparty.

It should be noted that the idea of analyzing the prices of cryptocurrencies based on risk premium has been explored across the literature [155]. We have not seen the analogy with CDSs yet, and this analogy provides valuable insights.

Another benefit of this analogy is that it allows for the pricing of different blockchain networks, relatively to another chain, and in particular relative network failure[18] risks.

5.7.1 Credit Default Swap Basics

Modern CDSs are attributed to Blythe Masters, a JP Morgan banker, in 1994. A CDS is a contract between a protection seller and a protection buyer. CDSs are in widespread use, especially after the GFC. The protection seller agrees to compensate the buyer in the event of a credit event on a third party, called the reference entity. While CDSs are designed to insure the buyer in the event of default on a bond issued by the reference entity, it is not necessary to hold one of such bonds to purchase a CDS.[19]

Credit events commonly include bankruptcies, failure to pay, or restructuring. The price of the insurance is called the protection premium, or spread, and is paid by the buyer to the seller periodically. CDSs are commonly priced either by computing a premium to the underlying bond of the reference entity and assuming no-arbitrage[20] or by using probability of default [157–159]. The CDS is therefore a representation of the credit risk.

The premiums are usually quoted in basis points and are expressed as the percentage of the notional amount of the contract being paid annually. CDSs typically have a term of five years in TradFi.

[18] We refer to network failure in the broadest sense: technical issues, loss of users, depletion of liquidity, and security shortfalls are all encompassed in our definition in this context.

[19] This is discussed in Michael Lewis' famous book, *The Big Short* [156].

[20] We discuss this concept more formally in Section 12.2.1.1.

5.7.2 Interchain Basis

Before examining how wrapped tokens might price network risk, we first establish the concept of interchain basis, the price differential between wrapped tokens and their underlying assets.

We will refer to basis in this section as a difference in pricing, the spread, between two digital assets representing the same underlying.

An analogy can be drawn with the onshore-offshore basis that exists for some FX markets, where the value of the domestic currency against the United States Dollar is slightly different in the onshore market, compared with international, offshore, markets. This basis is often the result of regulations that prevent ease of bringing liquidity inside and outside the country. In such analogy, the onshore price is the wrapped token, and the offshore price is the underlying. The convertibility of the currency is the key factor that determines how large the basis is, and how stable it is. Less convertible currencies with stronger capital controls will lead to larger and less stable basis; while more easily convertible currencies will lead to smaller, stable basis.

One of the main benefits of wrapped tokens compared with using native coins on their original chains is to benefit from potential speed improvements on a given blockchain compared with another. This means that when analyzing a potential price difference between a wrapped token and its underlying asset, one must consider the network effects and transaction efficiencies of the respective blockchains. A similar argument can be made with regard to sidechains.

One of the most notable examples is Polygon, which is a sidechain of Ethereum. Wrapped Ether on Polygon should theoretically trade at a premium compared with Ether on Ethereum because of the faster transaction times and lower transaction fees, making it more desirable.

Empirical evidence does not support this hypothesis over sustained periods.

This implies that the market did not reach consensus of the relative convenience of wrapped tokens compared with their underlying.

5.7.3 Network Default Swaps

A wrapped token is analogous to a CDS. Such tokens allow assets from one blockchain to remain tradable on another. The wrapped token value thus tracks the underlying asset while reflecting the risk profile of the issuing network. As a result, we argue that wrapped tokens can serve as a hedge against network-specific risks and that this should manifest as a small discount or premium relative to the underlying asset, depending on the market's relative perception of risk on each network.

When applied to an individual wrapped token, the basis carries two risks of default at the same time:

Guaranteed entity corresponds to the parent blockchain of the coin.

Protection seller corresponds to the custodian that will manage the wrapped token.

There are often multiple wrapped tokens bridging two networks. By averaging their prices, we can mitigate idiosyncratic risks from different custodians.[21]

[21]There are past, and unfortunately current, examples of wrapped tokens trading at a discount specifically due to custodian risks.

Currently, wrapped token arbitrage opportunities resolve rapidly and do not persist, indicating that markets view most blockchains as stable and assign them similar failure risk. If a sufficiently liquid network were to fail, its wrapped token on a more stable chain would decouple and trade at a premium. Conversely, a wrapped token issued on a less stable network may trade at a discount. Using the same rationale as CDS for corporate bonds, one could theoretically construct network default swaps, equating the interchain basis to the relative failure probability between two chains.

The implicit corollary of the previous observation is that, as of now, it is implied that no blockchain is at greater failure risk than another.

Remark 5.6 *(Theoretical Framework)*: Our Network Default Swaps framework is a theoretical lens for understanding wrapped tokens. This framework presents wrapped tokens as implicit CDS instruments that could potentially price relative network failure risk and formalizes the interchain basis as a measure of blockchain risk differentials. However, this remains an open research question.

There are two main limitations to solely relying on one specific wrapped token to assess network risk:

- Idiosyncratic risks linked to that wrapped token, such as custodian risk, which we discuss in Section 6.4.2
- Other liquidity effects, including network congestions

An ideal assessment would rely on multiple wrapped tokens and adequate time to smooth out temporary liquidity effects.

Open Problems

These thought experiments are guided explorations into the concepts discussed in this part of the book.
Hints are available at www.tomespel.com/books/mfin25.

Problem II.1: A token on a blockchain changes from payment token to governance token. How does this affect the valuation of the blockchain?

Problem II.2: The ZBOT Law suggests network value grows as $N \log N$. On blockchains like Bitcoin, the same user can generate multiple wallets at zero cost. How does this affect network valuation?

Problem II.3: Two wrapped tokens trading of the same underlying asset, trading on the same blockchain, trade persistently at different prices. How does this impact the valuation of the underlying asset? Can we trade this as an arbitrage?

Problem II.4: Two blockchains networks are connected via a new bridge. How does this impact the valuation of each network?

PART

Three

Market Structure

"Logic, reason and common sense are your best tools for synthesizing reality and understanding what to do about it."

Ray Dalio, Principles: Life and Work

CHAPTER 6

Carry and Storage

Digital assets present unique custody considerations and infrastructure requirements that differ fundamentally from traditional securities. This chapter examines carry and storage costs in DeFi, their impact on valuation models, and the specific risks they introduce to pricing frameworks.

- Analyze DeFi lending mechanisms and implications of margin trading, including liquidation cascades.
- Develop cost of carry models for digital assets, incorporating convenience yields and blockchain-specific characteristics.
- Examine digital asset custody arrangements and their implications for storage costs and counterparty risk.

We begin by exploring lending practices in DeFi and their impact on asset pricing.

6.1 LENDING AND MARGIN

There are two main ways lending can be observed in the DeFi space: conventional loan agreements and margin trading.

Conventional lending and borrowing involves a borrower paying interest in exchange for cryptocurrency assets. One specificity of DeFi is that the lending rates are often quoted in hours, alongside the more conventional annual equivalent. Most of the time, the loans are collateralized and can offer leverage up to 5×. In the context of lending and borrowing, this is often quoted as a loan-to-value (LTV) ratio, which is the ratio of the value of the loan to the value of the collateral. To illustrate, a 5× leverage[1] means that the LTV is 80%. Loan contract terms, such as maturity, are set in advance, and borrowers can usually use the borrowed funds for any purpose, including trading or investing. Borrowers can therefore express a short view by selling the asset and buying it back at maturity.

[1]In this context, we mean that this implies one unit of capital contributed and four units borrowed.

DeFi greatly facilitates peer-to-peer lending, in particular via layer 3 applications such as Aave [160] and Compound [161]. Most of these dApps rely on collateralization.[2] The main differences with loans in TradFi banking are

- the lending pool is fully collateralized; there is no fractional reserve banking;
- the interest rate is determined by the supply and demand for the asset and can differ between lending protocols.

Remark 6.1 *(Flash Loans)*: Not all DeFi lending is collateralized. One notable example is flash loans, which must be repaid within the same transaction block.

Some exchanges will offer margin accounts to investors. Margin accounts allow investors to borrow funds to open a long position greater than their own capital would have allowed. On margin, the agreement is ongoing for as long as the position is open and is marked to market at regular intervals. When the unrealized PnL of the position falls below a certain threshold, the exchange will issue a margin call, which requires the investor to either deposit more funds or close the position. If the investor fails to comply with the margin call, the exchange will proceed to liquidation. Because of the volatility of cryptocurrencies, marking to market is done at much higher frequency than in TradFi, and the liquidation can usually be triggered in a matter of minutes. The typical leverages available on such margin accounts can reach more than 100× on some leading platforms.[3] While margins are more common for derivatives, such as futures that we discussed in Section 3.2.4.3, they can also be offered on spot markets.

Remark 6.2: Margin trading carries substantial risk and can result in substantial losses, including total position wipeouts, for less experienced traders.

Margin accounts, which have grown in popularity for cryptocurrencies, result in two important differences compared with TradFi markets:

- Liquidations can more easily cascade as the forced sale of positions can itself move the price and trigger further liquidations, and these are referred to as cascading liquidations. We provide an illustration of these in Figure 6.1. Cascading liquidations are highly prevalent in cryptocurrency markets and therefore contribute to volatility.
- The derivatives market, which typically allows for the greatest levels of leverage on margin, is more liquid than the spot market, with strong retail participation.

As mentioned in Section 3.2.4.4, the perpetual futures contract is the most liquid contract for most cryptocurrencies.

[2] In practice, this means borrowers deposit assets on self-custodial wallets, and interact with the liquidity pool through smart contracts.
[3] This is far greater than what most TradFi brokers would offer for most stocks, in particular to retail investors.

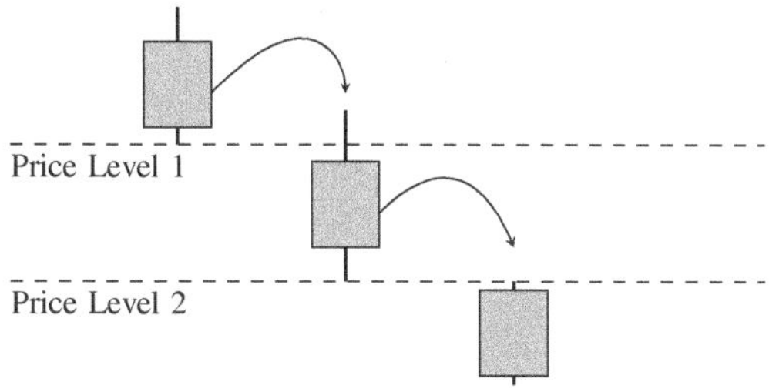

FIGURE 6.1 **Illustration of Cascading Liquidations.** Price drops trigger liquidations at successive price levels, causing further downward moves and additional liquidations.

Remark 6.3: There is a pronounced asymmetry between the potential leverage available, which can only support long positions, and the potential borrowing available, which can support short positions. This imbalance is also observed in TradFi markets, but is much more pronounced in DeFi markets. One may argue that it is more a product of recent strong asset price growth rather than a contributing factor.

6.2 CARRY AND FORWARD PRICING

We now turn to the fundamental pricing relationships that govern these assets. The concept of carry, the cost or benefit of holding an asset over time, forms the backbone of forward pricing across both traditional and digital markets.

We introduced forward contracts in Section 3.2.4.2 as a way to lock in a price for an asset at a future date. We will now discuss them in more detail with the concept of carry.

6.2.1 Forward Pricing Framework

In this section, we describe forward contract prices. Before we begin, let us recall an important result in pricing theory that shows the relationship between futures prices and forward prices.

Proposition 6.1: The price of futures contracts and forward contracts for the same underlying and maturity are equivalent under no-arbitrage conditions.

Proof. Under no-arbitrage conditions, we show that the daily settlement of the profits and losses of the futures contract is equivalent to holding the position to maturity. The intuition is that the daily settlement allows the investor to reinvest the profits at the risk-free rate.

We direct the reader to Geman, who provided the detailed proof of this result [162]. ■

We present no-arbitrage more formally in Section 12.2.1.1. Under no-arbitrage conditions, the forward price is determined by the spot price and the cost of holding the asset for the duration of the contract. For financial assets, this is usually the borrowing rate, usually expressed as a continuous compounding rate.

Definition 6.1 *(Forward Price [Without Cost of Holding])*: The forward price F of an asset at time t is the price agreed upon today for delivery at maturity M, which is determined by the spot price S and the discounting rate r as follows:

$$F(t; M) = S(t)e^{\int_t^M r(u)du}$$

where $M > t$ represents the maturity date of the forward contract.

It is important to note that the forward price does not reflect a prediction of the price of the underlying in the future; it is entirely determined by the current spot price and the costs to hold the asset until maturity [163]. When there is a cost associated with holding the asset, such as storage, a corrective term is added to the forward price, as per Definition 6.2.

Definition 6.2 *(Forward Price [with Cost of Holding])*: The forward price F of an asset at time t is the price agreed upon today for delivery at maturity M, which is determined by the spot price S, the discounting rate r, and the cost of holding q as follows:

$$F(t; M) = S(t)e^{\int_t^M (r(u)-q(u))du}$$

For financial assets, the cost of holding is usually negligible. This is not the case for commodities, and it is known as the cost of carry [164], which we define in Definition 6.4.

6.2.2 Foreign Exchange Forward Pricing

We first discuss a special case of the forward price, which is the forward price in FX markets, in Definition 6.3.

FX currency pairs are expressed under the convention BASE/QUOTE, such that USD/HKD has the US dollar (USD) as base and the Hong Kong dollar (HKD) as quote. It is the price paid in quote to acquire one unit of the base currency. Quotations against USD are called direct pairs, and quotations between non-USD pairs are called crosses.

For cryptocurrencies, all quotes against USD or stablecoins are typically expressed with the cryptocurrency instrument as the base, such as BTC/USD. This is the same convention as for the commodities markets, such as gold XAU/USD.

Remark 6.4: There are market conventions as to which pairs are quoted in which direction, such that USD/HKD is quoted, but not HKD/USD. These conventions also apply to crosses, where there is a hierarchy of which currency takes precedence as the base. These conventions are less clear for cryptocurrencies, but the rule of thumb is that the strongest cryptocurrency[4] is the base currency, which is usually Bitcoin (BTC) or Ethereum (ETH), depending on the market.

For FX forward contracts, the replication consists of borrowing in one currency and lending in another. For the pair BASE/QUOTE, the spot price allows an investor who has

[4]This is usually to avoid too many decimals in the prices!

borrowed the base currency to acquire the quote and lend it at the quote interest rate. This is reflected in the interest rate differential between the two currencies in Definition 6.3.

Definition 6.3 *(Forward Price [FX])*: The forward price F of a currency pair BASE/QUOTE at time t is the price agreed upon today for delivery at maturity M, which is determined by the spot price S as follows:

$$F_{\text{base/quote}}(t; M) = S_{\text{base/quote}}(t)\left(\frac{1 + r_{\text{base}}}{1 + r_{\text{quote}}}\right)^{M-t}$$

where r_{base} and r_{quote} are the discretely compounded interest rates, here assumed annualized for the period from t to maturity M, of the base and quote currencies, respectively.

We note in Definition 6.3 that the forward price is expressed under discrete compounding, as per Definition 12.6, as opposed to the exponential form of the forward price in Definition 6.2 using continuous compounding. This is a matter of convention in the FX markets, where the forward points are also expressed as a linear function of the interest rate differential between the two currencies, as per Definition 3.9. It is possible to use continuous compounding instead, as per Equation 12.4, but this is not the quoting convention in FX markets.

We will provide several examples of simple carry contracts in Chapter 15.

6.3 COST OF CARRY AND CONVENIENCE YIELD

While forward pricing provides the theoretical framework for valuing future delivery contracts, carry represents the net cost or benefit of holding an asset over a specific period. In traditional markets, carry typically includes the following:

- Storage costs for physical commodities
- Financing costs (the interest paid to borrow funds to purchase the asset)
- Income from the asset (dividends, coupons, or lending fees)
- Convenience yield (the benefit of holding the physical asset)

The cost of carry is the cost arising from holding an asset over time. It is usually associated with commodities and reflects the expenses of the holder, such as storage, insurance, and costs of financing. For TradFi financial assets, such as stocks, the cost of carry is often negligible, although it may include financing costs.

For DeFi assets, carry takes on unique characteristics. While there are no physical storage costs, custody and security considerations create operational expenses. Additionally, digital assets can generate income through staking, lending protocols, or liquidity provision, creating positive carry opportunities that differ from traditional markets.

Definition 6.4 *(Cost of Carry)*: The cost of carry is the total cost of holding a position in an asset, including storage, insurance, and financing costs. Let an asset with price S at time t and future price F at maturity date M. We define the cost of carry C as follows:

$$F(t; M) = S(t)e^{C(t;M)}$$

Remark 6.5: We note that the cost of carry in Definition 6.4 is not expressed linearly but in the exponential form, like a compounding rate as per Section 12.2.4. This is because it is viewed as an opportunity cost on capital, which accrues over time.

In the context of markets such as FX, the cost of carry as per Definition 6.4 is also associated with the forward points, which are linear as per Definition 3.9. It then refers to an interest rate differential between two currencies and represents the so-called carry trade.[5] That terminology might appear misleading, given the fact that the costs of holding the assets are markedly low. However, it represents the cost of opportunity for the investor, who divested capital in one currency to invest in another.

In commodities markets, the cost of carry is most often positive, which corresponds to a contango market, where the future price is higher than the spot price.[6] We examine this in more detail in Section 3.2.4.2.

Markets in backwardation present the opposite opportunity, when the cost of carry is negative, and the future price is lower than the spot price. This typically occurs when there is a benefit to holding the physical asset rather than a futures contract.

In that case, the underlying asset trades at a premium to the derivative, and the difference is called the convenience yield, as per Definition 6.5.

Definition 6.5 ***(Convenience Yield)*****:** The convenience yield y in the context of derivatives is the net economic benefit b derived from holding the cash asset instead of its derivative, minus its cost of holding q:

$$y = b - q$$

The concept of convenience yield is attributed to Kaldor [165] and Working [166], who introduced it in the context of commodities in the late 1940s [162]. It was most notably highlighted in the context of cryptocurrencies by Geman and Price [167, 168].

Remark 6.6: Both definitions of convenience yield y, which include the cost of holding the asset [162, 169] or exclude it [163, 170], coexist. In the latter case, it corresponds to b in Definition 6.5, and is sometimes referred to as pure convenience yield.

We prefer the former definition since, in some cases, the cost of holding can be negative, meaning that the holder receives a benefit from holding the asset. This can be in the form of staking for some tokens. Representing y as the net benefit of holding the asset, including the cost of holding, allows us to capture this effect.

The pure benefit of holding the asset, b, can be viewed by some as a market anomaly. It is, however, crucial in the context of commodities, where it tends to be linked to the inventory levels of the underlying. Convenience yields can be expressed for cryptocurrencies, most notably for Bitcoin [167, 168], which has had futures contracts since 2017.

---

[5]The carry trade is a strategy where an investor borrows in a low-interest-rate currency and invests in a high-interest-rate currency. The PnL of the investor arises from the interest rate differential.

[6]There are even situations of hypercontango, when the cost of carry becomes so high that spot prices can become negative. This was briefly the case in 2020 in the oil market, due to a lack of storage.

Remark 6.7: Positive convenience yields arise when two criteria are met:

- The cost of storage is low, meaning it is not too costly to hold inventory.
- The inventory levels are low, which corresponds to the commodity being scarce.

In these circumstances, given the low inventories and cheap storage, investors are willing to pay a premium to hold the asset themselves, which is the convenience yield from Definition 6.5.

By convention, the convenience yield is expressed as a percentage of the spot price [162]. We can derive a more general equation for the forward contract, which extends on Definition 6.2.

Definition 6.6 ***(Forward Price [with Convenience Yield])*****:** The forward price $F(t; M)$ of an asset at time t is the price agreed upon today for delivery at maturity M, which is determined by the spot price S, the discounting rate r, and the convenience yield y as follows:

$$F(t; M) = S(t)\left(1 + \int_t^M (r(u) - y(u))du\right)$$

When convenience yield exceeds the cost of carry, the market enters backwardation. Conversely, when the cost of carry exceeds the convenience yield, the market is in contango, with futures prices higher than spot prices.

Remark 6.8 ***(Convenience Yield in DeFi)*****:** In the context of DeFi, the convenience yield can be linked to staking rewards, since the underlying asset can be staked directly. We present this in more detail in Chapter 17. This corresponds to a pure benefit $b > 0$. If costs of storage remain low $q \simeq 0$, this can lead to a positive convenience yield $y > 0$.

On the other hand, because storage costs are linked to expected gas usage, typically in the form of smart contracts, q can exceed b, leading to a negative convenience yield $y < 0$. This is especially the case when gas fees are associated with operating the contract, such as for custodians described in Section 6.4.2.

In most cases, we will use average values $\bar{r}, \bar{y}$ over the contract period, resulting in a simplified representation of Definition 6.6:

$$F(t; M) = S(t)\left(1 + \left(\bar{r} - \bar{y}\right)(M - t)\right)$$

We can obviously expand the convenience yield to include the average cost of holding $\bar{q}$, as per Definition 6.5, which results in the following [163, 170]:

$$F(t; M) = S(t)\left(1 + \left(\bar{r} + \bar{q} - \bar{b}\right)(M - t)\right)$$

In some cases, the cost of carry c from Definition 6.4 is more narrowly defined as the pure costs of holding the assets $r + q$, minus the pure economic benefit b [163]. This leads to Definition 6.7.

Definition 6.7 ***(Forward Price [with Pure Cost of Carry]):*** Let an asset with price S at time t and future price F at maturity date M. We can express the price of the forward contract F with the pure cost of carry c, alongside the net pure economic benefit b:

$$F(t; M) = S(t) \exp\left(\int_t^M (c(u) - b(u))du\right)$$

Definition 6.7 is more often used in theoretical contexts and aligns with Definition 6.4 when the pure economic benefit b is zero, which is the case for many financial products.

6.4 DIGITAL ASSET CUSTODY

The custodian for digital assets is not in charge of the asset, but rather the private key that allows access to the asset. This is a fundamental difference from traditional custodians who hold physical assets or securities.

6.4.1 Wallet Types

In Section 1.2.1, we introduced the concept of wallet as a cryptographic key, called the private key, which enables the holder to authorize outbound transactions on the blockchain. As opposed to a bank account, which has a number and an associated name, a wallet is simply that cryptographic key. From that key can be generated one or many, depending on the blockchain, public addresses which can be used to receive funds.[7] It is because of this reliance solely on the private key that digital assets are described as bearer assets.

Digital assets can be stored in two main types of wallets: hot wallets and cold wallets:

Hot wallets are connected to the internet and are quick and easy to use. They allow for faster transactions and day-to-day payments. These will include software wallets such as the ones on mobile phones, or on exchanges.

Cold wallets are offline and are usually considered more secure. They include more sophisticated hardware wallets, or hard paper copies of the private key; refer to Figure 6.2. They are typically used for long-term storage and are impractical for day-to-day transactions.

Some recent developments have led to the creation of multi-signature[8] wallets, which require several private keys to authorize transactions. These solutions are either in the form of smart contracts or as an additional software layer on top of native wallet management software.

6.4.2 Custodial Models and Exchange Custody

In the context of DeFi, the custodian's main role is to safeguard a set of private keys. Some custodians will own a handful of wallets and have separate records for asset reconciliation;

[7]The reverse is not possible for obvious security reasons.

[8]Those are also called multisigs.

FIGURE 6.2 **Photograph of a Hardware Wallet** for retail investors. Most hardware wallets are designed to serve as cold wallets, and are used to store private keys offline.
Source: Photograph reproduced with the consent of its creator. Ledger.

others will solely store private keys securely on behalf of their clients. We will mostly focus on the former type of custodian, which is the most common in practice and which is the one that is relevant for asset pricing.

The custodian can be described as a liquidity interface, which we discussed in Section 7.3. As more TradFi institutions are entering the DeFi space, they are also becoming custodians of digital assets.

6.4.2.1 Third-party Versus Protocol-based Custody While in most circumstances the custodian is a third party, it is also possible on some blockchains that support smart contracts to have on-chain custodians, which are smart contracts that hold assets on behalf of users. Examples include Hashed Time Lock Contracts (HTLCs), ERC-4626 tokenized vaults on the Ethereum blockchain, and DEXs. One can also argue that in the case of staking for PoS blockchains, the protocol itself is custodian of the staked coins.

Such custodian still has associated risks, namely that the code of smart contracts is hacked, or that the private keys are compromised. The fact the custodian is purely on-chain does not bear influence on pricing methodologies; it just mitigates settlement risks without impacting counterparty risk.

Remark 6.9 ***(Federations as Custodians)*:** The federation in the context of sidechain bridges is also a form of custodian. It actually is a double-custodian, one on the mainnet and one on the sidechain.

6.4.2.2 Exchanges TradFi exchanges are usually not custodians of the assets, but rather intermediaries. In DeFi, most Centralized crypto EXchanges (CEXs) often also assume the role of broker and custodian. This is because many users, in particular retail investors, keep their digital assets on exchanges instead of transferring them to their own wallets. This has led to comparisons whereby exchanges behave like DeFi banks, holding large retail deposits [171].

To illustrate, on the Bitcoin blockchain, many of the largest wallets are linked to cryptocurrency exchanges. Readers may consult live wallet explorers listed at `www.tomespel.com/books/mfin25`.

Because of the breadth of services offered by DeFi CEXs, they are closer to the role of full-service retail banks in TradFi [171] with both custody, lending, and trading—including on margin—services. On the other hand, DEXs, which have been growing in popularity recently,[9] are more akin to TradFi exchanges, where the role of the custodian is more limited. These exchanges tend to cater to a more sophisticated group of investors, with deeper knowledge of the underlying technology and risks.

6.4.3 Storage Risk and Asset Pricing

From an asset pricing perspective, where a digital asset is stored should be relevant for risk discounting. One can expect assets held in cold wallets to trade at a premium, but in practice, there is no difference in valuation between the two types of wallet despite their distinct risk profiles.

One of the reasons why that is the case is that blockchain technology reduces the settlement risk. For transactions between two digital assets, such as a stablecoin versus a cryptocurrency, it will simply not proceed if the counterparty lost their private key or got their assets stolen, as described in Section 8.2.1.1. This is also called Delivery Versus Payment (DvP).

Remark 6.10: The only point of relevance would be at the liquidity interface between TradFi and DeFi, as described in Section 7.4, where there is settlement risk.

However, in the case of tokenized assets, there is a significant emphasis on the type of storage, when the underlying are digital assets themselves. In that case, the storage risk is embedded within the broader custodian risk.

[9] We introduced DEXs in Section 1.2.5 in the context of layer 3 and dApps.

CHAPTER 7

Liquidity Interface

Liquidity pathways between TradFi and DeFi create critical pricing channels and risk propagation mechanisms. This chapter examines how these interfaces function, their impact on spreads, and their role in connecting traditional and digital asset markets.

- Analyze TradFi liquidity interfaces and their adaptation to accommodate digital asset exposure.
- Examine the role of stablecoins and tokenized assets as primary bridges between on-chain and off-chain liquidity.
- Explore tokenized assets and their impact on bringing traditional securities on-chain.

We focus on secondary markets where liquidity considerations and spread decomposition prove most relevant. We begin by reviewing TradFi liquidity pathways.

7.1 TRADITIONAL FINANCE PATHWAYS

In TradFi, an investor may seek exposure to a particular asset class. They can do one of the following:

- Invest directly.
- Purchase a derivative directly.
- Purchase an ETF or other type of fund that includes the asset.

These three options each represent a liquidity path, with different degrees of control over the investment, liquidity, and resulting spreads.

In the case of foreign assets, which are posited to have the closest liquidity surface to digital assets, it is necessary to add FX as a layer.

The link between the derivatives and ETFs with the target foreign asset is weaker because few allow redemption in kind.[1] For this reason, the link is represented as dashed in Figure 7.1.

[1]Redemption in kind means that the investor in a fund can redeem the value of their share directly in the underlying.

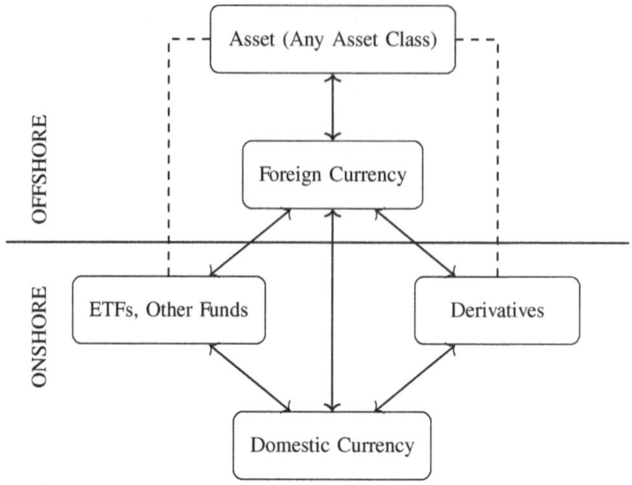

FIGURE 7.1 The **Liquidity Interface of Foreign Assets** is the set of pathways that allow liquidity to flow between a domestic (onshore) cash investor and a foreign (offshore) asset in TradFi.

7.2 STABLECOINS

Before introducing the liquidity interface for digital assets in Section 7.4, we must introduce one of its key components.

7.2.1 Definition and Classification

Definition 7.1 ***(Stablecoins)*****:** Stablecoins are digital assets designed as a stable store of value.

Remark 7.1 ***(Stablecoins Are Not Coins)*****:** Stablecoins are most often tokens that exist on multiple separate blockchains at any point in time.

There are four main types of stablecoins [104], classified as a function of the collateral:

- Collateralized by fiat currency. They represent the majority of the market.[2] When the peg arrangement is a ratio of 1:1, it is called a currency board.
- Collateralized by real assets.
- Collateralized by digital assets.
- Non-collateralized.

Remark 7.2 ***(Stablecoins as Custodial Arrangements)*****:** The best way to represent a stablecoin is that it is a custodial arrangement, like for any other tokenized asset as described in Section 7.3. The issuer represents the underlying as an IOU, which is the stablecoin itself. Trust resides in the issuer's commitment to redeem the IOU when necessary.

[2]As of April 2022, it was estimated that fiat-backed stablecoins accounted for more than 80% of the total capitalization of stablecoins [172].

7.2.2 Market Development and Regulation

Stablecoins have grown rapidly, particularly those linked to the US dollar. The first stablecoin, BitUSD, was issued in July 2014 [172]. Their capitalization increased more than ninefold in 2020, reaching $20 billion in December 2020 [172], arguably dominated by Tether[3] [172, 173] offshore and USD Coin onshore in the United States. We argue that they have become the most critical component of the liquidity interface between TradFi and DeFi.

The 2025 US GENIUS Act is regarded as a significant milestone for stablecoins, as it was the first major framework for their issuance and usage.

Markets need to trust that the entity managing the stablecoin has sufficient reserves to defend its value. This is even more critical in the case of pegs. TerraUSD, a once prominent stablecoin, notoriously broke its peg in 2022 [174, 175]. Furthermore, stablecoins are difficult to regulate, which makes the trust in the organization that issues them critical.

7.2.3 Economic Characteristics and Pricing

Stablecoins usually do not yield interest.[4] The revenue model for the issuers is to invest the reserves in low-risk assets and to keep the dividends. Because of these dynamics, stablecoins are usually assumed to not be economically viable in a negative interest rate environment.[5]

Stablecoins that yield interest are usually referred to as yieldcoins. Mechanisms for paying interest typically include accumulation, payment in another coin, or staking. The issuer will often engage in market price stabilization around the peg or target price.[6]

7.3 TOKENIZED ASSETS

Layer 2 solutions have enabled tokenization of both financial and real-world assets (RWAs). The outcome of the process is either the creation of fungible tokens that represent fractional ownership or the creation of an NFT. For the purposes of financial mathematics, we will only consider the fungible tokens.

Definition 7.2 *(Fractional Ownership)*: Fractional ownership is the process whereby investors will own a fraction of the claims on an underlying asset.

Note that in Definition 7.2, the underlying asset can be either on-chain or off-chain.

The custodian of digital assets serves as both the main and only interface for liquidity and represents the primary counterparty risk for all token holders. This arrangement is similar to that of stablecoins, where the issuer constitutes the main counterparty risk.

---

[3]Tether is officially a currency board. However, there are concerns about the stability of the peg [176, 177].

[4]Some jurisdictions, like the United States [178], explicitly bar stablecoins from paying interest to their holders.

[5]We note that there were stablecoins on JPY during negative rates, but they were not as prominent as the USD ones.

[6]For tokens with accumulation, the target price will typically reflect the daily compounding.

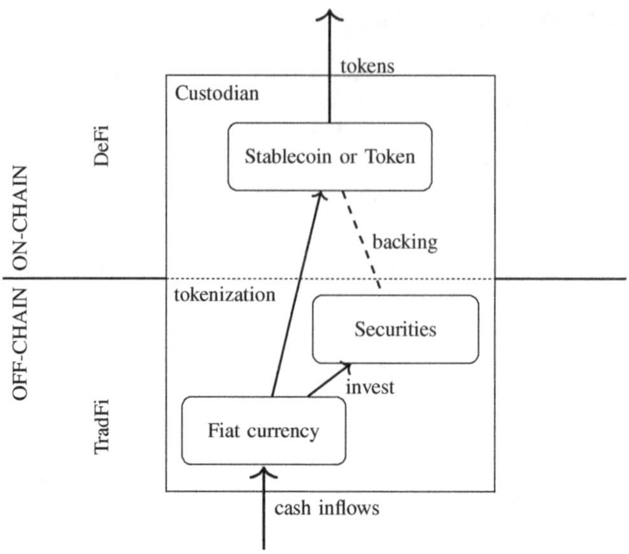

FIGURE 7.2 **Role of the Custodian as Liquidity Interface.** The custodian sits at the boundary between on-chain and off-chain assets, enabling tokenization of fiat and securities into stablecoins and other tokens. The reverse process is also possible, where the custodian will redeem the tokens for cash by selling the securities. The custodian is the main counterparty risk for all token holders.

This process is analogous to the process of securitization in TradFi, with the tokens analogous to fractional claims on the asset-backed security, as illustrated in Figure 7.2. DeFi here serves as a technology that enables, among other things, peer-to-peer transactions and automated delivery versus payment (DvP).

A key part of the tokenization process for off-chain assets, sometimes referred to as ramping [179], occurs when the custodian records and locks assets as collateral for the emission of new tokens. Several blockchains advertise themselves as platforms to support tokenization, such as Ethereum, Solana, and Algorand.

7.3.1 Tokenized Bonds

TradFi assets can be tokenized, such as bonds. The main purpose of these tokens is to bridge assets that are off-chain onto a blockchain, typically to enable peer-to-peer transactions or to serve as collateral. When the underlying asset is a bond, the tokenized bond typically pays lower interest. This difference, which we refer to as the tokenization yield, represents the premium for holding the asset on-chain versus holding the underlying asset directly.

Definition 7.3 ***(Tokenization Yield)*****:** The tokenization yield y_{token} is the difference between the yield of a tokenized bond and the yield of a similar bond that is not tokenized:

$$y_{\text{token}} = y_{\text{bond}} - y_{\text{tokenized}}$$

where y_{bond} is the yield of the underlying bond and $y_{\text{tokenized}}$ is the yield of the tokenized version.

Remark 7.3: The tokenization yield introduced in Definition 7.3 can be seen as a convenience yield from the perspective of a blockchain user, as per Definition 6.5.

Tokenization yields are typically small and can be negative. The latter is the most common case, occurring when the costs of tokenization and the custodial arrangement exceed the benefits of holding the asset on-chain. Because coupon payments have historically not been straightforward to perform on-chain due to lack of standardization, most tokenized bonds accrue interest. This is similar to accumulation funds in TradFi. However, the negative tokenization yield can still be observed as the difference between the token price return and the underlying asset.

7.3.2 CBDCs and Tokenized Deposits

We are discussing three types of tokens with similar characteristics but with different risk profiles: central bank digital currencies (CBDCs), stablecoins, and tokenized deposits.

The economics of most stablecoins closely resemble those of banking deposits. Stablecoins usually tend to not pay interest, and the difference with the yield of the underlying, the negative tokenization yield, is the revenue for the issuer. Banks also monetize deposits on their balance sheet by capturing the spread between the interest they pay on those deposits and the returns they earn on the assets they invest in.

The main difference between stablecoins and either tokenized deposits or CBDCs is the counterparty risk, which is the nature of the claim of the holder. Deposits sit on the balance sheet of a private regulated institution that can deploy the capital in a broader range of investments [180].[7] They are claims on the balance sheet as a whole. Tokenized deposits would also remain on a specific institution's balance sheet. Stablecoins are supposed to be backed by a designated pool of underlying investments instead, and the issuer can be any private entity.[8] Some prominent cryptocurrency exchanges, such as Binance, have issued their own stablecoins.

If a central bank were to issue a CBDC, the claims would be on the balance sheet of the central bank, like cash for fiat currencies. Because of the central bank's role in the economy, CBDCs would effectively have the lowest level of counterparty risk.[9] They are also expected to be more broadly accepted than any other privately issued tokenized deposit [171].

Remark 7.4: It is not a given that CBDCs would compete with and replace stablecoins. On paper, the latter has greater counterparty risk, while neither is expected to pay interest. The difference lies in the liquidity of the token, and in the case of stablecoins, the assets used to back them. Regulations may also play a role, in favor of the CBDC onshore, but potentially against it offshore.

7.3.3 RWA Tokens

RWA tokens have thus far been used predominantly for art and real estate [181–184] but can theoretically be used for any form of real asset. They are analogous to the structures in TradFi that allow for fractional ownership, such as real estate investment trusts (REITs).

[7]For banks in TradFi, deposits are one among other ways to raise capital.

[8]Some countries, like the United States, have introduced legislation to regulate stablecoin [178] issuers.

[9]Lower counterparty risk is not free in finance, a fact that was highlighted already at the time of Bagehot in *Lombard Street* [185] in 1873. Cash pays no interest, while bank deposits often do.

In practice, RWA tokens have not been widely adopted and tend to represent full rather than fractional ownership.

However, from a pricing perspective, even fungible tokens typically represent fractions of the same real asset. The lack of liquidity for such tokens places them outside the realm of financial mathematics.

7.4 DEFI LIQUIDITY INTERFACE

In the context of DeFi, we examine how an investor can seek exposure to various types of on-chain assets. It is evident from Figure 7.3 that stablecoins are critical in the liquidity interface. They serve as the primary gateway between DeFi and TradFi.

The conversion between stablecoins and USD[10] exhibits reasonable liquidity, depending on jurisdictions. This service is most commonly provided by exchanges or through peer-to-peer solutions.

Crypto-stocks are publicly listed companies that investors perceive as exposed to the DeFi ecosystem, either through the assets on their balance sheet, or because the products they sell are closely related to digital assets. They were prevalent before the introduction of the ETFs. Some of these crypto-stocks include so-called crypto treasury companies, which are listed companies that hold significant amounts of cryptocurrency as part of their treasury reserves.

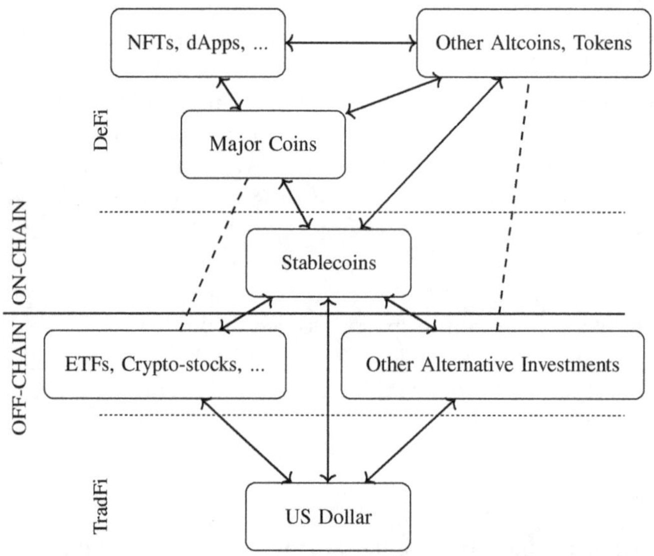

FIGURE 7.3 The **Liquidity Interface of Digital Assets** is the set of pathways that allow liquidity to flow between TradFi and DeFi. The links between ETFs and Major Coins and between Other Alternatives and Altcoins are dashed because redemption in kind is uncommon.

[10]There exist stablecoins for all major fiat currencies.

While investors can gain exposure to digital assets using TradFi instruments, such as ETFs, most of these investment vehicles still need to use stablecoins to convert USD to digital assets. Some funds, particularly ETFs, can accommodate redemption in kind,[11] but this remains uncommon. ETFs serve as the primary liquidity gateway for institutional investors, as they are fully compliant and integrated within the TradFi system, being traded on regulated exchanges.

The links and flows between TradFi and DeFi are still an active field of research [186, 187].

[11]Redemption in this instance means collecting the cryptocurrency instead of fiat currency. This remains uncommon and is a one-way process, meaning that an investor cannot purchase a USD-listed ETF on Bitcoin by providing the fund manager with the Bitcoin.

CHAPTER 8

Cost of Liquidity

Market participants rarely transact at theoretical mid prices; instead, they face transaction costs reflecting market microstructure effects. This chapter develops frameworks to decompose digital asset prices into consensus value, the mid price, and liquidity cost components, examining how DeFi markets differ from traditional finance in their cost structures.

- Decompose asset prices into mid price and cost of liquidity components.
- Analyze risk factors embedded in spreads, including peg risk, network failure risk, and liquidity risk.
- Explore the blockchain paradox, revealing how transaction costs in DeFi behave differently from TradFi.

We begin with the mathematical framework for price decomposition analysis.

8.1 PRICE DECOMPOSITION FRAMEWORK

8.1.1 Order Books and Market Structure

In a perfectly efficient market, with perfect information diffusion and no transaction costs, there would be a single market-clearing price where all transactions occur. As a result, the difference between all selling interests and all buying interests should be zero.

Definition 8.1 *(Bid and Ask)***:** The collection of selling interests in a financial market is called the asks or the offers, with the best ask being the lowest price. The collection of buying interests in a financial market is called the bids, with the best bid being the highest price.

This difference between the best selling offer and the best buying offer is called the spread, as per Definition 8.2.

Definition 8.2 *(Spread)***:** The spread is the difference between the best ask and best bid prices:

$$\text{Spread} = P_{\text{ask}} - P_{\text{bid}}$$

Remark 8.1: In some markets, such as when quoting bond yields, the spread is expressed with the opposite sign convention. This is because higher-valued bonds correspond to lower yields, meaning an aggressive seller will quote a lower yield to attract buyers.

Digital asset markets, and in particular cryptocurrency markets, have adopted the FX convention of calling the bids "left hand side" and the asks "right hand side." This arises from the representation of all the open interests with increasing prices, called the order book, where bids are on the left and asks are on the right, as per Figure 8.1.

This representation is carried over in many trading interfaces, with the buy button on the right-hand side and the sell button on the left-hand side, which correspond to the price of the best offer and the best bid respectively. The most common quoting convention, as described in Section 6.2, is to have the price of the digital asset (base) expressed in USD (quote).

The collection of transactions are called the prints. When a bid is transacted, it means a trader has agreed to sell their asset at the bid price, and the corresponding open interest is removed from the order book. This transaction is called a "given" and is referred to as "hitting" the bid. Conversely, a trader who "lifts" the ask is printing a "lift." As a result, the record of transactions on a market are often called the "paid and given."

Remark 8.2 ***(Why Prints?)*****:** This term comes from late nineteenth-century equities trading, where all trades were distributed using telegraph lines with a ticker tape machine. The term ticker, or ticker symbol, also derives from the use of this machine, where stock names were shortened to save space. References to the tape can be found in Lefèvre's classic *Reminiscences of a Stock Operator* [188].

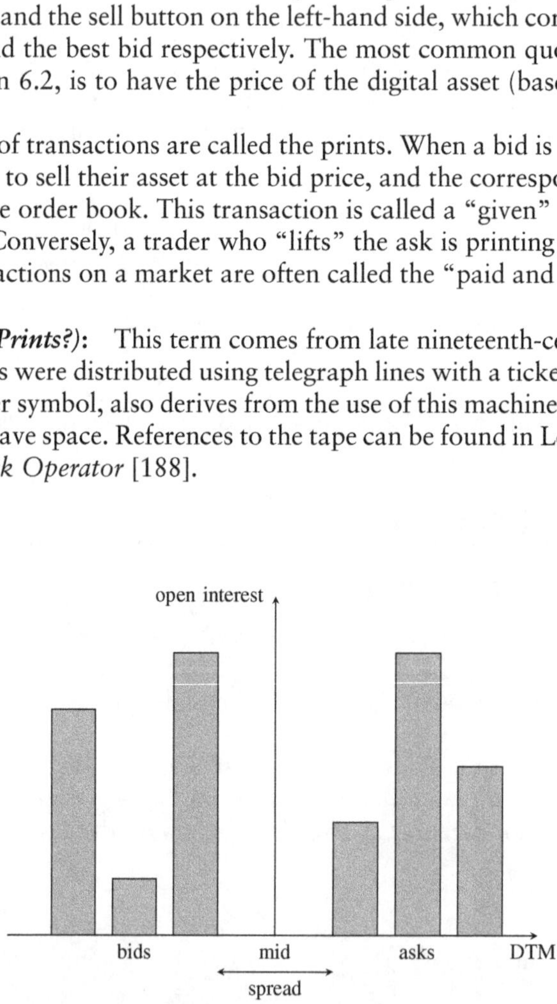

FIGURE 8.1 **Schematic Order Book.** Bids and asks are shown with price and volume. The spread is the gap between best bid and best ask, with the mid price in the center. DTM stands for Distance to Mid, and is usually expressed in price pips.

8.1.2 Economic Surplus and Market Making

The spread can be construed as a measure of the market's inefficiency and reflects the costs associated with trading and the risks we discuss in Section 8.2. It is also called the liquidity premium, or cost of liquidity. The tighter the spread, the more efficient the market is.

There is, however, another interpretation of the spread that relates to the concept of economic surplus. The spread is what a trader pays to acquire or dispose of an asset; it is the immediate financial benefit of providing liquidity to the market. This is therefore the economic surplus that the trader receives for the ability to take on or dispose of the risk of holding the asset.

Market makers are a group of market participants whose main business is to provide liquidity to financial markets at all times, and the spread is not only a function of their revenue but a measure of the added value of their service to the market. They endorse the risk linked to the inefficiency of the market and receive compensation for it through the spread.

In DeFi, these market makers can be smart contracts in the form of AMMs, or individual investors who post liquidity on DEXs.

8.1.3 Mathematical Framework

We will now construct mathematically the aforementioned framework.

Definition 8.3 ***(Price Decomposition)*:** The traditional price decomposition is given by the following equation:

$$P = P_{\text{total}} = P_{\text{mid}} + P_{\text{liquidity}}$$

where P_{mid} is the mid price and $P_{\text{liquidity}}$ is the cost of liquidity.

Definition 8.4 ***(Mid Price)*:** The mid price is the average of the best bid and best ask prices:

$$P_{\text{mid}} = \frac{P_{\text{bid}} + P_{\text{ask}}}{2}$$

Definition 8.5 ***(Cost of Liquidity)*:** The cost of liquidity $P_{\text{liquidity}}$ is the share $\omega \in [0; 1]$ of the spread paid by or received by the investor:

$$P_{\text{liquidity}} = \pm\, \omega \cdot \text{Spread}$$

Remark 8.3: While spreads are assumed positive, it is possible under certain circumstances that they turn negative. This creates an arbitrage, which is usually resolved fairly quickly by arbitrageurs.

For most products, it is assumed that the cost of liquidity is split equally between the buyer and the seller.

When that is the case, we have the following equations:

$$P_{\text{ask}} = P_{\text{mid}} + \frac{\text{Spread}}{2}$$
$$P_{\text{bid}} = P_{\text{mid}} - \frac{\text{Spread}}{2}$$

which correspond to $\omega = 1/2$ in Definition 8.5. However, this is not always the case, as we will see in the following sections.

8.2 COMPONENTS OF THE SPREAD

Having established the mathematical framework for price decomposition, we now examine the specific risk factors that contribute to spreads in DeFi.

We can list the following risks that are embedded in the spread:

- Peg risk
- Network failure and chain security risk
- Liquidity risk that captures the cost of liquidity

8.2.1 Settlement and Counterparty Risk

8.2.1.1 Counterparty and Settlement Risk This risk is deemed nonexistent in DeFi because DvP is guaranteed by the protocol. It is actually an important risk in TradFi.

8.2.1.2 Custodian Risk We do not add a standalone custodian risk and break it down either as a breach of trust, which we encompass in the peg risk, or a failure to safeguard the asset, which we encompass in the network failure risk.

8.2.2 Peg Risk

In this section, we present the peg risk mostly in the context of stablecoins, but it also applies to NFTs and in particular RWAs.

All pegs have eventually failed. One of the most famous examples was the depegging[1] of the US dollar from the gold standard in 1971,[2] which led simultaneously to the end of the Bretton Woods system. Currency pegs are subject to extensive academic research, and the consensus is that they are not sustainable in the long run [189–191].

Cryptocurrencies themselves have seen notable peg failures, starting with IRON, which failed in 2021 [192, 193]. One of the largest recent peg failures is the Terra stablecoin [174, 175, 194] in 2022, which was the fourth largest stablecoin by market capitalization at that time. Even the largest stablecoin, USDT, has lost its peg on several occasions, such as in 2022 after the collapse of FTX [176, 177].

[1]The process of depegging a currency is also often called floating.

[2]It was after that time that the US dollar, and very soon most major currencies, became fiat currency.

The peg risk in the context of DeFi typically refers to either of the following:

- The risk that the peg of a stablecoin is not maintained
- The risk that the peg of a sidechain is not maintained

Both are, in essence, a form of counterparty risk to the entity that maintains the peg. This is identical to conventional currency pegs in TradFi. However, while in TradFi that risk is typically not priced outside of distressed market conditions, we argue it should be priced at all times in DeFi for four reasons:

- The entities that maintain the peg typically have less control over monetary supply than central banks for fiat currency.
- The backing of the peg is typically not as transparent as for fiat currency or is subject to less outside controls.
- Transactions on DeFi can be conducted 24/7, and contract durations are typically shorter than in TradFi. This means that investors can react more quickly to headlines and trade accordingly.
- Because of generally higher volatilities in DeFi markets and a recent history of failures [176, 177], investors are more prone to panicking and therefore exerting pressure on the peg.

While we will still refer to peg risk as a form of counterparty risk, we want to highlight that one of the greatest risks to cryptocurrency pegs is the risk of bank runs [175, 193]. Even if the peg is fully backed by assets, the liquidity in TradFi might be insufficient to meet the demand for redemptions, which is a form of liquidity risk on the underlying reserve assets. We still believe it is a form of counterparty risk, as it is the counterparty's responsibility to adequately allocate the backing assets such that it can meet redemption demands.

8.2.3 Network and Technical Risk

8.2.3.1 Network Failure and Chain Security Risk A network can fail if there is either a protocol error or if there are no miners or validators able to process transactions. The compensation received by the network to prevent such failure is the network fee. We provide an overview of the role of fees in Section 9.1 and will only discuss the implications for pricing in the following sections.

Remark 8.4: On most networks, users can pick among different transaction priorities that each have a different fee. We will only discuss network fees as if there was only one possible fee f, acknowledging that all these fee tiers are proportionally linked. Higher priority tiers typically cost a fixed multiple of the base fee, maintaining consistent ratios across different congestion levels.

The network failure risk also encompasses security risks linked to a hack of the network that would prevent it from operating properly. If a systematic flaw were to be exploited in the protocol, the most likely course of action is that while a patch or a fork is being implemented, transactions on the network would be impossible.[3]

8.2.4 Liquidity Risk

The liquidity risk can be defined as the potential inability to buy or sell the asset at a specified future moment in time. It tends to be more pronounced for non-fungible assets, such as NFTs.

In TradFi, this risk is fully carried by market makers, whose role is to provide two-way prices to market participants. In that context, market makers are also called liquidity providers (LPs). In brokerage markets such as FX, market makers are compensated through the spread. Such brokerage markets are uncommon in DeFi, where more open structures with many participants have been historically favored. However, these might emerge over time, given that liquidity requirements diverge between smaller and very large participants.

In DeFi there are several forms of market making. On CEXs, both individual investors and professional market makers post visible liquidity on order books. On DEXs, automated market makers (AMMs) provide liquidity through smart contracts, allowing investors to trade against a pool of assets. Even with AMMs, there is still liquidity risk, since despite being immutable, the underlying smart contracts can be compromised or self-destruct.

In practice, liquidity risk takes two dimensions:

Size leads to the observation that smaller positions might have lower liquidity risk than larger ones.

Slippage is how the price moves when a trade is executed as a result of the depletion of liquidity. Some DEXs are specifically designed to minimize slippage. This is related to the concept of best execution, an important parameter in TradFi regulations.

Liquidity risk is primarily prevented by adequate depth of liquidity in the market. It is influenced by the market makers, market fragmentation, and overall trading volumes. In TradFi, the risk becomes negligible as market activity increases, which is visible in the contraction of interbank spreads for the most liquid assets such as major currencies in FX.

While DeFi has a high concentration of liquidity on CEXs, some tokens are only tradable on DEXs, where there is greater fragmentation. NFTs tend to be illiquid due to the lack of market makers for these digital assets.

DeFi also faces the unique challenge of network congestion. When there is excessive market activity, transaction times can increase significantly, and gas fees can become prohibitive. In other words, while TradFi liquidity risk stems from insufficient market depth, DeFi faces the additional risk that excessive network activity can prevent trade execution even when liquidity exists. We illustrate this convexity of liquidity risk in Figure 8.2.

Remark 8.5 ***(MEV and Hidden Execution Costs)*****:** Beyond traditional liquidity risk, DeFi markets face costs related to maximum extractable value (MEV) where sophisticated

[3]This is because transactions between the time of the hack and the patch are likely to be absent from the fork after the patch is deployed.

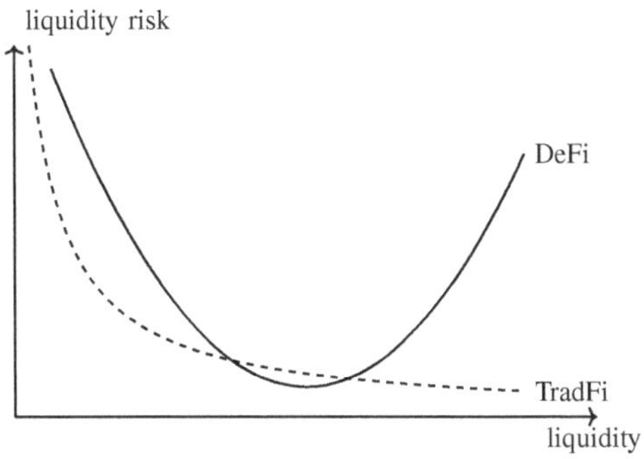

FIGURE 8.2 **Illustration of Liquidity Risk** as a function of liquidity in DeFi and TradFi. A convexity is observed in DeFi, when excess liquidity creates network congestion.

actors extract value through transaction ordering, effectively widening spreads for unprotected trades. This leads to hidden execution costs, which are not captured in the visible spread. We omit detailed maximum extractable value (MEV) analysis as it requires game-theoretic treatment beyond our pricing framework's scope. MEV is still an active research area in DeFi [195–197].

The relationship between network activity and transaction costs in blockchain networks creates a fundamental difference from TradFi markets that warrants closer examination.

8.3 THE BLOCKCHAIN PARADOX

In most TradFi markets, transaction costs for a given volume decrease as market volumes increase. This is empirically observed as a result of increased competition and efficiency in processing transactions [198, 199].

In DeFi, the transaction cost is set by the protocol. Most networks charge by transaction size, which reflects transaction complexity, rather than the actual volume transferred. Assuming that the volume per transaction is relatively stable, this means the size in bytes per transaction is also stable.

However, the cost of transactions is not a fixed fee. It is a function of how congested the blockchain network is [199, 200]. This is a feature of protocols, designed to incentivize more validators or miners to come online when the volume of transactions spikes. To a lesser extent, this also encourages market participants to bundle transactions, thereby increasing the volume per transaction.[4]

This leads to a paradoxical result for blockchains.

Proposition 8.1 ***(Blockchain Paradox)*****:** The fee f on a blockchain increases as the market volume V_{market} on that blockchain increases:

$$\frac{\partial f}{\partial V_{\text{market}}} \geq 0$$

[4]We believe this effect is marginal, since bundling can also increase transaction complexity, and in turn the size in bytes of each transaction.

This has historically been one of the main incentives to create sidechains, which we introduced in Section 2.2, to reduce congestion on the mainnet. For a given asset that may be traded on different blockchains, the average cost of transactions does decrease as the asset becomes more popular because more transactions move to sidechains with lower fees. However, a wrapped token is not strictly equivalent to the original asset, as it is subject to the risks of the sidechain. This creates basis risk.

Remark 8.6 ***(Long-term Decrease in Mainnet Fees)*****:** Because of supply and demand dynamics for the available space on each block to record transactions, mainnet fees on a given blockchain are unlikely to decrease substantially in the long term except through the introduction of protocol changes, or a large migration of users to sidechains that would reduce transactions on the mainnet. The former was observed on Bitcoin, most notably with the SegWit update in 2017. The latter has not been observed for major coins thus far. The balancing of these forces makes the blockchain paradox of Proposition 8.1 less visible in the long term.

We must distinguish between mainnet fees, which are directly observed on the blockchain, and effective fees, which are the typical fees paid by blockchain users.

Definition 8.6 ***(Effective Fee)*****:** The effective fee is the volume-weighted average fee $\bar{f}$ paid by all blockchain users, at all layers and for any asset it supports:

$$\bar{f} = \frac{\sum_{i=1}^{N} f_i V_i}{\sum_{i=1}^{N} V_i}$$

where f_i is the fee paid on transaction i out of N total transactions, and V_i is its volume. This metric is typically calculated for each block.

Remark 8.7: We can alternatively refer to the effective fee of Definition 8.6 as the blockchain fee. However, we also want to encompass wrapped tokens, which can be bridged to unaffiliated blockchains.

On the mainnet, only the mainnet fee f_{mainnet} is observed:

$$f_{\text{mainnet}} = \frac{\sum_{i \in \text{mainnet}} f_i V_i}{\sum_{i \in \text{mainnet}} V_i}$$

Remark 8.8 ***(Long-term Decrease in Effective Fees)*****:** The blockchain paradox described in Proposition 8.1 is only verified in the short term, typically over periods of days to weeks. Over longer time horizons, we observe a general decrease in effective fees paid for transactions on blockchains. This results from the introduction of sidechains and layer 2 solutions, which allow transactions to be offloaded from the mainnet to cheaper networks.

In practice, network participants also use sidechains to settle transactions faster, such as the Lightning Network for Bitcoin. This means that the effective fee $\bar{f}$ paid on average differs from the mainnet fee f_{mainnet} on the mainnet and is usually lower.

Proposition 8.2: The effective fee $\bar{f}$ is always less than or equal to the mainnet fee f_{mainnet}:

$$\bar{f} \leq f_{\text{mainnet}}$$

Proof. Assume $\bar{f} > f_{\text{mainnet}}$. Given that sidechains have increased risk compared to the mainnet, this would create an arbitrage opportunity for users to move their transactions to the mainnet where fees are lower, contradicting the assumption that users act rationally to minimize costs. ■

The blockchain paradox is acutely observed during periods of high volatility, particularly with meme coins, where transaction fees can spike dramatically in response to increased congestion [201]. These spikes also align with major events on the mainnet, as was observed on Bitcoin.

This dynamic relationship between network activity and fees requires a more sophisticated mathematical treatment, which we develop in Chapter 9.

CHAPTER 9

Fee Models

Network fees in DeFi are dynamic and can significantly impact pricing, unlike TradFi where transaction costs are often negligible. This chapter develops mathematical models to capture fee dynamics and their effects on digital asset valuation.

- Explain the economic and technical role of network fees in blockchain systems.
- Develop mathematical models for fee dynamics, including congestion and oscillation effects.
- Present extensions and practical considerations for modeling fees in digital asset markets.

We begin by examining the basic structure and incentives behind blockchain fees.

9.1 FEES

The relationship between network activity and transaction costs described in the Blockchain Paradox in Section 8.3 highlights the central role that fees play in blockchain economics.

Fees are an important part of the blockchain ecosystem for two reasons:

- Fees are necessary to provide an incentive for miners or validators to approve transactions.
- For blockchains with a finite total number of coins mined, such as Bitcoin, fees are designed to provide a long-term incentive for the network to be maintained.

In other words, fees are compensation paid by network users to mitigate network failure, which we discuss in our risk decomposition in Section 8.2.3.1.

Fees can be substantial for a transaction and cannot always be ignored in pricing. While transaction costs are often ignored in most pricing theory in TradFi, we cannot make this approximation in DeFi. We provide a more robust mathematical model in Sections 8.2.3.1 and 9.2.

There are two notable differences between fees in DeFi and those in TradFi:

- The fee is most commonly paid in the native coin of the blockchain, which can be referred to as payment-in-kind (PIK). In TradFi, such costs are typically settled in local fiat currency.

- In some blockchains, transaction fees paid by users constitute only a portion of the total compensation received by miners and validators for processing a block.

Definition 9.1 ***(Block Reward)*:** The block reward is the total compensation paid to miners or validators for successfully creating a block, consisting of the following:

- Transaction fees collected from users
- New coins created through monetary emission (if applicable)

Remark 9.1: Not all transaction fees are awarded to miners or validators. Some blockchains, such as Ethereum, permanently remove a portion of the paid fees. That process is known as burning. This mechanism helps regulate the circulation of coins.

Proposition 9.1: The only mechanism of continuous coin issuance on a blockchain is through the block reward paid to miners and validators.

We provide a schematic illustration of the fee trajectory in Figure 9.1. Numerous online platforms offer visualizations of blockchain fee data, and readers are encouraged to consult those listed at `www.tomespel.com/books/mfin25`. Fee-to-reward ratios are also available.

Remark 9.2: This does not imply that fees are necessarily inflationary:

- One argument is that the issuance of new coins is the direct result of activity on the network.
- Another argument is that an increased coin supply may be required to maintain liquidity on a growing network, without imposing large increases in fees on participants.
- As noted in Section 2.1.1.1, some blockchains permanently burn a proportion of collected fees to stabilize the circulating supply of coins.

We can therefore draw similarities between network fees and the principal interest rate set by a country's central bank. However, an important difference is that coin issuance mechanisms are typically fixed in the protocol, whereas monetary policy can change.[1]

9.2 OSCILLATING FEES MODEL

In DeFi, the interplay between network congestion and user behavior produces a characteristic oscillatory fee pattern that can be modeled mathematically.

Blockchain fees f generally increase with market volumes V_{market} by design. In the short term, both mainnet and effective fees are denoted by f in this model.

Proposition 9.2 ***(Simplified Fees Model)*:** Let $f \in \mathcal{L}^1(\mathbb{R})$ be the transaction fees on a blockchain as a function of market volumes V_{market}:

$$f(V_{\text{market}}) = u + v \cdot V_{\text{market}}$$

[1] The trade-off is between greater certainty and predictability versus flexibility and responsiveness to liquidity situations.

We have $(u, v) \in \mathbb{R}_+^2$ constants.

In Proposition 9.2, u represents base fees and v is akin to a congestion coefficient.

Proof. From Proposition 8.1 we have

$$\frac{\partial f}{\partial V_{\text{market}}} \geq 0$$

For the linear model this implies $v \geq 0$. The base fee $u \geq 0$ represents a nonnegative minimum network fee even at zero volume. ■

Remark 9.3: While we use a linear approximation for tractability, actual blockchain fees often exhibit nonlinear behavior, with exponential growth during severe congestion:

$$f(V_{\text{market}}) = u + v \cdot V_{\text{market}} + g \cdot V_{\text{market}}^{\gamma}$$

where $\gamma > 1$ captures congestion nonlinearity and $g \geq 0$ is typically small under normal conditions. A more refined model might include quadratic or higher-order terms; in practice, mainnet fees can increase nonlinearly as market volumes grow, as illustrated in Figure 9.1.

While Proposition 9.2 expresses fees as a function of market volumes V_{market}, volumes themselves exhibit temporal patterns. We therefore model V_{market} as a function of time:

$$V_{\text{market}}(t) = \bar{V} + \hat{V}(t)$$

where $\bar{V}$ is the average volume and $\hat{V}(t)$ denotes a time-dependent deviation. Hence $f(t) = f(V_{\text{market}}(t))$.

We propose a time-dependent model $f(t)$ designed to capture a key feature of blockchain fees that reflects the blockchain paradox described in Proposition 8.1. This directly models temporal fee behavior while implicitly capturing underlying volume dynamics.

Following Propositions 8.1 and 9.2, market participants reduce or delay transactions when fees become excessive. Conversely, they take advantage of lower fees, increasing activity. During busy periods, participants often favor sidechains (see Section 2.2).

These oscillations are clearly observable in blockchain fee data, as illustrated in Figure 9.1, most notably for Ethereum.

Remark 9.4: There is typically, over an extended time horizon, a decreasing trend in effective fees paid. Oscillations are observed on a shorter time scale for both mainnet and effective fees, such as a day or a week. Readers are advised to consult live online monitors listed at `www.tomespel.com/books/mfin25`.

The feedback between fees and volume creates oscillations; high fees reduce activity, leading to lower fees, which increase activity, returning to high fees. To model this, let $\hat{f} : t \mapsto f(t) - \bar{f}$ denote the deviation from average fees $\bar{f}$.

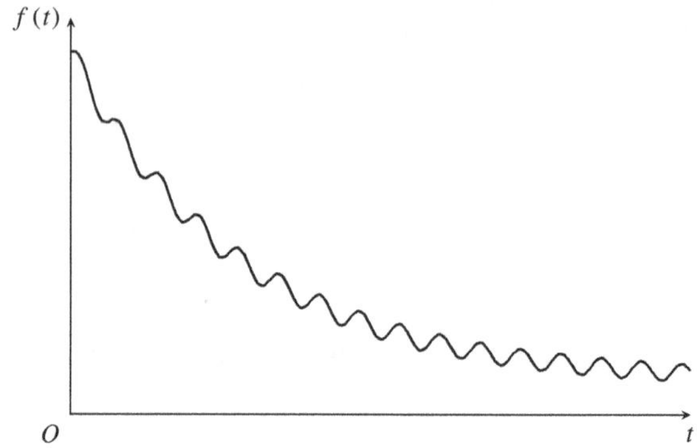

FIGURE 9.1 **Illustration of Typical Effective Fee Decay** with short-term oscillations and long-term decreasing trend. The long-term decreasing trend is often attributed to increased efficiency, network upgrades, and increased usage of sidechains that alleviate congestion on the mainnet.

Remark 9.5: Note that $\bar{f}$ is not the same quantity as the effective fee discussed in Definition 8.6.

The observed oscillations arise from momentum, since volume responds to fees with a lag. We model the centered fee deviation $\hat{f}(t)$ by the second-order linear differential equation:

$$\frac{\partial^2 \hat{f}(t)}{\partial t^2} = -k^2 \hat{f}(t)$$

which is the harmonic oscillator linear differential equation (LDE), where $k^2 \geq 0$ is a reaction constant.

Remark 9.6: We have a similar LDE for market volumes as a partial derivative of time. Because we established in Proposition 9.2 the linear relationship between fees and volumes, and because we are only interested in fees, we write the LDE for the centered fees $\hat{f}$.

Proposition 9.3 ***(Oscillating Fees Model)*:** Blockchain transaction fees are a harmonic oscillator with respect to time t:

$$f(t) = \bar{f} - A\cos(k \cdot t)$$

with $k \geq 0$, $A \geq 0$ constants and $\bar{f}$ the average fee.

Remark 9.7 ***(Phase Shift)*:** A more general solution would be $f(t) = \bar{f} - A\cos(kt + \phi)$. For simplicity, we set $t = 0$ at the fee minimum, which eliminates the need for a phase shift term ϕ in Proposition 9.3.

Proof. We know that the LDE for the centered function for fees is given by the following:

$$\frac{\partial^2 \hat{f}(t)}{\partial t^2} = -k^2 \hat{f}(t)$$

We now write the general solution of the LDE for the centered function for fees:

$$\hat{f}(t) = \tilde{A}\cos(k \cdot t) + \tilde{B}\sin(k \cdot t)$$

with $\tilde{A}$ and $\tilde{B}$ constants.

We assume fees are minimal when volumes are lowest. Setting this point as $t = 0$ for convenience, we have $\hat{f}(0)$ at a local minimum. For a minimum at $t = 0$ we have the following:

$$\frac{\partial \hat{f}}{\partial t}(0) = -k\tilde{A}\sin(0) + k\tilde{B}\cos(0) = k\tilde{B} = 0$$

Therefore $\tilde{B} = 0$.

At this minimum, fees should increase with time initially (as volumes pick up):

$$\frac{\partial^2 \hat{f}}{\partial t^2}(0) = -k^2\tilde{A} > 0$$

which requires $\tilde{A} < 0$. We also set $\tilde{A} = -A$ with $A \geq 0$:

$$\hat{f}(t) = -A\cos(k \cdot t)$$

Adding the average fee $\bar{f}$ produces the claimed expression. ■

Remark 9.8: We can solve this equation with boundary conditions that we observe on network fees:

$$A = \bar{f} - \min_{V_{\text{market}}} f(V_{\text{market}})$$

Definition 9.2 ***(Oscillating Fees Period)*****:** We define the blockchain fee oscillation period as $T = \frac{2\pi}{k}$.

The oscillation period in Definition 9.2 is the time it takes for the fees to complete one full cycle of oscillation.

Typical oscillation periods align with macroeconomic factors, such as time of the day for different liquidity regimes, or seasonality by time of the year. The intraday and intraweek variations are well known and are used by market participants to optimize their trading strategies.

Under this model, the fees will oscillate in perpetuity as market participants adapt their behavior; refer to Figure 9.2. The oscillating fees model offers a practical and effective basis for daily modeling of transaction fees, where we can neglect other trend effects, which we discussed in Remark 8.8. In practice, while there is a short-term oscillation of both mainnet and effective fees, the long-range trend is that effective fees are decreasing despite the market volumes increase, as per Figure 9.1 and Remark 8.6.

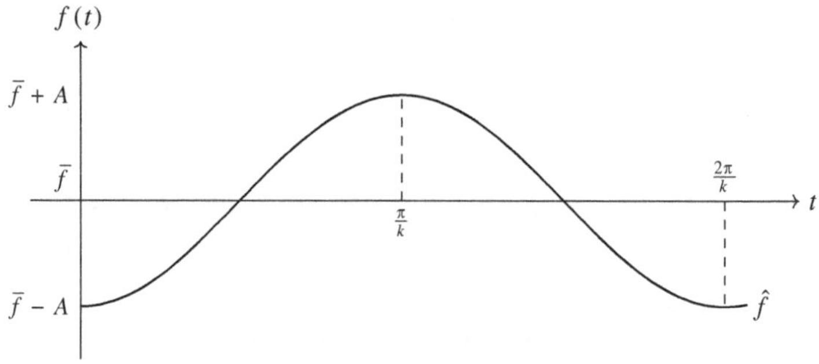

FIGURE 9.2 Illustration of the **Solution of the Oscillating Fees Model** presented in Proposition 9.3. The fees $\hat{f}$ are a harmonic oscillator with respect to time t.

9.3 EXTENDED FEE MODELS

However, this model has several shortcomings; we propose the following extensions to address them:

1. It is reasonable to assume that over time, fees will stabilize under a trend, which may be linear or not. One way to address this is to introduce a trend function of volumes $\mu \in \mathcal{C}^2(\mathbb{R})$ and to consider the LDE as the perturbation:

$$f(t) = \mu(t) + \hat{f}(t)$$

   Common trend functions for μ include linear and square root.
2. The oscillations might decrease over time, especially if the market volumes increase under a trend as per item 1. This can be addressed by introducing a damping factor $\xi \in \mathbb{R}_+^*$ in the LDE:

$$\frac{\partial^2 \hat{f}(t)}{\partial t^2} = -\xi \frac{\partial \hat{f}(t)}{\partial t} - k^2 \hat{f}(t)$$

   In physics, the previous equation is known as the damped harmonic oscillator.
3. The model does not account for the fact that the oscillations of fees are not necessarily symmetric around the average fee. This can be addressed by introducing an amplitude function $\Gamma \in \mathcal{C}^2(\mathbb{R})$, which can be a function of both V_{market} and time t, alongside the trend function μ introduced in item 1:

$$f(t) = \mu(t) + \Gamma(V_{\text{market}}(t), t) \cdot \hat{f}(t)$$

Remark 9.9: The functions introduced in points 1–3 can be combined together. We can also adjust them as functions of both the market volumes and time t.

One implication of the oscillating fees model is that it is possible to arbitrage fees on a given blockchain. These opportunities arise because transaction fees are borne by the sender only. Market makers can also alter settlement terms for off-chain contracts to take advantage of lower fees for delivery.

Remark 9.10: This could theoretically also be encoded in a smart contract, but this is still uncommon at the time of writing for two reasons:

- Oracles are complex to set up.
- The additional execution and contract development fees remain high for simple transactions.

Open Problems

These thought experiments are guided explorations into the concepts discussed in this part of the book.
Hints are available at `www.tomespel.com/books/mfin25`.

Problem III.1: Design a trading strategy that can profit from oscillating fees. Can it persist?

Problem III.2: A stablecoin trades persistently as a premium to its peg. Under which circumstances can the convenience yield still be negative?

Problem III.3: Cascading liquidations create a violent market crash, with strong sell volumes. Yet the order book shows strong buying interest. How is this possible?

Problem III.4: A new ETF launches and fully tracks a stablecoin that trades on two blockchains with different fee structures. What is the optimal allocation to minimize tracking error?

Problem III.5: A wrapped token issuer claims a perfect peg with a physical asset as underlying. Under which circumstances will the token trade at discount to the equivalent futures contract, with the same underlying, off-chain?

PART Four

Price Returns

"Without embracing uncertainty, we can't rationally bet on our beliefs."

Annie Duke, Thinking in Bets

CHAPTER 10

Price Process

Digital assets exhibit price dynamics that are analogous to TradFi modeling approaches. This chapter develops mathematical frameworks to capture volatility patterns, correlation structures, and microstructure effects specific to cryptocurrency markets.

- Present mathematical foundations for representing price processes in digital asset markets.
- Examine stylized facts specific to cryptocurrency markets, including volatility clustering, leverage effects, and heavy-tailed distributions.
- Discuss the Hurst exponent as a measure of long-range dependence in cryptocurrency time series.

We begin with the mathematical foundations of price processes and their application to digital assets.

10.1 MATHEMATICAL FRAMEWORK FOR PRICE PROCESSES

The mathematical representation of the price $P_t := P(t)$ of an asset is called the price process, which we define more formally in Definition 10.1.

Definition 10.1 ***(Price Process)*****:** A price process $(P_t)_{t \geq 0}$ is a stochastic process that represents the price of an asset as a function of time.

Remark 10.1: The price process need not be continuous and is often observed at discrete times. For this reason, this chapter adopts the notation $(P_t)_{t \geq 0}$, commonly associated with discrete-time processes.

As just indicated, the price process is stochastic rather than deterministic. When no closed-form solution to a pricing equation exists, numerical methods provide useful approximations.

The most common numerical methods are the following:

Finite difference methods are numerical methods that provide a local approximation of the solution to partial differential equations. The fundamental principle is to discretize the equation around the points where a solution is needed and to approximate the derivatives using nearby grid values.

Monte Carlo simulations are mainly used to price derivatives [202, 203]. They consist of repeating simulations with random components and taking the average outcome. While computationally intensive, by the Law of Large Numbers, they converge to the expected value. Some applications also include common risk measures, such as value-at-risk (VaR) or Greeks of a financial instrument.

Remark 10.2 *(Non-Markov)*: One application of Monte Carlo simulations is to simulate entire random paths of the price process, which are often called non-Markov. The Heath-Jarrow-Morton (HJM) model, discussed in Section 16.4, is one such case.

These methods rely on boundary conditions, which can be constructed from historical data, assumptions, and known patterns from technical analysis.

10.2 PRICE RETURNS

The primary object of study for price processes is typically returns, since returns are easier to model and analyze than raw price series.

Definition 10.2 *(Price Return)*: Let $(P_t)_{t\geq 0}$ be the price process of an asset. The return of the asset at time t is defined as follows:

$$R_t = \frac{P_t - P_{t-1}}{P_{t-1}}$$

Remark 10.3 *(24/7 Trading in Cryptocurrency Markets)*: Unlike traditional financial markets, cryptocurrency markets operate continuously. Most models in this section assume discrete, daily returns, but they can be adapted to other sampling intervals, including intraday returns.

An important property of returns is that they can be analyzed statistically and may be locally stationary. Over a given interval, their statistical properties can be approximately constant, which is generally not true for raw price series.

For assets with lower volatility, or in high-frequency contexts, the log-return is often preferred [204].

Definition 10.3 *(Price Log-return)*: The log-return of an asset with price P_t at time t is defined as follows:

$$r_t = \log\left(\frac{P_t}{P_{t-1}}\right)$$

Log-returns offer the advantage that they are additive and easier to manipulate.

Proposition 10.1: For small price variations, price returns are approximations of price log-returns.

Proof. We recall Definition 10.3

$$r_t = \log\left(\frac{P_t}{P_{t-1}}\right)$$
$$= \log\left(\frac{P_t - P_{t-1}}{P_{t-1}} + 1\right)$$

and write

$$\varepsilon = \frac{P_t - P_{t-1}}{P_{t-1}}$$

with $|\varepsilon| < 1$, such that we can rewrite the log-return:

$$r_t = \log(\varepsilon + 1)$$

We assume that ε is very close to 0, at least $|\varepsilon| \ll 1$, and expand the logarithm in a Taylor series:

$$r_t = \log(\varepsilon + 1)$$
$$\approx \varepsilon + \mathcal{O}\left(\varepsilon^2\right)$$

This gives us the original definition of the price return, as in Definition 10.2:

$$\log\left(\frac{P_t}{P_{t-1}}\right) \approx \frac{P_t - P_{t-1}}{P_{t-1}}$$

■

The mathematical modeling of price returns is discussed more specifically in Section 11.1.

10.3 EMPIRICAL PROPERTIES OF FINANCIAL TIME SERIES

10.3.1 Stylized Facts

As noted in Section 10.2, returns are a primary object of study in mathematical finance. This has led to a set of empirical regularities known as stylized facts [205–208].

Definition 10.4 ***(Stylized Facts [Finance]):*** Stylized facts are empirical observations on financial time series that are consistent across different markets.

Remark 10.4: Stylized facts are often treated as established regularities despite being empirical observations. The concept originated in economics; a mathematical parallel would be to regard them as conjectures or axioms.

Most stylized facts observed in TradFi also hold for cryptocurrencies. The degree to which a model reproduces stylized facts is a common benchmark of its adequacy [209]. We present some of the most significant stylized facts from Cont's categorization [205].[1] The following numbering is for convenience of reference only and is not canonical.

[1]We recommend readers consult Cont's analysis and references in his paper [205].

SF1 No autocorrelation: returns are uncorrelated over time.

SF2 Heavy tails: the return distribution exhibits heavy tails, both with and without Gaussianity conditioning [210, 211].

SF3 Gain/loss asymmetry: drawdowns are typically of greater amplitude than run-ups.

SF4 Volatility clustering: returns display irregular bursts that tend to be clustered [134, 210, 212].

SF5 (Inverse) Leverage effect: there exists a correlation between volatility and price returns. We discuss the nature of that correlation in Remark 10.5. The direct leverage effect, observed on stocks, means that negative returns are associated with increased volatility [213, 214].

SF6 Volume/volatility correlation: trading volume and volatility are correlated.

Remark 10.5 *(Leverage Effect)*: The leverage effect refers to the empirical observation that negative returns are associated with increased volatility, while positive returns are associated with decreased volatility. This was first identified for stocks by Black in 1976 [215] and is often attributed to the increase in default risk for leveraged positions following a price decline.

However, the nature of the correlation depends on the asset class and market conditions, with commodities displaying an inverse[2] leverage effect [216, 217].[3] This increase in volatility as prices go up is attributed to hedging behavior and inventory levels. A growing body of research on cryptocurrencies suggests an inverse leverage effect [211, 216, 218–222], or at least a weak direct leverage effect [208].

Some authors argue that an inverse leverage effect may not persist in the long term for cryptocurrencies:

1. Much of the available data coincide with prolonged upward trends in cryptocurrency prices; consequently, volatility spikes are more likely to be observed in prevailing positive-return environments.
2. Options on some cryptocurrencies exhibit a smirk, as discussed in Section 3.2.5. The leverage effect for equities is reflected in the IV skew; an evolution from smile to smirk may signal changes in the underlying asset's volatility dynamics.
3. Leverage levels in cryptocurrency markets can be very high and may trigger liquidation cascades, as discussed in Section 6.1. This mechanism can amplify dynamics beyond those typically observed in equity markets.

As mentioned earlier in Definition 10.4, stylized facts are empirical. Their presence and characteristics are not always intrinsic to the properties of the asset and have more to do with the behavior of market participants.

[2]Sometimes it is called negative leverage effect. We will avoid this terminology as it is prone to confusion, given that the direct leverage effect corresponds to negative correlation, while the inverse leverage effect corresponds to positive correlation.

[3]The presence of the inverse leverage effect was evidenced to have changed through time, with it disappearing for oil in recent years [217, 223].

It is also interesting to note which stylized facts common in TradFi are not observed in cryptocurrencies:

- Aggregational Gaussianity: the distribution of returns is Gaussian at short time scales. This property has not been consistently observed for cryptocurrencies, in part due to persistent skew [212, 224].
- Some autocorrelation has been observed in cryptocurrency returns over longer horizons, which challenges SF1 [212].

10.3.2 Long-range Dependence Analysis

Beyond the immediate statistical properties captured by stylized facts, financial time series often exhibit long-term memory effects.

10.3.2.1 Hurst Exponent The Hurst exponent is commonly used in time series analysis. It is named after British hydrologist Hurst (1880–1978), who introduced it in 1951 [225, 226] in the context of reservoir sizing. Mandelbrot [227] made significant contributions to Hurst's work in 1972. The Hurst exponent quantifies long-term memory[4] in a time series and has been applied to stochastic processes in finance [228–232].

Definition 10.5 *(Hurst Exponent [Discrete])*: The Hurst exponent H is defined via the rescaled range of a time series $(P_t)_{t=1}^{N}$ with N observations:

$$\frac{R(N)}{S(N)} \propto N^H$$

where $X_t := \sum_{u=1}^{t} (P_u - \bar{P}(N))$ are the cumulative deviations, $\bar{P}(N)$ is the sample mean, and the range $R(N)$ and standard deviation $S(N)$ are defined as follows:

$$R(N) := \max_{1 \le t \le N} X_t - \min_{1 \le t \le N} X_t$$

$$S(N) := \sqrt{\frac{1}{N}\sum_{t=1}^{N}(P_t - \bar{P}(N))^2}$$

Remark 10.6: It is because of Definition 10.5 that the Hurst coefficient is called the Hurst exponent. This definition is also called the R/S definition, or rescaled range definition.

Corollary 10.1 ***(Computation of Hurst Exponent)***: *Using the notations of Definition 10.5, an estimate of H is computed as follows:*

$$H = \frac{1}{\log N}\left(\log \frac{R(N)}{S(N)} - \log C\right)$$

with $C \in \mathbb{R}^+$ *a constant.*

[4] Also called persistence.

The Hurst exponent takes values in [0, 1] and has a critical value at $H = 0.5$:

- $H < 0.5$ indicates anti-persistent behavior, with the series being trend-reversing.
- $H = 0.5$ indicates the series' behavior is random.[5]
- $H > 0.5$ indicates persistent behavior, with the series being trend-following.

Mandelbrot and Wallis [227, 228, 233, 234] coined the term Joseph[6] effect to describe persistence in time series, and Noah[6] effect to describe anti-persistence. These terms were also extended to macroeconomics, where Joseph effects refer to persistency of time series,[7] while Noah effects refer to abrupt and unpredictable changes. We show a comparison between these two effects in Table 10.1.

10.3.2.2 Applications to Cryptocurrency Markets The Hurst exponent is computed to assess the persistence in the context of cryptocurrency prices [231, 235], in particular for the identification of stylized facts [236].

Using Corollary 10.1, the Hurst exponent may be estimated by regressing over different horizon values T [237, 238]; with a fixed sampling interval Δt, this is equivalent to regressing over window sizes N since $T = N\Delta t$. The most common representation is a plot of the R/S ratio versus N on a log scale, as illustrated in Figure 10.1. A linear section is expected, whose slope provides an estimate of H. An alternative methodology is detrended fluctuation analysis (DFA) [238–240], which often handles nonstationarity more robustly; we omit further details here.

Another application of identifying persistence is to discuss the efficiency of a given financial market.[8] Under the theoretical framework that efficient markets are random walks, a proxy for market efficiency at a given price horizon would be to compute the Hurst exponent. Since the Efficient Market Hypothesis (EMH) suggests that prices should follow a random walk with $H = 0.5$, deviations from this value indicate market inefficiency. This motivates a simple efficiency metric derived from the Hurst exponent, which we present in Corollary 10.2.

TABLE 10.1 Comparison of Joseph and Noah Effects in the Context of Price Return Persistence

	Joseph Effect	Noah Effect
Hurst Exponent	$H > 0.5$	$H < 0.5$
Persistence	Trend-following	Trend-reversing
Memory	Persistent	Anti-persistent
Time Series Pattern	Smooth, gradual changes	Abrupt, unpredictable changes
Macroeconomic Analogy	Credit cycles	Shocks, volatility spikes

[5] In other words, it means that the series does not have any long-term memory and is a random walk.
[6] Noah and Joseph are biblical references.
[7] Credit cycles are a form of Joseph effects [234, 241].
[8] This concept relates to the Efficient Market Hypothesis (EMH).

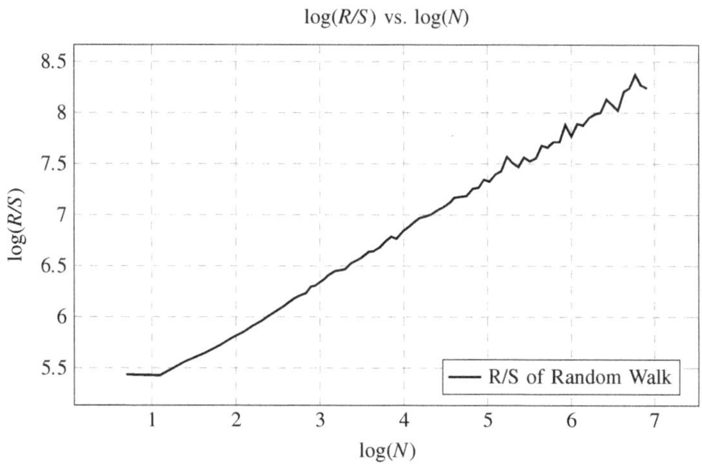

FIGURE 10.1 **Estimation of the Hurst Exponent of a Random Walk** by plotting $\log(R/S)$ as a function of $\log(N)$. In this example we simulated a random walk of length $N = 1{,}000$. We observe a slope of $H \approx 0.5$, which is expected given the characteristic value of the Hurst exponent H for purely random processes.

Note: In the context of stochastic processes, simulated paths are sometimes also called trajectories or realizations.

Corollary 10.2 *(Market Efficiency Score)*: *The market efficiency score E is defined as*

$$E = 1 - |1 - 2H|$$

with H the Hurst exponent.

CHAPTER 11

Price Return Models

This chapter develops canonical models for price returns, emphasizing their application to digital assets. We examine model properties, calibration challenges, and implications for risk management and derivative pricing in cryptocurrency markets.

- Present autoregressive models for return dynamics and discuss stationarity requirements.
- Introduce continuous-time price processes and compare their modeling trade-offs.
- Develop stochastic volatility frameworks and address practical calibration issues.

We begin with discrete-time autoregressive models and their application to cryptocurrency returns.

11.1 AR MODELS

Empirical analysis of price returns has evidenced autocorrelation, which is not expected for shorter horizons, as per SF1 in Chapter 10. This has led to the introduction of autoregressive models (AR models) that are used to model price returns [242]. These models are discrete.

Stationarity is an important concept in time series analysis, as it implies the stability of the statistical properties over time. While there are several formal definitions of stationarity, we will refer to weak stationarity[1] in this chapter.

Definition 11.1 *(Stationarity [Weak])*: A time series is said to be weakly stationary (WSS) if it satisfies both the following conditions:

- Its mean is constant.
- The covariance between two lagged values is only a function of the lag.

Definition 11.1 leads to Corollary 11.1 on the variance of the time series.

[1]This is also referred to as second-order stationarity or wide-sense stationarity (WSS) in the literature. WSS is often implied when discussing financial time series and is therefore the most common stationarity assumption in mathematical finance [242, 243].

Corollary 11.1: *Variance is also therefore constant over time under weak stationarity.*

Proof. The variance is defined as the covariance of a time series with itself. ■

In practice, Corollary 11.1 means that price return models assuming weak stationarity correspond to constant volatility.

11.1.1 ARMA

The Mixed AutoRegressive Moving Average (ARMA) model combines an autoregressive (AR) component and a moving average (MA) component. It is widely used to model return time series in finance because of its simplicity and its ability to capture correlations. It is often used alongside GARCH models for volatility, as discussed in Section 11.3.1, to model price returns R_t.

The AR component models the relationship of the current value with its past values [242–246] and has an order often denoted as p.

Definition 11.2 ***(AutoRegressive [AR] Model):*** An AutoRegressive (AR) model of order p, with notation AR(p), is defined as follows:

$$R_t = \mu + \sum_{i=1}^{p} \varphi_i R_{t-i} + \varepsilon_t$$

with $\mu \in \mathbb{R}$ the mean, $(\varphi_i)_{i \in \mathbb{N}} \in \mathbb{R}^{\mathbb{N}}$ the coefficients, and ε_t a white noise.

Remark 11.1 ***(White Noise):*** A white noise, as described in Definition 11.2, is a sequence of uncorrelated random variables with zero mean and finite variance. They are independent and identically distributed.

In other words, this means that R_t is a linear combination of past values.

Remark 11.2: We note from Definition 11.2 that an AR(0) model is a pure white noise. As a result, there is no coefficient φ_0 by convention, since we would have $\varphi_0 = 1$.

AR models have been used to model volatility for various assets, including cryptocurrencies [136].

Remark 11.3: Another common notation of the AR model is by introducing the lag operator L such that we have the following:

$$R_t = \mu + \sum_{i=1}^{p} \varphi_i L^i R_t + \varepsilon_t$$

There are constraints on the values of the coefficients φ_i to ensure stationarity [247].

Proposition 11.1: The AR model is stationary if the roots of the characteristic polynomial P:

$$P(z) = 1 - \sum_{i=1}^{p} \varphi_i z^i = 0$$

are outside the unit circle.

The proof of Proposition 11.1 is outside the scope of this material, but we can take the example of an AR(1) to develop some intuition.

Proposition 11.2: An AR(1) model is stationary if $|\varphi_1| < 1$.

We illustrate Proposition 11.2 in Figure 11.1.

Proof. We compute the expected value $\bar{R}$ based on Definition 11.2:

$$\begin{aligned} R_t &= \mu + \varphi_1 R_{t-1} + \varepsilon_t \\ \mathbf{E}R_t &= \bar{R} = \mathbf{E}\left(\mu + \varphi_1 R_{t-1} + \varepsilon_t\right) \\ &= \mu + \varphi_1 \bar{R} \\ &= \frac{\mu}{1 - \varphi_1} \end{aligned} \tag{11.1}$$

We now assume $\varphi_1 \neq \pm 1$, which is a characteristic value, as per Equation 11.1.

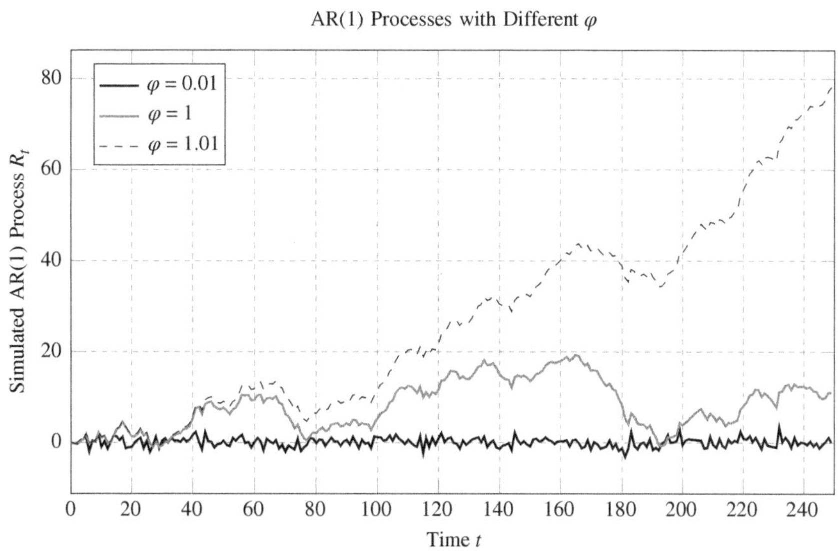

FIGURE 11.1 **AR(1) Processes with Different Coefficients** φ, with the same simulated noise. The black line represents a stationary process, while the gray and dashed lines represent nonstationary processes as per Proposition 11.2.

Writing σ_ε^2 the variance of ε_t, we can compute the variance σ_R^2 of the AR(1) model, by applying Huygens' formula:

$$\begin{aligned}\sigma_R^2 &= \mathbf{Var}R_t = \mathbf{E}\left(R_t^2\right) - \bar{R}^2\\ &= \mathbf{E}\left(R_t\left(\mu + \varphi_1 R_{t-1} + \varepsilon_t\right)\right) - \bar{R}^2\\ &= \mu\bar{R} + \varphi_1\mathbf{E}\left(R_t R_{t-1}\right) + \mathbf{E}\left(R_t\varepsilon_t\right) - \bar{R}^2\end{aligned}$$

We know $\mathbf{E}\left(R^2\right) = \mathbf{E}\left(R_t^2\right) = \mathbf{E}\left(R_{t-1}^2\right)$, assuming the independence of ε_t and R_t, and $\mathbf{E}\varepsilon_t = 0$:

$$\sigma_R^2 = \mu\bar{R} + \varphi_1\mathbf{E}\left(R_t R_{t-1}\right) + \sigma_\varepsilon^2 - \bar{R}^2 \tag{11.2}$$

We express $\mathbf{E}\left(R_t R_{t-1}\right)$ from Equation 11.2:

$$\begin{aligned}\mathbf{E}\left(R_t R_{t-1}\right) &= \mathbf{E}\left(\left(\mu + \varphi_1 R_{t-1} + \varepsilon_t\right) R_{t-1}\right)\\ &= \mu\mathbf{E}\left(R_{t-1}\right) + \varphi_1\mathbf{E}\left(R_{t-1}^2\right) + \mathbf{E}\left(R_{t-1}\varepsilon_t\right)\\ &= \mu\bar{R} + \varphi_1\mathbf{E}\left(R_{t-1}^2\right)\\ &= \mu\bar{R} + \varphi_1\mathbf{E}\left(R^2\right)\end{aligned} \tag{11.3}$$

We can then combine Equations 11.2 and 11.3, using Equation 11.1 and the assumption that $\varphi_1 \neq \pm 1$:

$$\begin{aligned}\sigma_R^2 &= \mu\bar{R} + \varphi_1\left(\mu\bar{R} + \varphi_1\mathbf{E}\left(R^2\right)\right) + \sigma_\varepsilon^2 - \bar{R}^2\\ &= \mu\bar{R} + \varphi_1\left(\mu\bar{R} + \varphi_1\left(\sigma_R^2 + \bar{R}^2\right)\right) - \bar{R}^2 + \sigma_\varepsilon^2\\ \sigma_R^2(1-\varphi_1^2) &= \mu\bar{R}(1+\varphi_1) - \bar{R}^2(1-\varphi_1^2) + \sigma_\varepsilon^2\\ \sigma_R^2 &= \bar{R}\mu\frac{1+\varphi_1}{1-\varphi_1^2} - \bar{R}^2 + \frac{\sigma_\varepsilon^2}{1-\varphi_1^2}\\ &= \bar{R}\mu\frac{1+\varphi_1}{(1-\varphi_1)(1+\varphi_1)} - \bar{R}^2 + \frac{\sigma_\varepsilon^2}{1-\varphi_1^2}\\ &= \frac{\sigma_\varepsilon^2}{1-\varphi_1^2}\end{aligned} \tag{11.4}$$

According to Equation 11.4, the variance is positive and finite if and only if Equation 11.5 is verified:

$$\begin{aligned}1-\varphi_1^2 &> 0\\ |\varphi_1| &< 1\end{aligned} \tag{11.5}$$

Because of Corollary 11.1, we can conclude on Proposition 11.2 with Equation 11.5. ■

The MA component represents the relationship of the current value with the past errors and has an order often denoted as q. As opposed to the AR model, there is no constraint on the coefficients to ensure stationarity [243, 246].

Definition 11.3 ***(Moving Average [MA] Model)*****:** A Moving Average (MA) model of order q, with notation MA(q), is defined as follows:

$$R_t = \mu + \sum_{i=1}^{q} \theta_i \varepsilon_{t-i} + \varepsilon_t$$

with $\mu \in \mathbb{R}$ the mean, $(\theta_i)_{i \in \mathbb{N}} \in \mathbb{R}^{\mathbb{N}}$ the coefficients, and ε_t a white noise.

Remark 11.4: With the lag operator L, the MA model can be written as follows:

$$R_t = \mu + \sum_{i=1}^{q} \theta_i L^i \varepsilon_t + \varepsilon_t$$

The ARMA model is a combination of the AR and MA models and is defined in Definition 11.4.

Definition 11.4 ***(ARMA Model)*****:** An AutoRegressive Moving Average (ARMA) model of order (p, q), with notation ARMA(p,q), is defined as follows:

$$R_t = \mu + \sum_{i=1}^{p} \varphi_i R_{t-i} + \sum_{i=1}^{q} \theta_i \varepsilon_{t-i} + \varepsilon_t$$

with $\mu \in \mathbb{R}$ the mean, $(\varphi_i)_{i \in \mathbb{N}} \in \mathbb{R}^{\mathbb{N}}$ the AR coefficients, $(\theta_i)_{i \in \mathbb{N}} \in \mathbb{R}^{\mathbb{N}}$ the MA coefficients, and ε_t a white noise.

The conditions on the coefficients φ_i for stationarity presented in Proposition 11.1 apply. It follows from the definition that

- ARMA(p, 0) is an AR(p) process,
- ARMA(0, q) is an MA(q) process, and
- ARMA(0, 0) is a pure white noise process.

By convention, the μ defined in Definitions 11.2–11.4 is set to 0 in finance under the assumption that returns are centered.

11.1.2 ARIMA

While ARMA models remain heavily relied upon, in particular alongside GARCH models, variants exist. One of the downsides of ARMA models is the assumption of stationarity [243], which does not always hold for highly volatile time series like digital assets.

Popular alternatives are AutoRegressive Integrated Moving Average (ARIMA) models. ARIMA models are used to model nonstationary time series [248, 249]. The main idea of ARIMA(p,d,q) models is to introduce a differencing operator, such that the d-th difference of such a process is an ARMA process. We illustrate this in Figure 11.2.

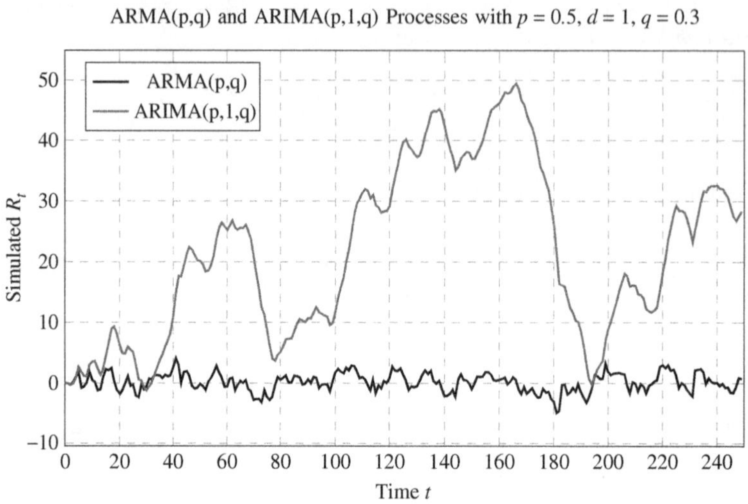

FIGURE 11.2 **ARMA(p,q) and ARIMA(p,1,q) Processes** simulated using the same white noise. The ARMA(p,q) process (black) is stationary, while the ARIMA(p,1,q) process (gray) is nonstationary. The ARIMA(p,1,q) process can be easily simulated in Python from the ARMA(p,q) by applying a cumulative sum function.

For a formal definition of the ARIMA(p,d,q) process, we refer the reader to Box et al. [249]. There are several specific cases of ARIMA processes that we want to highlight to the reader:

- ARIMA(0,1,0) is a random walk process, which is a nonstationary process.
- ARIMA(p,0,q) is an ARMA(p,q) process, which can be stationary depending on the value of p.
- ARIMA(0,0,0) is an ARMA(0,0) process, which is a pure white noise.

Even though ARIMA models are more effective at capturing nonstationarity, it is still common to segment the time intervals in different liquidity regimes in the context of financial mathematics. Most notably, ARIMA models have been successfully applied to Bitcoin [250–252].

11.1.3 Calibration

A first step in calibration is model selection. Stationarity tests such as the Dickey-Fuller (DF) test [253, 254] and its Augmented variant (ADF) are commonly used to detect unit roots and guide the choice between ARMA and ARIMA [255].

An ARMA model would be selected for stationary time series and an ARIMA for nonstationary ones. We provide a more detailed comparison in Table 11.1.

There is a comprehensive methodology due to Box and Jenkins [256, 257] for identification and parameter estimation; parameters are often estimated by maximum likelihood [257, 258].

The Box-Jenkins methodology, because of its comprehensiveness and its systematic approach, is often viewed as the industry standard [259, 260].

TABLE 11.1 Comparison of AR, ARMA, and ARIMA Models for Price Return Modeling

	AR(p)	ARMA(p,q)	ARIMA(p,d,q)
Stationarity	Assumed	Assumed	Not required, achieved after differencing
Nonstationarity handling	No	No	Yes (via differencing)
Applications	Volatility modeling	Most common with GARCH	Price returns modeling
Components	Past values only	Past values and past errors	Past values, past errors and differencing
Coefficient constraints	$\|\varphi_i\|$ constraints	$\|\varphi_i\|$ constraints	No constraints on MA
Memory	Short term	Short to medium term	Long term
Complexity	Low	Medium	Medium to high

11.2 CONSTANT VOLATILITY MODELS

Models for price processes are often classified by assumptions on volatility σ. Constant volatility models assume $\sigma(t) = \bar{\sigma}$ is constant. This approximation is useful under stationary conditions and is referred to as a stable volatility regime. Table 11.2 provides a comparison.

11.2.1 Geometric Brownian Motion

The Geometric Brownian Motion (GBM) is the most common price model used in finance. It is used to represent directly the price process of the asset.[2] It is continuous and has a closed-form solution, which we present in Theorem 11.1.

The intuition behind the GBM is that there is a drift term and a stochastic term. We mention the concept of Wiener process, which is an alternative name for Brownian motion.[3]

Definition 11.5 ***(Wiener Process)*:** A Wiener process W_t is a continuous-time stochastic process with the following properties:

- $W_0 = 0$.
- W_t has independent increments.
- W_t has normally distributed increments, meaning that for $0 \leq t < s$, $W_s - W_t \sim n(0, s - t)$.

---

[2]One notable usage of the GBM model is the Black-Scholes equation for the European option price.

[3]Wiener process is more commonly used in mathematics, while Brownian motion is more commonly used in physics. One can describe the Wiener process as the mathematical theory that describes Brownian motions, but in practice these terms are often used interchangeably.

TABLE 11.2 Comparison of Constant Volatility Models for Price Process Modeling

	GBM	OUP
Volatility	Constant	Constant
Mean reversion	No	Yes
Markov property	Yes	Yes
Closed-form solution	Yes	Yes
Distribution	Log-normal	Normal
Complexity	Low	Low to medium

Remark 11.5 ***(Absolute Wiener Process)*****:** In dimension $d = 1$, we call the absolute value of the Wiener process W_t a Bessel process of dimension one X_t:

$$X_t = \sqrt{W_t^2} = |W_t|$$

Bessel processes are commonly used to model volatility in finance, since the latter can only be positive. More generally, Bessel processes form a broader class of processes defined for a specified dimension [261–263].

Definition 11.6 ***(Geometric Brownian Motion)*****:** A GBM is a stochastic process defined as follows:

$$dP_t = \mu P_t dt + \sigma P_t dW_t$$

with μ the drift, σ^2 the volatility, and W_t a Wiener process.

Figure 11.3 illustrates the GBM process, with different values of the drift μ and volatility σ.

The proof of most results in this section use Itô's lemma, a fundamental result in stochastic calculus, which is beyond the scope of this chapter. We will simply present the lemma in differential form, also referred to as the Itô formula, and refer the reader to the literature for a more detailed discussion.

Lemma 11.1 ***(Itô's Lemma [Differential Form])*****:** *Let X_t be a stochastic process of the form defined by the stochastic differential equation*

$$dX_t = a(X_t, t)dt + b(X_t, t)dW_t$$

with W_t a Wiener process, $(a, b) \in \mathcal{C}^0$ and Lipschitz, and let $f(x, t)$ be a twice-differentiable function. Then, the differential of $f(X_t, t)$ is given by

$$df(X_t, t) = \frac{\partial f}{\partial t}dt + \frac{\partial f}{\partial X}dX_t + \frac{1}{2}\frac{\partial^2 f}{\partial X^2}(dX_t)^2$$

Further details on Itô calculus can be found in the corresponding section of the comprehensive books by Øksendal [264] or Shreve [265].

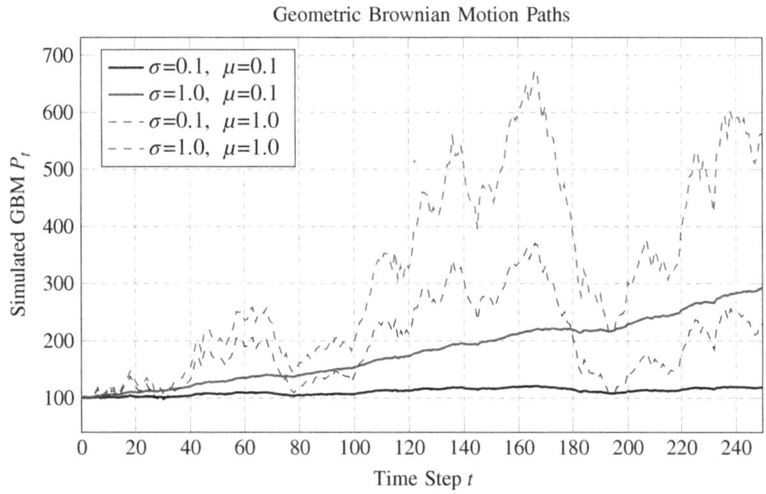

FIGURE 11.3 Geometric Brownian Motion Paths P_t simulated with the same Wiener process W_t. The paths show the effect of different values for parameters drift μ and volatility σ.

We can now solve the GBM equation to derive the closed-form solution.

Theorem 11.1 ***(Closed Form of the Geometric Brownian Motion)*****:** *The closed-form solution of the GBM is given by*

$$P_t = P_0 e^{\left(\mu - \frac{1}{2}\sigma^2\right)t + \sigma W_t}$$

with P_0 the initial price, μ the drift, σ^2 the volatility, and W_t a Wiener process.

Proof. The proof is straightforward with Itô's lemma. The idea of the proof is to introduce $df(P_t) = \frac{dP_t}{P_t}$. We can now directly write the SDE as follows:

$$\begin{aligned} dP_t &= \mu P_t dt + \sigma P_t dW_t \\ \frac{dP_t}{P_t} &= \mu dt + \sigma dW_t \\ df(P_t) &= \mu dt + \sigma dW_t \end{aligned}$$

We can now apply directly Itô's lemma, which introduces quadratic variation in the derivation of the stochastic process. We recognize that $f(P_t) = \ln P_t$:

$$\begin{aligned} df(P_t) &= \frac{\partial f}{\partial P_t} dP_t + \frac{1}{2}\frac{\partial^2 f}{\partial P_t^2}(dP_t)^2 \\ &= \frac{1}{P_t} dP_t - \frac{1}{2}\frac{1}{P_t^2}(dP_t)^2 \end{aligned}$$

and we can use known properties of Brownian motion, such as $dWdt = 0$ and $(dW)^2 = dt$. Also, $(dt)^2 = 0$:

$$
\begin{aligned}
(dP_t)^2 &= (\mu P_t dt + \sigma P_t dW_t) \cdot (\mu P_t dt + \sigma P_t dW_t) \\
&= \mu^2 P_t^2 (dt)^2 + 0 + \sigma^2 P_t^2 (dW_t)^2 \\
\frac{(dP_t)^2}{P_t^2} &= \sigma^2 dt
\end{aligned}
$$

We can now combine the results:

$$
\begin{aligned}
df(P_t) &= \frac{1}{P_t} dP_t - \frac{1}{2}\frac{1}{P_t^2}(dP_t)^2 \\
&= \mu dt + \sigma dW_t - \frac{1}{2}\sigma^2 dt \\
d \ln P_t &= \left(\mu - \frac{1}{2}\sigma^2\right) dt + \sigma dW_t
\end{aligned}
$$

We can now solve the closed form by introducing the boundary condition $P_0 = P(t = 0)$ and knowing $W_0 = W(t = 0) = 0$:

$$
P_t = P_0 \exp\left(\left(\mu - \frac{\sigma^2}{2}\right) t + \sigma W_t\right)
$$

■

Another interesting property of the GBM is that it is a Markov process. This means that the future price only depends on the current price, not on the previous prices.[4]

The GBM is commonly used to price Decentralized Finance (DeFi) options using the Black-Scholes model and to model the price processes of cryptocurrencies [266].

11.2.2 Ornstein-Uhlenbeck Process

Ornstein-Uhlenbeck Processes (OUPs) are named after physicists Ornstein (1880–1940) and Uhlenbeck (1900–1988). One feature of OUPs is that they are mean-reverting, which is a property observed in many financial time series.

Definition 11.7 ***(Ornstein-Uhlenbeck Process)*****:** An OUP is a stochastic process defined as follows:

$$
dP_t = \theta \left(\mu - P_t\right) dt + \sigma dW_t
$$

with θ the rate of mean-reversion, μ the drift, σ^2 the volatility,[5] and W_t a Wiener process.

We illustrate examples of simulated OUP processes in Figure 11.4, with different values of the mean reversion speed θ and long-term mean μ.

The OUP is also a Markov process. It is less popular than the GBM because of the mean-reverting property, although it is used for interest rates and for high-frequency

[4]This leads to simplified computations when computing the expected value of the price.
[5]It is also called dispersion in the context of OUP, in reference to physics.

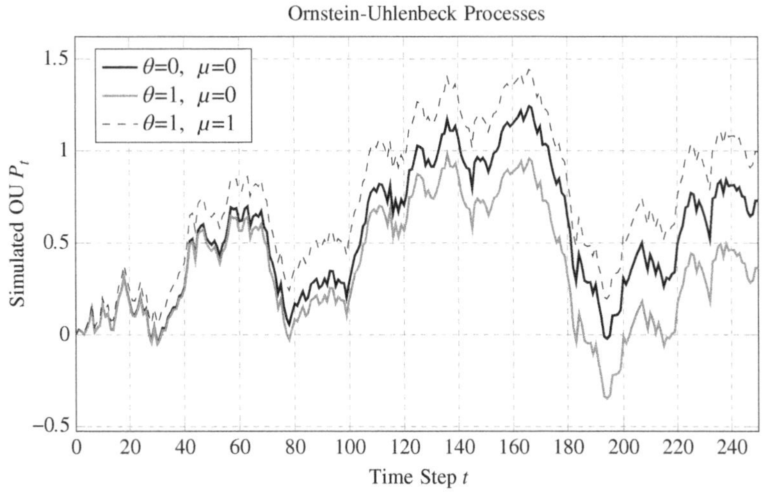

FIGURE 11.4 Ornstein-Uhlenbeck Processes P_t simulated with varying mean reversion speed (θ) and long-term mean (μ). The Wiener process W_t is the same for all simulated paths.

trading. In the context of DeFi, it is used for stablecoins and other pegged assets and can be used to model yields. Another application of OUPs in both TradFi and DeFi is to model spreads.

In the context of interest rates and other yield instruments, the OUP is referred to as the Vasicek model [267, 268]. The concept of long-term variance, or long-term volatility, is a notable feature of Vasicek processes. We define it in Definition 11.8.

Definition 11.8 ***(Long-term Variance of the OUP)*:** The long-term variance of the OUP is defined as follows:

$$\sigma_{\text{long}}^2 = \frac{\sigma^2}{2\theta}$$

with σ the volatility and θ the rate of mean-reversion.

The long-term variance would be used in practice during the model calibration phase, by looking at a steady state or longer-horizon data. There is a similar concept in the Heston model, which we discuss in Section 11.3.2.

Remark 11.6 ***(Class of Short Rates Models)*:** A notable extension of the Vasicek model, commonly used for short-term interest rates, is the Hull-White model. It is a popular model in the context of short-term interest rates [269, 270], alongside the Cox-Ingersoll-Ross (CIR) model presented in Section 16.1.

The HJM model discussed in Section 16.4, which aims at modeling the full term structure, is considered a generalization of the Vasicek model [271, 272].

11.2.3 Lévy Process

Both the GBM and the OUP are Lévy processes. Lévy processes have stationary and independent increments [273, 274] and are named after mathematician Lévy (1886–1971).

While both GBM and OUP use Wiener processes to model the stochastic component, Lévy processes are a generalization. These processes and their extensions are used in the context of commodities pricing, with one notable extension being the Carr-Geman-Madan-Yor (CGMY) model [275–278].

Because Wiener processes follow by construction a normal distribution, they are not able to reflect heavy tails, which is a known property of financial time series, as per SF2 [279]. An alternative is to introduce a stochastic component that follows a different distribution.

11.3 STOCHASTIC VOLATILITY MODELS

In Section 11.2, we assumed that the volatility σ was constant over time. This is an imperfect approximation, and it is known that volatility clustering exists in financial time series, as per SF4 [212]. Because of SF5, first observed by Black in 1976 [215], there is also a known relationship between the returns and the volatility.

We provide in this section some of the most commonly used models for stochastic volatility. We argue that given the large fluctuations in volatility for cryptocurrencies, these models are more appropriate than constant volatility models. A comparison of the main stochastic volatility models is provided in Table 11.3.

11.3.1 GARCH Model

The Generalized Autoregressive Conditional Heteroskedasticity (GARCH) model was introduced by Bollerslev [280] in 1986 and independently by Taylor [281, 282] in 1987. It is a generalization[6] of the Autoregressive Conditional Heteroskedasticity (ARCH) model introduced in 1982 by Engle[7] [283].

Both ARCH and GARCH models are discrete models [284, 285] and are primarily used to model volatility such that it displays clustering, SF4. The main idea of the GARCH model, as per Definition 11.9, is that the residual term ε_t in a price model is normally

TABLE 11.3 Comparison of Stochastic Volatility Models for Volatility Modeling

	GARCH	Heston
Time	Discrete	Continuous
Mean reversion	No	Yes
Markov property	No	Yes
Closed-form solution	No	Yes
Distribution	Normal innovations	Square-root process
Complexity	Medium	High

[6]The "G" in GARCH stands for "generalized."
[7]Engle was actually Bollerslev's PhD supervisor.

distributed, but the variance σ_t^2 is not constant over time. In this context, ε_t is also called the innovation process.

Remark 11.7: The canonical notation for the innovation process is $\varepsilon_t | \mathcal{F}_{t-1}$, with $\mathcal{F}_{t-1}$ being the information set available at time $t-1$. In GARCH models, the innovation process ε_t is said to be conditioned on $\mathcal{F}_{t-1}$, with the latter usually being functions of the past observed returns. These definitions are out of the scope of this chapter,[8] and we will use the simplified notation ε_t.

Definition 11.9 ***(GARCH Model):*** A GARCH model of order $(p, q) \in \mathbb{Z}_+^2$, with notation GARCH(p,q), is defined as follows:

$$\varepsilon_t \sim n(0, \sigma_t^2)$$

$$\sigma_t^2 = \omega + \sum_{i=1}^{p} \alpha_i \varepsilon_{t-i}^2 + \sum_{j=1}^{q} \beta_j \sigma_{t-j}^2$$

with σ_t^2 the conditional variance at time t, $\omega > 0$ a constant, $(\alpha_i)_{i=1}^p \in \mathbb{R}_+^p$ the ARCH coefficients, and $(\beta_j)_{j=1}^q \in \mathbb{R}_+^q$ the GARCH coefficients.

A variant GARCH called Exponential GARCH (EGARCH), which models the log-variance, was introduced by Nelson in 1991 [286] and is also popular. This creates an asymmetry in the model, which is useful to capture the leverage effect, Stylized Fact SF5.

Remark 11.8: As per Definition 11.9, if $q = 0$, we have a pure ARCH model. Consequently, it is assumed $q > 0$ for GARCH models.

Because GARCH models primarily deal with volatility, they are not often used on their own to model price processes. Instead, they are often combined with ARMA models, introduced in Section 11.1, to produce ARMA-GARCH models. These blended models are used for price returns, with ARMA models capturing the returns and GARCH models capturing the innovation, as illustrated in Figure 11.5.

GARCH models are used for cryptocurrencies [287–289], including for seasonality analysis [290–293].

11.3.2 Heston Model

The first modern stochastic volatility model is attributed to Hull and White [294] in 1987, but their model does not capture correlation between returns and volatility, as per SF5, the leverage effect. Stein and Stein in 1991 [295] would introduce OUP to model the volatility, while still not capturing the leverage effect.

Following these two models, Heston introduced in 1993 a new model [296], which is still arguably the most popular stochastic volatility model and is used in both TradFi and DeFi. The main idea of the Heston model is to generalize the GBM by making the variance stochastic [296, 297]. It also reflects the leverage effect.

[8] Tsay's [285] treatment of GARCH models is an excellent reference for the interested reader.

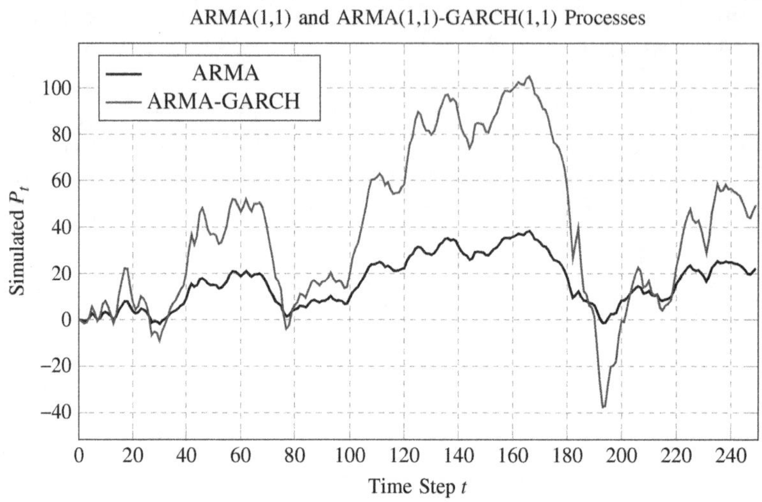

FIGURE 11.5 **ARMA(1,1) and ARMA(1,1)-GARCH(1,1) Processes.** In this example we kept the same underlying ARMA(1,1) process and introduced a GARCH(1,1) process with coefficients $\omega = 1.0$, $\alpha_1 = 0.2$, and $\beta_1 = 0.7$. The ARMA-GARCH process is more volatile than the ARMA(1,1) process, which is expected as it captures the volatility clustering.

Definition 11.10 ***(Heston Model)*:** The Heston model is a stochastic process defined as follows:

$$dP_t = \mu P_t dt + \sqrt{v_t} P_t dW_t^P$$

with the variance process v_t following a square-root process

$$dv_t = \kappa(\theta - v_t)dt + \xi\sqrt{v_t}dW_t^v$$

with κ the mean-reversion rate, θ the long-term variance, μ the drift, and ξ the volatility of variance. We introduce two distinct Wiener processes W_t^P and W_t^v respectively, with correlation ρ:

$$dW_t^P dW_t^v = \rho dt$$

Remark 11.9: The model in Definition 11.10 is sometimes referred to as the single Heston model, following the introduction of the double Heston model in 2009 [298, 299].

There is an alternative to Definition 11.10 that uses independent Wiener processes, which is more common because it can more easily be transcribed for computer simulations.

Definition 11.11 ***(Heston Model [Alternative])*:** The Heston model is a stochastic process defined as follows:

$$dP_t = \mu P_t dt + \sqrt{v_t} P_t \left(\rho dW_t^v + \sqrt{1-\rho^2} dZ_t\right)$$

with the variance process v_t following a square-root process

$$dv_t = \kappa(\theta - v_t)dt + \xi\sqrt{v_t}dW_t^v$$

with κ the mean-reversion rate, θ the long-term variance, μ the drift, ξ the volatility of variance, and ρ the correlation. We introduce two independent Wiener processes, W_t^v and Z_t.

Proof. We show Definition 11.10 is equivalent to Definition 11.11, using their notations. We start by identifying dW_t^P in Definition 11.11:

$$dW_t^P = \rho dW_t^v + \sqrt{1-\rho^2}dZ_t$$

$$dW_t^P dW_t^v = \rho(dW_t^v)^2 + \sqrt{1-\rho^2}dZ_t dW_t^v$$

and we know $dZ_t dW_t^v = 0$, by independence, and $(dW_t^v)^2 = dt$:

$$dW_t^P dW_t^v = \rho dt$$

which is in Definition 11.10. ■

Remark 11.10: To capture SF3, which is often extended as volatility increasing when returns decrease, ρ in Definition 11.10 would often be negative.

The variance v_t in the Heston model can be rewritten in terms of volatility $\sigma(t) = \sqrt{v_t}$, which follows a stochastic process,[9] as we present in Proposition 11.3.

Proposition 11.3 ***(Heston Model Volatility Dynamics)*****:** The volatility $\sigma(t) = \sqrt{v_t}$ in the Heston model follows:

$$d\sigma(t) = \frac{\kappa(\theta - \sigma^2(t))}{2\sigma(t)}dt + \frac{\xi}{2}dW_t^v - \frac{\xi^2}{8\sigma(t)}dt$$

with κ the mean-reversion rate, θ the long-term variance, and ξ the volatility of variance.

Proof. We use Itô's lemma[10] with $f : x \mapsto \sqrt{x}$:

$$\begin{aligned} df(v) &= \frac{\partial f}{\partial v}dv + \frac{1}{2}\frac{\partial^2 f}{\partial v^2}(dv)^2 \\ d\sigma(t) &= \frac{1}{2\sqrt{v_t}}dv_t + \frac{1}{2}\cdot\left(-\frac{1}{4}v_t^{-3/2}\right)(dv_t)^2 \end{aligned} \tag{11.6}$$

We derive from Definition 11.10 the quadratic variation of the variance process. We use known properties: $(dt)^2 = 0$, $dt \cdot dW_t^v = 0$, and $(dW_t^v)^2 = dt$:

$$\begin{aligned} (dv_t)^2 &= \left(\kappa(\theta - v_t)dt + \xi\sqrt{v_t}dW_t^v\right)^2 \\ &= \kappa^2(\theta - v_t)^2(dt)^2 + 2\kappa(\theta - v_t)\xi\sqrt{v_t}dt \cdot dW_t^v + \xi^2 v_t(dW_t^v)^2 \\ &= \xi^2 v_t dt \end{aligned} \tag{11.7}$$

[9]This representation shows how volatility behaves in the Heston model, though the variance formulation is more common [296, 300].
[10]Refer to the proof of Theorem 11.1.

We can now combine Equations 11.6 and 11.7:

$$
\begin{aligned}
d\sigma(t) &= \frac{1}{2\sqrt{v_t}}\left(\kappa(\theta - v_t)dt + \xi\sqrt{v_t}dW_t^v\right) - \frac{1}{8}v_t^{-3/2}\xi^2 v_t dt \\
&= \frac{\kappa(\theta - v_t)}{2\sqrt{v_t}}dt + \frac{\xi}{2}dW_t^v - \frac{\xi^2}{8\sqrt{v_t}}dt \\
&= \frac{\kappa(\theta - \sigma^2(t))}{2\sigma(t)}dt + \frac{\xi}{2}dW_t^v - \frac{\xi^2}{8\sigma(t)}dt
\end{aligned}
$$

■

Remark 11.11: The complete dynamics include an additional drift term $-\frac{\xi^2}{8\sigma(t)}dt$ arising from the quadratic variation. This term is often omitted in practice, since it is typically small relative to the main drift term when ξ is small.

There is one important condition in the Heston model used at the calibration stage. Because the variance $v_t > 0$, we must observe the following condition [301, 302]:

$$2\kappa\theta > \xi^2$$

which is referred to as the Feller condition.[11]

Another attractive feature of the Heston model is that it has an explicit closed-form solution [296]. However, one of its main limitations is that variance can become negative during simulation, in particular when the Feller condition is not respected, which is not realistic.

11.3.3 Rough Volatility Models

Rough volatility models are a modern framework that captures jumps in volatility, which is linked to SF4. Rough volatility theory is attributed to Comte and Renault [303] in 1998 who introduced the Fractional Stochastic Volatility (FSV) model. The main idea is to replace the GBM with a fractional Brownian motion[12] process, which better captures long-term memory properties of volatility.

Table 11.4 provides a comparison between rough volatility models and classical stochastic volatility models.

Local volatility models are stochastic volatility models, which were developed as an extension of the BSM model for options pricing. They are used to model the IV surface, which we discussed in Section 3.2.5. Goodness of fit of these models is assessed by comparing with observed volatility surfaces on the market [209].

The Bergomi model in 2005 is one of the most popular to date [305, 306]. It aims to represent the forward volatility curve, which is the IV of options with different maturities, and the volatility skew [307, 308]. We refer the reader to Bergomi's book [308] for more details about his model. The concepts to discuss this model in more detail are not addressed

[11] This is also a reference to the underlying theory of the CIR process, discussed in Section 16.1 [300, 301, 304].

[12] Fractional Brownian motions are a type of Brownian motion, like the GBM introduced in Section 11.2.1, defined by their Hurst exponent, which we introduced in Section 10.3.2.1.

TABLE 11.4 Comparison of Rough Versus Classical Volatility Models

	Classical Models	Rough Models
Memory	Short term	Long term
Markov property	Yes	No (returns)
Brownian motion	Standard	Fractional
Hurst exponent	$H = 0.5$	$H < 0.5$
Path behavior	Smooth	Rough
Vol. of vol.	Constant or smooth	Time-varying
Complexity	Medium to high	Very high

here. A notable variant of the Bergomi model, called the rough Bergomi model,[13] was introduced by Bayer et al. [306, 309] in 2016.

Rough volatility is arguably one of the most popular and active fields of research in financial mathematics, with significant advancements in TradFi [309–312]. It has also been applied successfully to cryptocurrencies [313–316].

Remark 11.12: For a comprehensive read on the topic of rough volatility, we refer the reader to the eponymous book *Rough Volatility* [312], whose authors comprise many of the leading researchers on that topic and leading figures in contemporary quantitative finance.

[13]Research has evidenced that the rough Bergomi model would have performed well in highly distressed markets during the Great Financial Crisis (GFC) [309].

Open Problems

These thought experiments are guided explorations into the concepts discussed in this part of the book.
Hints are available at `www.tomespel.com/books/mfin25`.

Problem IV.1: Three trading bots use different methods to calculate returns and size their positions. One uses log returns, another uses simple returns, and the third uses arctan returns. During a sudden crash, all place trades in the same direction, but the one with simple returns outperforms. Why?

Problem IV.2: Under what circumstances would a stablecoin display a Joseph effect?

Problem IV.3: A bridge between two blockchains ceases to work during a market crash. The price of the wrapped token on the isolated chain becomes more stable than the native token on the original chain. Explain why.

Problem IV.4: Two traders fit the price returns of the same cryptocurrency. One uses an ARIMA process, the other an ARMA process. Both turn a profit. Can they trade at the same horizon?

PART Five

Pricing Theory

"To understand how something works, figure out how to break it."

Nassim N. Taleb, The Bed of Procrustes

CHAPTER 12

Discounting and Staking

Digital assets require adaptations to traditional concepts of discounting and time value of money. In DeFi, network time operates independently of physical time, and staking mechanisms create unique risk-free rate structures. These concepts form the foundation for the pricing framework developed in Chapter 14.

- Develop mathematical frameworks for pricing theory incorporating staking, fees, and interest rate mechanisms specific to digital assets.
- Establish network time and market time concepts, examining their implications for staking rewards and fee structures in pricing applications.

We begin by examining different time coordinate systems and their applications in blockchain pricing.

12.1 CLOCKS

While physical time is the standard in quantitative finance, blockchain systems benefit from choosing time coordinates that simplify most computations and assumptions in pricing.

Time changes have been used in TradFi, including in the context of commodities pricing [263, 277, 317]. We note that these concepts can be easily applied beyond the field of pricing for digital assets and cryptocurrencies, in particular the concept of market time.

12.1.1 Network Time

We introduce the concept of network time t_B for pricing applications, as opposed to physical time t, which is off-chain.

Definition 12.1 *(Network Time)*: The network time on a blockchain is the duration since the genesis block.

We can represent mathematically the number of blocks as a counting sequence, $(B_i)_{i\in\mathbb{N}}$. Because blockchains have the concept of genesis block, meaning they have no existence before that block, we can even assume that the first block is at time $t_B = 0$.

Remark 12.1: One may refer to network time as blockchain time instead, given that it is based on the addition of blocks to the blockchain. However, we suggest not using this terminology, since it can be confused with block time, which corresponds to the physical time it takes to create one block.

Definition 12.2: The unit of network time is the number of consecutive blocks recognized by a majority of participants on a blockchain.

Remark 12.2 ***(Interpolation to Continuous Time):*** The BSM model and other pricing models require continuous time to apply Itô calculus and solve stochastic differential equations. This allows us to define network time for any real value, not just at block boundaries.

While network time is defined by its discrete increments, we can extend it to a continuous domain for continuous-time stochastic calculus applications. For physical time $t \in [t_i, t_{i+1})$, where t_i is the timestamp of block i, we have the following:

$$t_B(t) = i + \frac{t - t_i}{t_{i+1} - t_i}$$

which is a piecewise-linear interpolation. For all block timestamps, we have $t_B(t_i) = i \in \mathbb{N}$. This interpolation preserves the property that $t_B(t_i) = i \in \mathbb{N}$ for all block timestamps.

Remark 12.3 ***(Why Not Epochs?):*** For some blockchains, the concept of epoch is used. The definition of an epoch will vary greatly from one blockchain to another, making it less practical. To illustrate, one Bitcoin epoch corresponds to the time between two halvings, which is set to 210,000 blocks and has been historically around every four years. In contrast, a Cardano epoch is defined as a fixed period of physical time, currently set at five days.

We introduced network time t_B in Definition 12.2 such that the unit of time is the number of blocks where $t_B \in \mathbb{N}$, as per Proposition 12.1. An illustration of network time is provided in Figure 12.1.

Proposition 12.1: In network time, the interval between two blocks is exactly 1.

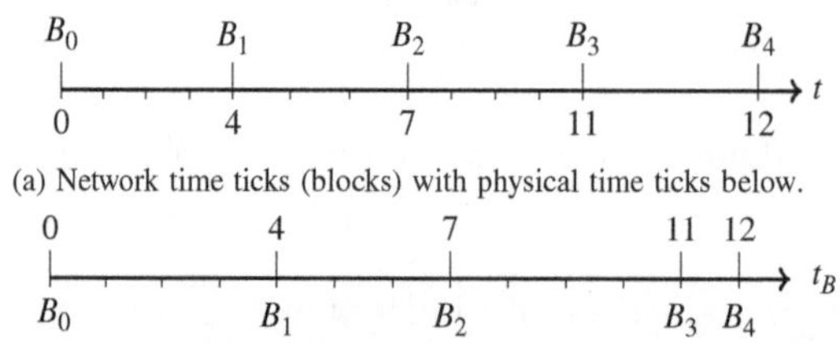

(a) Network time ticks (blocks) with physical time ticks below.

(b) Physical time ticks with network time ticks (blocks) below.

FIGURE 12.1 **Network Time and Physical Time** represented aligned with each other. In 12.1a, the number of evenly spaced ticks of physical time is different between two ticks of network time, and vice versa in 12.1b.

Proposition 12.1 means that the increment in network time corresponds to block time in physical time. We note that for some protocols where block time and hash rate are linked, we could also draw an equivalence with number of hashes, the computer operations, instead of physical time.

Remark 12.4 ***(Block Timestamps and Settlement)*****:** While transactions are effectively only recorded on the blockchain for times $t_B \in \mathbb{N}$, we still prefer to define the time as continuous. This is because transactions are still agreed between parties between blocks, and the recording is effectively only the settlement of such transactions.

Proposition 12.2: Let $\mathcal{B} = \{B_0, B_1, B_2, \ldots\}$ be the sequence of blocks and $T = \{t_0, t_1, t_2, \ldots\}$ be their corresponding timestamps in physical time. There exists a bijection $\phi : \mathcal{B} \to T$.

Proof. By construction, each block B_i is created at a unique physical time t_i. We can define the function ϕ such that $\phi(B_i) = t_i$ accordingly. ∎

Corollary 12.1: *Each block corresponds to exactly one timestamp.*

Corollary 12.1 highlights the uniqueness of block timestamps. This is a necessary approximation where the mathematical framework diverges from reality. In practice, new blocks added to the blockchain will slowly be recognized by network nodes due to the inherent propagation mechanism.

By convention, consensus is reached when the majority of nodes have added and recognized the block, which we used in Definition 12.2. Alternatively, another convention could be that whenever at least one node recognizes the block, it is considered added to the blockchain.

Regardless of the convention chosen, Corollary 12.1 is essential for establishing an adequate mapping between network time and physical time under Corollary 12.2.

Corollary 12.2: *Under deterministic block times, there exists a bijection between continuous physical time and continuous network time.*

Remark 12.5 ***(Stochastic Nature of the Bijection)*****:** We state Corollary 12.2 with the assumption of deterministic block times. In practice, block arrivals follow stochastic processes, which makes network time a counting process rather than a smooth bijection. However, this approximation remains reasonable over shorter time intervals where the stochastic variations average out.

A mathematically rigorous formulation of Corollary 12.2 is that the mapping between the two continuous time scales constitutes a bijection.

Proof. We assume deterministic timestamps (t_i) for blocks. Let $\varphi : \mathbb{R}_+ \to \mathbb{R}_+$ be the function mapping physical time t to network time t_B. We know each block B_i has a unique timestamp t_i from Proposition 12.2.

For any physical time $t \in [t_i, t_{i+1})$, we define $\varphi(t) = i + \frac{t-t_i}{t_{i+1}-t_i}$. This linearly interpolates network time values between blocks:

- **Injectivity.** If $\varphi(t_1) = \varphi(t_2)$, then t_1 and t_2 must be in the same interval $[t_i, t_{i+1})$ with the same fractional position, hence $t_1 = t_2$.
- **Surjectivity.** For any network time $t_B \in \mathbb{R}_+$, let $i = \max\{k \in \mathbb{N} \mid k \leq t_B\}$ and $\alpha = t_B - i$. Then $t = t_i + \alpha(t_{i+1} - t_i)$ satisfies $\varphi(t) = t_B$.

Therefore φ is bijective. ■

In practice, some blockchains have stochastic block times, while our framework assumes deterministic block timestamps (t_i). This approximation holds for the following reasons:

- While block times are stochastic for many blockchains, some have bounded ranges around a target block time, such as Solana.
- The approximation is reasonable over short time intervals where the stochastic variations average out.
- One could model block times as a stochastic process, but this adds complexity that is unnecessary for our pricing framework where we work in network time units.

12.1.2 Market Time

We discuss the concept of market time t_M for pricing applications. The concept parallels network time, but the unit of time corresponds to the arrival of new information to market participants. It is sometimes also called the innovation process, as it brings new information to the market.

Definition 12.3 ***(Market Time)*:** Market time is a time coordinate where the unit corresponds to the arrival of new market information.

Remark 12.6: We assume both time coordinates are continuous, and we can do a similar proof as for network time to show the mapping is bijective. We are interested in the ticks, which are the units of time, in the following section.

There is no consensus in the literature if market time is a continuous or a discrete time coordinate.

Remark 12.7: Market time is most commonly used in the context of high-frequency trading.

In the specific context of blockchain networks, a new block is new information, and therefore there is a direct mapping between the ticks in network time and the ticks in market time.

Assuming market time is continuous, we can use similar arguments to Corollary 12.1 to show bijectivity with both physical time and network time.

12.2 PRICING ASSUMPTIONS

12.2.1 Axioms

We introduce two important concepts in pricing, which we formulate as axioms:

- No-arbitrage in Section 12.2.1.1
- Time Value of Money (TVM) in Section 12.2.3

12.2.1.1 No-arbitrage and Replication

Definition 12.4 ***(No-arbitrage)*:** No-arbitrage is the absence of risk-free profit opportunities.

Corollary 12.3: *Two identical assets will have the same price.*

Corollary 12.4 ***(Replication)*:** *Two assets with the same payoffs will have the same price.*

Remark 12.8: Corollary 12.4 is also called the Law of One Price. We chose to present it as a corollary to the no-arbitrage definition, as it is its direct consequence.

Corollary 12.4 leads to the concept of replication, which is the basis of several pricing models, including the Black-Scholes-Merton (BSM) model.

12.2.2 Terminology

Before proceeding further, we clarify three key concepts in quantitative finance that are often confused with one another:

Price is how much is agreed to pay for a contract at initiation.

Payoff refers to the cash flows of the contract, this is sometimes called the payout in the context of options.

Present Value (PV) is the value of the future payoff at the present time, and is discussed in Section 12.2.5.

A convention we will discuss in the next sections is that we aim to price contracts under no-arbitrage, such that at initiation, the price is equal to the PV of future payoffs. This is sometimes called fair pricing, and we present it in mathematical terms in Remark 12.18.

12.2.3 Risk-free Rate

Definition 12.5 ***(Risk-free Rate)*:** The risk-free rate is the rate of return of an investment with no risk of financial loss.

We refer to the risk-free rate of return of Definition 12.5 more simply as the risk-free rate. An asset that pays the risk-free rate is also called a risk-free asset. We emphasize that the risk-free rate does not have to be certain, in the sense of known in advance,[1] its existence is sufficient. The risk-free rate is essential to the definition of time value of money (TVM), discussed in Section 12.2.5.

Remark 12.9 *(Nominal and Real Risk-free Rate)*: The concept of risk-free rate takes its roots in early monetary theory. The concept of risk-free rate is theoretical in nature and can be approached under different angles:

Nominal Risk-free Rate The nominal risk-free rate is the rate of return on a risk-free asset without adjusting for inflation.

Real Risk-free Rate The real risk-free rate is the rate of return on a risk-free asset after adjusting for inflation.

We adopt, as does most of the financial literature, the first definition of the risk-free rate, as nominal. This means that Definition 12.5 can be interpreted as the return of an asset with a guaranteed payoff. If we were to uphold the second definition, it would be something closer to the return of an asset that holds its value over time.

To properly define TVM in the context of cryptocurrencies, we present several results linked to the risk-free rate, in particular Theorems 12.1 and 12.2.

Theorem 12.1 *(Unicity of Risk-free Rate)*: *There is only one risk-free rate per blockchain.*

Proof. Let R_1 and R_2 be the rates of return of risk-free assets A_1 and A_2 on the same blockchain. Assume $R_1 < R_2$. Then, there exists an arbitrage opportunity between A_1 and A_2, where an investor can borrow at the lower rate R_1 and invest at the higher rate R_2 without any risk, as per Definition 12.4. This is not possible in a no-arbitrage market; therefore, $R_1 = R_2$. ■

Remark 12.10: While the risk-free rate is unique, there can be theoretically several risk-free assets on a blockchain.

Theorem 12.2 *(Risk-free Rate of Blockchains)*: *The activity of validating or mining new blocks on a blockchain is risk-free for the purposes of pricing under network time.*

We implicitly make some assumptions when stating Theorem 12.2, including that validators act honestly and the protocol operates as designed.

Proof. We can verify the following with regard to the activity of mining or staking, introduced in Section 2.5:

- The activity of validating or mining new blocks on a blockchain guarantees the existence of a reward to honest validators, conditional on protocol rules. This guarantee is provided directly by the protocol.
- Under network time t_B, the payoff time is deterministic, corresponding to $t_B + 1$ for a notional amount staked at time t_B, assuming successful validation.

[1] This is also referred to as ex ante.

- The payoff function (per-block reward) is deterministic conditional on the protocol state; ex ante, it may be modeled as stochastic via network characteristics.[2]

Since honest validators receive rewards with no loss of principal and deterministic timing in network time, this activity satisfies the definition of risk-free for the purpose of pricing. ■

While the risk-free rate, and its corresponding asset, are a theoretical construction, the latter is most often approximated using safe government bonds, in particular the US Treasury bills.[3] In DeFi, Theorem 12.2 shows that the risk-free rate can be earned by network participants. We can even identify which instrument yields the risk-free rate on a blockchain as per Theorem 12.3.

Theorem 12.3 ***(Risk-free Rate for Native Coin)*:** *The payoff of the validator for the native coin on a blockchain with a staking consensus mechanism is the risk-free rate.*

Proof. We need to prove that the staking reward is a rate, and then prove that it is risk-free.

Proof of the rate. We assume validators operate the optimal number of validating nodes, which we describe in Remark 12.12, such that they maximize the reward per total amount staked. As a result, the payoff of the validator is proportional to the amount staked, meaning it is a rate.

Proof of the risk-free activity. We know from Theorem 12.2 that the activity of validating or mining new blocks on a blockchain is risk-free for the purposes of pricing.

The payoff of a validator is therefore risk-free, and the rate is the risk-free rate by unicity stated in Theorem 12.1. ■

As discussed following Theorem 12.2, we assume validators act honestly and protocols operate as designed. While slashing and protocol risks exist, we treat staking yields as risk-free for theoretical consistency within the blockchain ecosystem.

Remark 12.11 ***(Adjusting for Risk)*:** An easy and common way to adjust for the existence of the risk is to apply a nominal risk penalty, which would be subtracted from the staking rate, to obtain an adjusted risk-free rate. However, this is not necessary for our purposes, as we are only interested in the existence of a risk-free rate for pricing theory.

---

[2]Such characteristics, e.g., active validators or fees, may be stochastic. Ex post, conditional on realized protocol state, rewards are determined by the rules.

[3]In TradFi the risk-free rate is not achievable for most investors, but it is approximated by government bonds, usually US Treasury obligations. We can easily argue that no private lender in the DeFi market can be regarded as reputable as a government entity. A natural question concerns why the reference rate of a central bank cannot always be used as a risk-free rate. The rationale is that this rate is a policy tool, instead of a tradable market instrument. Furthermore, most investors cannot invest, as it is often only accessible to depository institutions.

This parallels the use of government bonds in TradFi as risk-free despite their inherent risks, making staking perhaps more accurately a "least-risk rate" as noted in Remark 12.14.

Remark 12.12 *(Optimal Number of Validators)*: The proof of Theorem 12.3 assumes that validators operate the optimal number of validating nodes. We define this as the following state of equilibrium:

- The marginal utility for participants, in terms of security and resiliency, of each additional validator has decreased to match the marginal cost.
- Each validator controls enough nodes to be profitable, earning exactly their opportunity cost.
- The blockchain maintains balance among the three pillars described in Section 2.1.2.

This equilibrium prevents both excessive concentration, which would violate decentralization, and excessive competition, which would make validation unprofitable. As a result, the staking rate equals the risk-free rate as validators cannot earn excess returns.

A common objection to staking being risk-free is the possibility of slashing, where a validator may lose their staked funds. As discussed in Section 2.5, slashing occurs when validators act dishonestly. In our analysis, we assume that validators adhere to protocol rules and that dishonest behavior is efficiently disincentivized by both the staking rewards and the threat of slashing.

Remark 12.13 *(Miners)*: We exclude from Theorem 12.3 the case of miners because the reward is not proportional to an amount of coins and it is therefore not a rate.

Remark 12.14 *(Risk-free or Least-risk Rate?)*: A reasonable interpretation of Remark 12.9 could be that we set the risk-free rate on mined blockchains to zero. In other words, we would say that there is nothing guaranteeing a payoff, except for holding the digital asset. This would however be inconsistent with financial practice:

- Even though holding cash is the best guaranteed payoff in TradFi, it can still be subject to inflation,[4] if we regard it as a real risk-free rate.
- Investors demand returns on holding any asset, and we can imagine very short-term instruments providing a payoff with marginally low risk.
- In TradFi, the risk-free rate is often represented by the yield on government bonds,[3] which are considered safe investments. In such cases, a more adequate name for risk-free rate might be "least-risk rate."

As mentioned in Remark 12.9, the concept of risk-free rate from Definition 12.5 is theoretical. We actually do not need to assume the existence of such rate for pricing theory, in particular for the Fundamental Theorem of Asset Pricing (FTAP), which we discuss in Section 14.2.

[4]In the context of coins, inflation corresponds to monetary emission by the protocol itself. Note that some protocols have capped monetary emission, such as Bitcoin, and therefore this argument would not apply.

Corollary 12.5: *The risk-free rate for digital assets that are mined is theoretical and cannot be achieved by investors.*

Proof. The only form of reward guaranteed by the protocol in a PoW network is the block reward.[5] However, this reward does not scale proportionally with the resources committed on-chain by miners. ∎

Remark 12.15 ***(Risk-free Rate Without Staking)*****:** We argue, as an extension of Corollary 12.5, that a risk-free rate for mined assets can be approximated by the market rate of the best and most reputable lender at every single point in time.[3] This is, however, an imperfect approximation, since these lenders are, by construction, risky, and it would be difficult to always lend from the top lender at every point in time.

The construction of a risk-free rate as one of the most reputable lenders at any given point in time, as we detail in Remark 12.15, has historically been the most accurate. Central banks are a relatively recent invention in economic history. The most reputable lender at any given point in time is the lender of last resort, often regarded as the "last man standing" in a crisis. This idea can be traced back to Bagehot in *Lombard Street* [185], as shown in Figure 12.2, in the mid-eighteenth-century London. The interpretation of Corollary 12.5

FIGURE 12.2 **Photograph on Lombard Street** in London, UK, in 2025. The street begins where the photograph was taken, at the intersection of Threadneedle Street and Poultry, in the heart of the City of London. The Bank of England, the UK's central bank, is on the left of the old Royal Exchange. Lombard Street itself continues on the right side of the image.
Source: With permission of Aurelien Dworniczek.

[5]Some protocols guarantee only the block reward, with additional compensation derived from transaction fees paid by users.

then goes that it is the subjectivity, in an environment where the soundness of different lenders is untested, that makes the risk-free rate impossible to achieve with certainty, in the context of blockchains without staking.

This result of Theorem 12.3 can be extended from the mainnet to sidechains as per Corollary 12.6.

Corollary 12.6: *The payoff of the validator for the native coin on a sidechain is the risk-free rate.*

Proof. A sidechain is an independent blockchain that is bound to its mainnet by a federation. The coin on the sidechain supports the blockchain of that sidechain and therefore is akin to native coin. ■

12.2.4 Compounding

Assume an instrument provides a payoff at simple rate R, which can be the risk-free rate or any other rate in this section. Given an initial notional S_0 we can write the payoff F as follows:

$$F = S_0(1 + R) \tag{12.1}$$

We can also rewrite Equation 12.1 assuming an annualized simple rate R and a term T:

$$F = S_0(1 + RT) \tag{12.2}$$

The representation of Equation 12.1 is called the simple or linear rate. It is convenient when there is only one payment and one term for interest to accrue. We now assume there are, say, two installments that compound. We would write Equation 12.3:

$$F = S_0\left(1 + \frac{R}{2}\right)\left(1 + \frac{R}{2}\right) \tag{12.3}$$

We can infer by recursion from Equation 12.3 the general term of discrete compounding, with N regular installments as follows:

$$F = S_0\left(1 + \frac{R}{N}\right)^N$$

As we did for Equation 12.2, we can rewrite this as a function of the term T.

We can generalize for any maturity T, with the same normalized simple rate R as Definition 12.6.

Definition 12.6 ***(Discrete Compounding)*:** Let F be the payoff of an instrument with N payoffs at normalized simple rate R over period T for notional S_0:

$$F(T) = S_0\left(1 + \frac{R}{N}\right)^{NT}$$

Remark 12.16: We treat NT as the effective number of compounding periods; i.e., either take $NT \in \mathbb{N}$, or interpret via the continuous-time extension in Equation 12.4.

A common assumption made in mathematical finance is that of continuous compounding. This means that interest accrues continuously, instead of at regular intervals, accruing infinitesimal interest. In Definition 12.6, this means that the number of installments $N \to \infty$:

$$\begin{aligned} F(T) &= \lim_{N \to \infty} S_0 \left(1 + \frac{R}{N}\right)^{NT} \\ F(T) &= S_0 e^{RT} \end{aligned} \tag{12.4}$$

The continuous compounding in Equation 12.4 is sometimes called the exponential rate, to differentiate it better from the discrete compounding rate of Definition 12.6.

The linear representation of Equation 12.1 is often used for simplicity in practical applications and for some quoting conventions. Discrete and continuous compounding rates, used in pricing, can be related to one another per Proposition 12.3.

Proposition 12.3 ***(Equivalence of Discrete and Continuous Compounding)*****:** We use notations of Definition 12.6. For RT close to zero, the linear and continuous compounding representations are approximately equivalent:

$$F(T) = S_0\,(1 + RT) \approx S_0 e^{RT}$$

Proof. Direct application of the Taylor expansion of the exponential function, near zero. ■

Remark 12.17: We note that Proposition 12.3 is only an approximation. In practice, there are different market conventions for different products on whether their rate is expressed in continuous compounding or not, with the latter being referred to as the simple rate.

We can take the example of a simple rate $R = 10\%$ and notice the difference over $N = 1, T = 5$ for a principal of 1:

$$\begin{aligned} F_{\text{simple}}(T) &= \left(1 + \frac{R}{N}\right)^{NT} \\ &= \left(1 + \frac{0.1}{1}\right)^{1 \cdot 5} \simeq 1.61051 \\ F_{\text{continuous}}(T) &= e^{RT} \\ &= e^{0.1 \cdot 5} \simeq 1.64872 \end{aligned}$$

For larger principal amounts, this difference becomes substantial. Therefore, the equivalence is only really used for small rates and short periods.

12.2.5 Time Value of Money

We can now properly introduce discounting and TVM.

If there exists an investment with continuously compounded rate of return R with payoff F for notional S_0 after duration T, the payoff is given by Equation 12.4. This means that receiving S_0 now is more profitable for an investor than at time T, since they can immediately purchase the instrument that provides payoff F at time T. This concept is called the time value of money (TVM).

Conversely, given the TVM, if a lump sum payment of value S_0 is received after time T, we cannot infer that it has the same value as if it were received today. We can actually compute an adjusted value of that future payment S_0 as of today, which is PV the present value (PV):

$$\begin{aligned} PV \cdot e^{RT} &= S_0 \\ PV &= S_0 e^{-RT} \end{aligned} \tag{12.5}$$

Remark 12.18 ***(Zero Net PV)*****:** The PV of a financial asset is not necessarily equal to its price. As a case in point, futures contracts have a quoted price but are typically described as having a PV of zero at inception. Under the no-arbitrage principle, the price of a contract equals the difference between the PV of the future payoff and the PV of the obligation, which is what is paid. This means the net PV, the difference of the two PVs, is zero. This is referred to as a net PV of zero at inception, or sometimes simply as PV of zero:

$$\text{Price}(t = 0) = \text{PV}_{\text{payoff}}(t = 0) - \text{PV}_{\text{obligation}}(t = 0)$$

A contract with zero net PV at inception is therefore said to be fairly priced.

We call discounting the process of valuing the future cash flows in the present using a reference rate of return R and define this idea more formally in Definition 12.7.

Remark 12.19 ***(Choice of Discounting Rate)*****:** The choice of discounting rate R corresponds to the expected rate of return of the investment. The latter reflects investor preferences or market expectations,[6] which are based on the market's perceived probabilities of future outcomes. We sometimes refer to this approach as pricing under the real-world probability measure $\mathbb{P}$, a concept that we will discuss in Section 14.3.

Definition 12.7 ***(Discounting)*****:** Let R be the discounting rate and $T \in \mathbb{R}_+$ the discounting period. The discounting factor $\mathcal{D}(R; T)$ is defined as follows:

$$\mathcal{D}(R; T) := e^{-RT}$$

We can rewrite Equation 12.5 using Definition 12.7:

$$PV = S_0 \mathcal{D}(R; T)$$

Remark 12.20: By construction, the discounting factor in Definition 12.7 is always strictly positive. When $\mathcal{D} > 1$, it means that money is worth more in the future than now, which is a deflationary environment with $R < 0$.

[6]It is often taken to be the risk-free rate, as is discussed in Remark 14.12.

Note that we have made the assumption that the discounting rate R is constant over the period T. This is not always verified, and we can generalize by introducing the instantaneous interest rate.

The instantaneous (forward) interest rate is the interest rate for a very short period, typically approaching zero, that we expect today will be applied at a future maturity M. We will discuss it in more detail in Chapter 13. It can be represented as the function $r : M \to r(M)$ such that we can rewrite Definition 12.7 as follows:

$$\mathcal{D}(r; M) := \exp\left(-\int_0^M r(u)du\right)$$

Remark 12.21 ***(Integrability of the Rate Function)***: In practice, $r : M \mapsto r(M)$ is such that $r \notin \mathcal{C}^0(\mathbb{R})$. This is because there are jumps that correspond to changes in the reference rate.[7]

We can still integrate r despite it not being continuous because it is piecewise continuous[8] except for a finite number of discontinuities on any finite interval, and these jumps are bounded.

Given our distinction between tokens and coins, the immediate consequence of Corollary 12.6, expressed with the concept of discounting is the following:

Corollary 12.7: *From the perspective of on-chain participants under $\mathbb{B}$, a token does not admit a risk-free rate and is discounted at the native coin's staking rate on that blockchain.*

The result of Corollary 12.7 is important for pricing, as it clearly establishes the difference between risk-free assets and risky assets on a given blockchain. Some of its main implications are the following:

- No layer 2 or layer 3 digital asset can offer a risk-free rate when pricing in the perspective of the mainnet.
- Wrapped tokens can never be risk-free assets, since they are not native to the blockchain on which they are transacted.

The argument for TVM, which allows us to discount, can only be used in the case of purely deterministic cash flows. In practice, cash flows are stochastic, and we need to introduce broader arbitrage pricing theory concepts in Chapter 14 to compute under expectation.

[7]These jumps correspond either to central bank policy changes, or changes in rate from one block to another in the case of staking, as discussed in Section 2.5.

[8]It is at least bounded and for most reference rates, constant in those open intervals.

CHAPTER 13

Forward Rate Curve

Interest rate expectations drive asset valuations across all financial markets. The term structure captures these market expectations across different maturities through mathematical relationships essential for pricing rate-dependent instruments. This chapter presents the TradFi foundations that will inform our DeFi extensions in subsequent chapters.

- Establish mathematical relationships between zero-coupon bonds (ZCBs), forward rates, and yield curves from TradFi.
- Present forward rate agreements (FRAs) and interest rate swaps (IRSs) as foundational instruments for rate modeling applications.

We begin with core terminology, presenting traditional concepts before exploring their extensions to DeFi in Chapter 14.

13.1 RATES AND CURVES

Thus far, we have mainly discussed the instantaneous (forward) rate $r : M \to r(M)$, which is the rate today that is expected to apply at a future maturity M.

Definition 13.1 ***(Forward Rate Curve)*****:** The (forward) rate curve is the function $r : M \to r(M)$ of the instantaneous forward interest rates as a function of their maturity M. It assumes continuous compounding.

Remark 13.1: Term structure is a more general relationship where the price of an asset is related to different maturities. While the forward rate curve is technically just the representation of the term structure for forward rate instruments, the terms are often used interchangeably by practitioners.

There is one specific value of the instantaneous forward rate observed at time 0 for maturity 0; it is called the short rate.[1] It is the only point that is a direct observation on the rate curve $r(M)$, $M \geq 0$.

[1] A common source of confusion is between the short rate, which is the instantaneous interest rate, and short-term rates, which are the interest rates for short-dated, also called near-dated, maturities. These are different mathematical objects!

Remark 13.2 ***(Notations)*****:** An alternative notation system in the literature is $f(0, M)$ for the instantaneous rate, with $r(t) \approx f(t, t)$ for the short rate. We will not discuss the short rate further and prefer to use $r(M) \approx f(0, M)$ to highlight that the forward rate is a function of maturity.

The most mathematically accurate notation would be that of Andersen and Piterbarg [318]. Namely, $F(0; 0, M)$ is the simple futures rate at time 0 that would apply between 0 and M. This notation can be useful when describing more complex interest rate products but is cumbersome for our purposes in this chapter.

As per Definition 13.1, the rate curve is a representation of the expectation as of today of future short rates. It is derived from observations and is mostly prevalent for pricing applications.

The yield curve, on the other hand, represents the term structure of interest rates for different maturities observed today. Its most common form is the par-yield curve, and it represents the average rate for a given maturity of bonds priced at par. It is commonly used by practitioners and typically assumes semiannual compounding.

It is often said that the forward rate generalizes the instantaneous rate to future maturities. However, because the forward rate is implied from the present, its term structure will change through time. We will discuss in this section how the forward rate curve is constructed based on observed yield curves.

We present a summary of the terminology discussed in this section in Table 13.1. In the following sections and for simplicity, we will predominantly use the continuously compounded zero-rate R introduced in Equation 12.4, which is linked to the instantaneous forward rate r as follows:

$$R(M) = \frac{1}{M} \int_0^M r(u)du \tag{13.1}$$

We will often omit the time t from our notation when $t = 0$. Equation 13.1 highlights that the zero-rate $R(M)$ represents the average, under continuous compounding, of instantaneous forward rates from now until maturity M.

TABLE 13.1 Key Terminology for Forward Rates

Object	Fixed	Variable	Compounding	Usage
Short Rate	Time (now)	Maturity	Continuous	Discounting
Inst. Forward Rate	Time (future)	Maturity	Continuous	Theoretical Pricing
Yield Curve	Time (now)	Maturity	Based on coupons	Quoting (Practitioners)
Zero Yield Curve	Time (now)	Maturity	Continuous	Theoretical Pricing and Quoting
(Forward) Rate Curve	Time (now)	Maturity (future)	Continuous	Theoretical Pricing

13.2 ZERO-COUPON BOND (ZCB)

The simplest financial instrument in fixed income is the zero-coupon bond (ZCB) [319], which we present in Definition 13.2.

Definition 13.2 ***(Zero-coupon Bond)*:** A zero-coupon bond pays its face value at maturity and does not pay any coupon during its life.

Remark 13.3: Face value is also referred to as par value, or principal.

Usually, a ZCB is bought at a discount, which reflects the interest rate. We illustrate the cash flow of a ZCB in Figure 13.1. Since the only cash flow occurs at maturity for the ZCB, the price is the PV, as per Remark 12.18.

Definition 13.3 ***(Price of Zero-coupon Bond)*:** The price of a ZCB with face value P_{face} and maturity M is given by the following formula:

$$P_{\text{ZCB}}(M; R) = P_{\text{face}} \cdot e^{-RM}$$

where R is the rate of the ZCB for that maturity.

We commonly refer to R as the ZCB rate, or simply zero-rate.

Definition 13.4 ***(Zero-rate)*:** The ZCB rate $R(M)$ for maturity M is called the zero-rate for that maturity.

The zero-rate is agreed in advance, which is why we do not use the expectation in Definition 13.3. It is therefore linked to the forward rate as per Proposition 13.1.

Remark 13.4 ***(Inflation-adjusted ZCB)*:** In some cases, there exist structured products such as inflation-linked ZCBs, where the bond's principal or interest payments are adjusted according to an inflation index. Typically, a fixed rate is agreed and discounted at initiation; the residual variation due to inflation is computed using a pre-agreed methodology and reflected in principal accrual, paid at maturity.

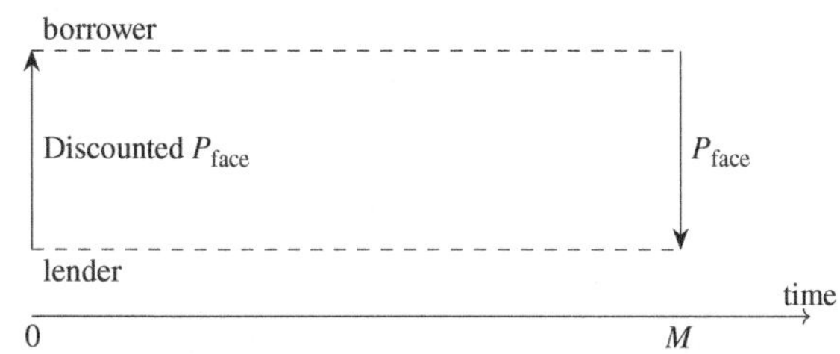

FIGURE 13.1 **ZCB Cash Flow Diagram.** The cash flow of a ZCB is a single payment at maturity M of the principal, which is discounted as per Definition 13.3. The lender receives the principal at maturity, while the borrower only receives the discounted principal at time 0.

Proposition 13.1 ***(Relationship Between Zero-rate and Forward Rate):*** The forward rate $R(M_1, M_2)$ between times $M_1 < M_2$ is given by

$$R(M_1, M_2) = \frac{R(M_2)M_2 - R(M_1)M_1}{M_2 - M_1}$$

where $R(M_1)$ and $R(M_2)$ are the zero-rates of zero-coupon bonds maturing at M_1 and M_2, respectively.

Proof. We construct two investment strategies:

- One is to invest in a ZCB maturing at M_2.
- The other is to invest in a ZCB maturing at M_1, then reinvest the proceeds at the forward rate $R(M_1, M_2)$ until time M_2.

At time M_2, the first strategy yields a payoff of $e^{R(M_2)M_2}$ per unit invested. The second strategy yields a payoff of $e^{R(M_1)M_1} \cdot e^{R(M_1,M_2)(M_2-M_1)}$ per unit invested.

Given no-arbitrage, we can equate the payoffs and conclude. ■

We note that the zero-rate is directly related to the TVM, which we introduced in Section 12.2.5.

The elegance of the representation of ZCBs is that any bond that pays coupons can be represented as a linear combination of ZCBs, with each coupon payment represented as a ZCB with the corresponding maturity. ZCB rates are usually quoted in compounding conventions.

Remark 13.5: The ZCB is not simply a theoretical construct; it is a ubiquitous financial instrument in its own right in TradFi. Most notably, US Treasury bills are ZCBs.

The yield curve constructed from the ZCBs, which we introduce in Definition 13.5, is a yield curve as it represents the zero-rates for different maturities.

Definition 13.5 ***(Zero-curve):*** The zero-curve is the function $R : M \to R(M)$ of zero-rates as a function of their maturity M.

The zero-curve is a specific type of yield curve, since ZCBs have no coupon payments. It therefore conveniently assumes continuous compounding.[2] Consequently, it is sometimes referred to as a pure illustration of the TVM. We discuss an equivalent to the zero-curve in the context of staking contracts in Chapter 17.

Remark 13.6: Alternative names for the zero-curve of Definition 13.5 are ZCB yield curve and spot rate curve.

We refer the reader to Hull's reference book [319] for a more detailed discussion of ZCBs and their properties.

---

[2] Recall that while the forward rate curve that is derived from the zero-curve does use continuous compounding, many yield curves are actually using coupon payment conventions for compounding, most often semiannual.

13.3 INTEREST RATE CURVE

The zero-curve discussed in Section 13.2 can be used to construct the (forward) interest rate curve [319], which is a curve that represents the future interest rates for different maturities.

As per Definition 13.1, when continuously compounded, the forward interest rate curve is defined as the instantaneous interest rate r at a given time in the future. It can therefore be derived from the zero-curve R, as per Figure 13.2 and Equation 13.1. This means that at maturity M, we have the following, starting from the discounting terms:

$$\begin{aligned}
\exp\left(-\int_0^M r(u)du\right) &= \exp\left(-R(M)\cdot M\right) \\
\int_0^M r(u)du &= R(M)\cdot M \\
\frac{\partial}{\partial M}\int_0^M r(u)du &= \frac{\partial}{\partial M}\left(R(M)\cdot M\right) \\
r(M) &= R(M) + M\frac{\partial R(M)}{\partial M}
\end{aligned} \tag{13.2}$$

The construction of the forward rate curve allows us to define an instrument called the forward-forward agreement (FFA), which is an OTC agreement for one party to borrow a principal at a future date, for a set period, at an interest rate that is agreed now. In the context of the FFA, principals are exchanged, as per Figure 13.3.

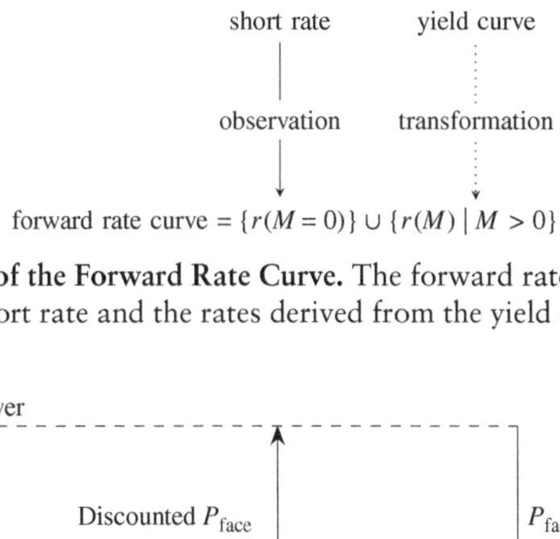

FIGURE 13.2 Construction of the Forward Rate Curve. The forward rate curve is constructed by combining the observed short rate and the rates derived from the yield curve for maturities $M > 0$.

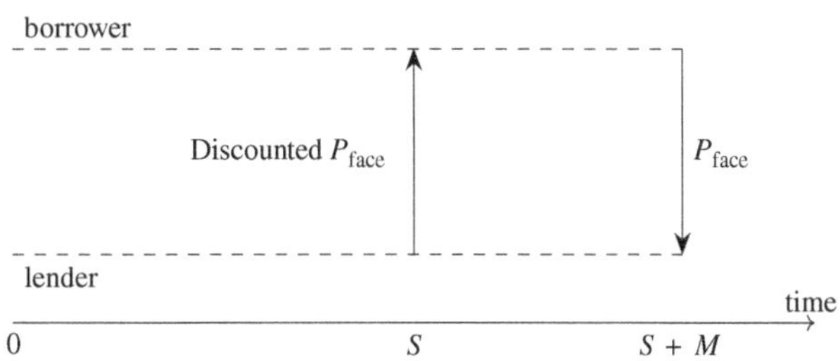

FIGURE 13.3 FFA Cash Flow Diagram. The contract is agreed at time 0, the borrower receives the discounted principal at time S, while the lender receives the principal at maturity M, at time $S + M$.

Remark 13.7: The FFA can be viewed as a ZCB in the future, as illustrated in Figure 13.3. It is not traded often in TradFi, but it is a common theoretical construct in the context of interest rate curves and derivatives pricing.

An extension of the FFA, where no principal is exchanged and only the difference between the agreed rate (called the fixed leg) and a floating rate (the floating leg) is exchanged, is called an FRA. The fixed rate is agreed at the time of the contract, while the floating rate is based on a benchmark rate observed at settlement. This type of contract is called fixed-for-floating, as opposed to floating-for-floating.

Definition 13.6 *(Forward Rate Agreement)*: An FRA is an OTC contract between two parties to exchange the difference between a continuously compounded fixed interest rate $\bar{R}$ and a continuously compounded floating interest rate R_b at a future date S for maturity M, without exchanging the principal P_{face}.

FRA rates are typically quoted using simple interest conventions.

Remark 13.8 *($n \times m$ Conventions)*: Most contract duration increments in TradFi are in months for short-term instruments. For FRAs, the notation commonly used is called $n \times m$. Under this notation, n is the number of months until the start of the contract, and m is the duration of the contract in months. We recognize $n + m = M$ with M the contract maturity.

To illustrate, an FRA that starts in 4 months with a duration of 2 months will be denoted as 4×2. Its maturity from today is $M = 6$ months.

We can write the payoff of the FRA at maturity M as follows, using the discounting operator from Definition 12.7. It is a linear equation given the quoting convention of the FRA.

Proposition 13.2: Using the notations of Definition 13.6, the payoff of the FRA at maturity M is valued at $t = 0$ as follows:

$$PV = \mathcal{D}(R_f, S) \cdot P_{\text{face}} \left(R_b - \bar{R}\right) M$$

with R_f the risk-free rate.

In such a contract, one party is a borrower of the fixed rate, while the other is a lender of the fixed rate, and the roles are swapped for the floating rate, as per Table 13.2. The FRA buyer is commonly the fixed rate borrower.

The cash flow diagram of an FRA is illustrated in Figure 13.4, and we note that there is no initial cash flow when the contract is executed. This is because, by convention, the net PV of such a contract is zero at inception, as for other forward contracts.

TABLE 13.2 Summary of Roles in an FRA

Role	Position	Fixed Leg	Floating Leg
Buyer	Long	Borrower	Lender
Seller	Short	Lender	Borrower

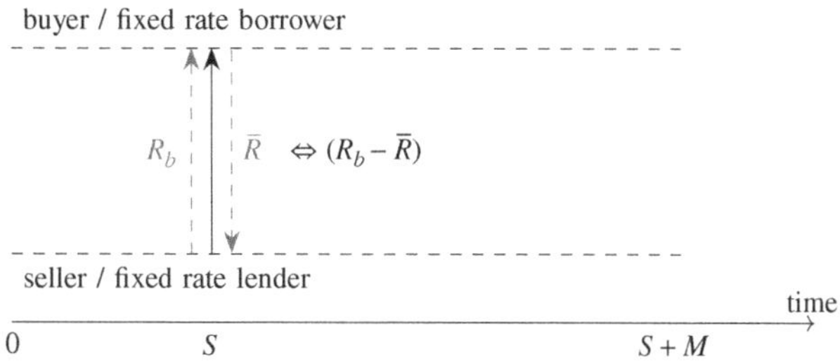

FIGURE 13.4 **FRA Cash Flow Diagram.** In this example, we assume the variable benchmark rate R_b, also called the floating leg, is lower than the fixed rate $\bar{R}$. The contract is agreed at time 0, and there is no exchange of principal. The lender of the fixed rate, who is the borrower of the variable rate for maturity M (as of time S), must pay the other party upfront at time S.

Remark 13.9: The FRA is settled at initiation of the contract. Because the principal is not exchanged, the FRA is called a cash-settled contract.

FRAs are a common financial instrument, and we refer the reader to Hull's book [319] for more details.

Remark 13.10: The zero-curve can conversely be seen as a special case of the forward rate curve, since it takes as values the average of the curve from 0 up to maturity M:

$$\begin{aligned} R(M) &= \frac{1}{M} \int_0^M r(u)du \\ &= \mathbf{E}\left[r(M)\right] = \bar{r}(M) \end{aligned}$$

Of particular importance, the instantaneous interest rates cannot be directly observed, neither can the forward rate curve. Only the yield curve is observable, by plotting the bond yields for different maturities.[3] The forward rate curve is derived, in the proper and figurative sense, from the yields of forwards, swaps, and other instruments such as the ZCB. We illustrate this relationship in Figure 13.5.

The shape of the interest rate curve is also important for understanding market expectations. In the context of interest rates, we can revisit Definition 3.7 as follows:

Definition 13.7 ***(Interest Rate Curve Shape)*****:** There are two main types of shape for the interest rate curve:

Contango is when future interest rates are expected to be higher than present interest rates.

Backwardation is when future interest rates are expected to be lower than present interest rates.

[3]This is however less common these days in TradFi, given that the market has shifted toward more complex instruments which rely on the forward rate curve instead.

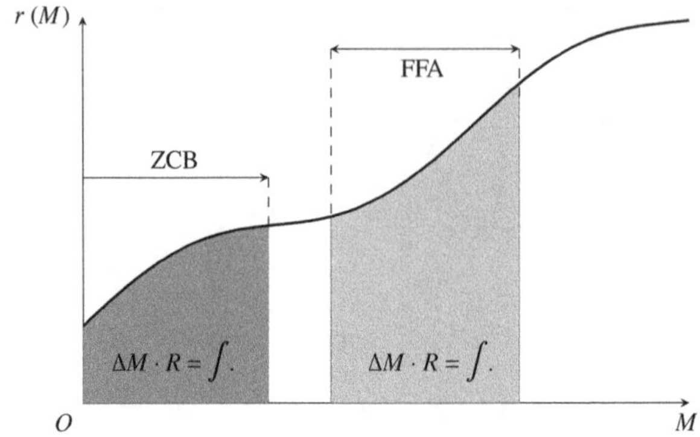

FIGURE 13.5 **Interest Rate Curve Illustration** with ZCB and FFA. The shaded area under the curve is the integral, which illustrates the relationship between the forward rate and the rate for each instrument.

The forward curve shape is expected to be in contango for long horizons, since investors expect compensation for the uncertainty of future payments. It is, however, not uncommon, particularly post-GFC, to observe pronounced short-term backwardation. This situation is often interpreted as a sign of economic uncertainty or expectations of dovish monetary policy, when interest rates are expected to decrease in the near future. It is also called an inverted forward curve, or inverted yield curve depending on the context.

The interest rate curve can even be negative, under two circumstances:

- As a result of quoting conventions, typically on the short term, for maturities earlier than the conventional settlement.[4]
- As a result of a pronounced short-term backwardation.

13.4 INTEREST RATE SWAP (IRS)

The IRS is a financial instrument that allows two parties to exchange interest rate risk. It is a vanilla fixed income contract in TradFi. IRSs are OTC products,[5] and are usually standardized under ISDA master agreements.[6]

Remark 13.11: Notably, despite being zero-sum games (the loss of one party is exactly the gain of the other), swap contracts are seen as hedging contracts rather than speculative

[4]This is more common in Foreign Exchange (FX) for pre-spot maturities, although this does not transpose to digital assets where settlement is instantaneous, in the form of Delivery Versus Payment (DvP), in most cases.

[5]Given the popularity of IRSs, there already exist centrally cleared IRSs, and we can expect exchange trading for specific maturities to continue to grow in the upcoming years. To this point, OTC non-deliverable IRSs, where the settlement is done in another currency than the one where one of the leg's interest rates is earned, seemed promising. If such contracts were to be brought to DeFi, one can expect they would take a similar form.

[6]ISDA master agreements do not lead to the same degree of standardization as, say, futures for forwards. But they greatly reduce the complexity of entering such contracts and leave minimal customization between parties, usually around maturity and selection of the rates.

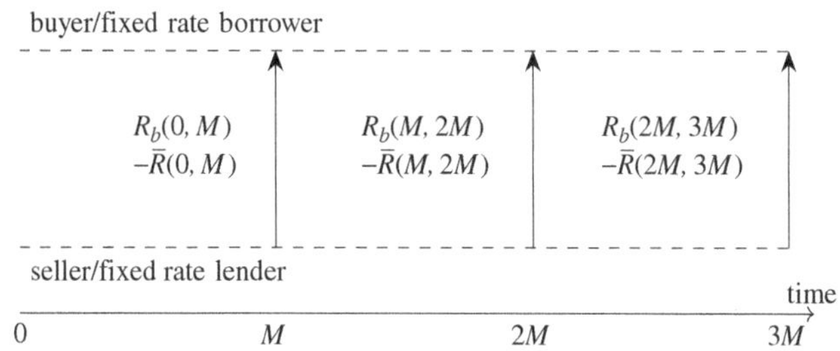

FIGURE 13.6 **IRS Cash Flow Diagram.** $R_b(M_1, M_2)$ and $\bar{R}(M_1, M_2)$ represent rates between M_1 and M_2 as per Proposition 13.1. In this example, we assume the variable benchmark rate $R_b(.,.)$ is consistently lower than the fixed rate $\bar{R}(.,.)$. The contract has three payment terms with each duration M.

TABLE 13.3 Comparison Between FRA and IRS

Feature	Forward Rate Agreement (FRA)	Interest Rate Swap (IRS)
Rate Type	Fixed-for-floating	Fixed-for-floating or floating-for-floating
Exchange of Principal	None	None
Periodicity	Only one	Often multiple
Settlement	Start of the period	End of each period

ones. This is because the process of swapping usually implies collateralization, even though each party takes a different view on the interest rate trajectory.

IRS can be viewed as a series of FRAs, where each FRA represents a single period of the swap, as per Figure 13.6. The main differences are shown in Table 13.3.

Remark 13.12: There is often some confusion with regard to the distinction between a single-period IRS and an FRA. The main difference in that edge case is the settlement, with IRS typically settling at the end of each period, while FRA settles at the start.

There are different valuation methods for the IRS, with the most popular one being based on decomposing it into multiple FRAs. This approach is often called a portfolio approach.

Proof. Assume an IRS with N terms of fixed periodicity M, with variable rates $(R_i)_{i \leq N}$ and fixed rate $\bar{R}$. For simplicity, we assume the principal is 1.

We construct a portfolio Π of N FRAs, such that for each period $i = 1, \ldots, N$, we enter into an FRA contract that pays the fixed rate $\bar{R}$ and receives the floating rate R_i:

$$\Pi = \sum_{i=1}^{N} \text{FRA}((i-1)M, i \cdot M; \bar{R}, R_i)$$

We notice that both cash flows for Π and the IRS are the same. Therefore, we know the portfolio of FRAs and the IRS have the same value by Corollary 12.4:

$$PV(\Pi) = PV(\text{IRS})$$

■

The principal is not exchanged for IRS, so the proof can be adapted by scaling the cash flows. The principal is fixed for the whole duration of the contract and does not accrue.

Remark 13.13: One can notice that there is, actually, a difference between how the FRAs settle (beginning of each period) and how each leg of the IRS settles (end of each period). This leads to a small pricing error, which corresponds to the fact that the FRA discounts back the payment of each leg to the starting period of the contract. Nevertheless, the portfolio methodology as illustrated in the proof is frequently employed to model IRSs.

Another popular valuation methodology is to view the IRS as a long-short position in two different bonds and discounting their cash flows [158, 320]. As for the FRA and as illustrated in Figure 13.6, there is no cash flow at inception since the net PV then is zero. We direct the reader to Boyle and McDougall's comparison of the two methodologies [320].

The FX counterpart of the IRS is another popular contract, called the currency swap. This type of swap is the most directly relevant to digital assets, and cryptocurrencies in particular. There are two notable differences with the conventional IRS:

- The principal is exchanged at the start and at the end of the contract, as opposed to only at the end for the IRS.
- The interest rates are denominated in different currencies, and therefore the payments are usually not netted. This means at the end of each period, both parties will exchange payments.

Remark 13.14: A currency swap, also called cross-currency swap (XCS), is different from an FX swap:

- The former, which is the one being discussed in this section, is an OTC interest rate product.
- The latter is an FX product, which can be seen as one spot, followed by one forward contract. A variant is to have two consecutive forwards with opposite directions.
- A currency swap involves exchanging principal and interest payments in different currencies, while an FX swap typically involves exchanging only principal payments.

There are two variants of the treatment of the principal:

1. The principals of the XCS are computed to be equal, using the spot FX rate at initiation, and are unchanged during the life of the contract. This is the simplest type of XCS but also the least common because there exists a spot exchange rate risk. It is this type of XCS that we represented in Figure 13.7.

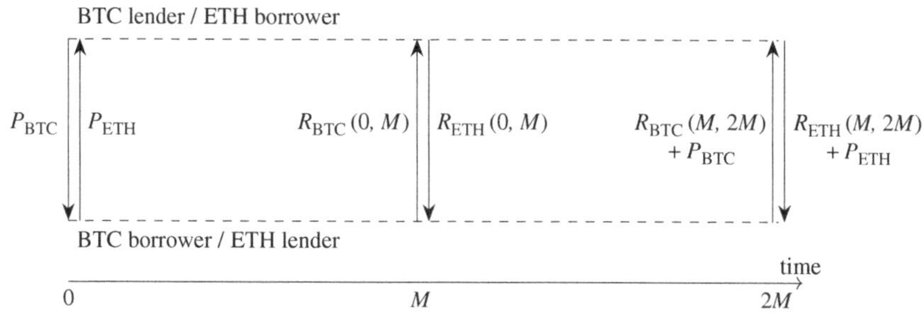

FIGURE 13.7 XCS Cash Flow Diagram. In this example, we represent a non-mark-to-market swap between BTC and ETH, with their corresponding exchange rates and principals. The contract has two payment terms with each duration M.

2. The value of the principal is continuously adjusted and settled using the spot rate at the end of each period, such that the XCS remains spot-neutral. These XCSs are also called mark-to-market XCSs and are the most common.

XCSs are commonly available as fixed-for-fixed, fixed-for-floating, and floating-for-floating.

Remark 13.15: The terminology swap in DeFi is more commonly used to describe peer-to-peer spot transactions on DEXs. We refer in this section to the financial instrument, not the settlement technology.

In DeFi, cross-cryptocurrency swaps still typically rely on a third party, which means that there is a counterparty risk attached to such contracts. These are becoming increasingly popular with exchanges, both DEXs and CEXs, as a way to incentivize the provision of liquidity. One leg would typically be a standard cryptocurrency and the other an exchange-issued token.

The lender of the standard cryptocurrency would pay zero interest on the exchange token, while the rate earned from the standard cryptocurrency may be either fixed or floating based on transaction fees earned by the exchange. In such cases, this is closest to a traditional bond instrument, with the exchange tokens, while tradable, being akin to IOUs.

Some DeFi exchanges will pay the interest earned on an accrued basis in the form of additional exchange tokens. This is not a common configuration in TradFi, since even in the case of the XCS, the interest is paid by the borrower in the currency borrowed.

It is technically possible to create cross-chain swaps, comparable to the TradFi equivalent, with either bridges or hashed time lock contracts (HTLCs). The latter is an escrow technology that enables the exchange of the token between two different chains without trusting a third party [321–323], allowing for the settlement of the principal. It is highly probable that such technologies, associated with smart contracts, will lead to an increased offering of swaps in the DeFi space in the future.

CHAPTER 14

Arbitrage Pricing Theory

Arbitrage pricing theory provides the mathematical foundation for no-arbitrage valuation, enabling us to price financial instruments as discounted expected values of future cash flows. This chapter develops these frameworks for digital assets, extending traditional martingale pricing theory to accommodate DeFi structures.

- Define the numéraire, money market account, and martingale pricing theory in TradFi.
- Construct risk-neutral measures and demonstrate their application to no-arbitrage pricing.
- Introduce the validator account and blockchain measure $\mathbb{B}$ as DeFi extensions of the validator account concept.
- Apply the extended framework to stablecoin valuation.

We begin with the formal definition of the numéraire and its role in relative pricing.

14.1 NUMÉRAIRE

Definition 14.1 *(Numéraire)*: A numéraire n is a tradable asset with strictly positive value that is used as a standardized unit of measure for value.

Examples of Definition 14.1 are the US dollar.[1] In the context of blockchain, the native coin of a blockchain is often used as a numéraire.

Corollary 14.1: *We can write the relative value S of a given asset in units of numéraire n:*

$$S^n(t) = \frac{S(t)}{n(t)}$$

Remark 14.1: As per Corollary 14.1, the value of numéraire n can be a function of time, which is not constant.

[1]In the context of commodities, which is closer to their modern use for digital assets, Geman, El Karoui, and Rochet are often credited for the introduction of the concept of numéraire [325].

We can broadly classify the changes of numéraire into two categories:

1. Changes of economic denomination, such as converting from fiat currency to cryptocurrency. Changes of numéraire with a financial asset introduce new risks, and in turn potential opportunities for arbitrage [324, 325].
2. Mathematical changes of numéraire, such as changes of probability measure, which are common in the context of risk-neutral pricing.

The main purpose of the latter is to ensure that prices under the new measure are martingales, which we introduce in Section 14.2.

14.2 MARTINGALES

We introduce martingales, which are mathematical processes that describe so-called fair games. Under martingales, the best prediction[2] of the future value of a process is equal to the current value, which is a direct consequence of the absence of arbitrage. This means that the market currently prices in all the information available. As we will establish in Corollary 14.4, the existence of a risk-neutral measure is equivalent to the absence of arbitrage opportunities.

Definition 14.2 *(Martingale)***:** A martingale is a stochastic process S such that, given all the information $\mathcal{F}_t$ available at time t, we have the following:

$$\forall 0 \leq t \leq T, \quad \mathbf{E}[S(T) \mid \mathcal{F}_t] = S(t)$$

Remark 14.2: The notation $\mathcal{F}_t$ in Definition 14.2 refers to the mathematical concept of filtration, here to represent all the information available at a given time t.

Definition 14.3 *(Equivalent Martingale Measure)***:** An equivalent martingale measure is a probability measure under which discounted asset prices, relative to a chosen numéraire, are martingales.

We discuss probability measures in more detail in Remark 14.3.

Pricing with martingales brings significantly more convenience when dealing with stochastic processes. In particular, it allows us to use several results in pricing theory and to simplify mathematical computations, such as the so-called Fundamental Theorem of Asset Pricing (FTAP). There are several phrasings of the theorem, some more mathematical than others, but we will use the formulation of Theorem 14.1 in this material.

Theorem 14.1 *(Fundamental Theorem of Asset Pricing)***:**

1. *A market is arbitrage-free, if and only if there exists an equivalent martingale measure.*
2. *A market is complete and arbitrage-free, if and only if there exists a unique equivalent martingale measure.*

[2] More formally, this is the expectation of future value conditioned by present information.

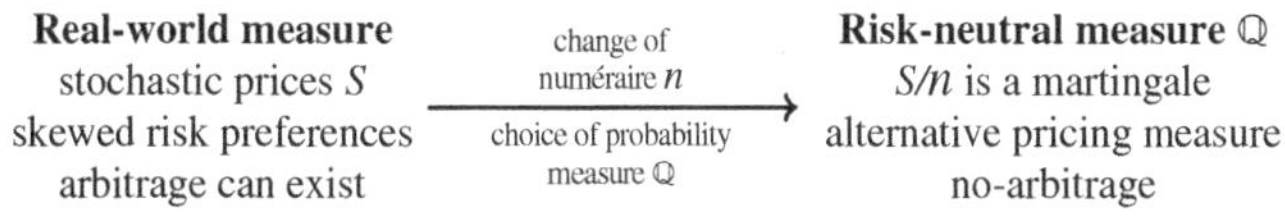

FIGURE 14.1 **Change of Numéraire and Probability Measure.** The transition from the real-world measure to the risk-neutral measure involves a change of numéraire and a choice of probability measure, ensuring discounted prices are martingales and arbitrage is excluded.

Proof. We admit the result in this introductory book. Comprehensive proofs can be found, but we direct the interested reader to Shreve's proof [326] in the coin toss space to build an intuition of how the results arise in finite probability spaces. The same author also provides a straightforward proof in continuous time [327] for the first part of the theorem statement.

The proof by Harrison and Pliska [328] provides a more general framework for the FTAP in continuous time and is often cited as the reference in the literature. ■

In practice, we will also commonly use the following Corollary 14.2 of Theorem 14.1.

Corollary 14.2: *Under the equivalent martingale measure, all discounted asset prices are martingales.*

Proof. Direct application of Theorem 14.1 and Definition 14.3. ■

Remark 14.3: Pricing with martingales gives a robust and consistent mathematical framework for no-arbitrage. If we were not using martingales for stochastic prices, it would be difficult to use these results for pricing, which we introduced in Section 12.2.1.1.

There are many possible changes of numéraire, but the ones we are interested in for quantitative finance all preserve the martingale and no-arbitrage property, as per Figure 14.1. Several pricing measures can be selected, including the risk-neutral measure, which we will discuss in Section 14.3, but all should preserve no-arbitrage.

Consequently, in mathematical finance, we try to work with equivalent martingale measures, which ensure that all discounted asset prices are martingales. To do so, we need to associate the change of numéraire with a change of probability measure, as per Figure 14.1. We will discuss the most common of such measures, called the risk-neutral measure, in Section 14.3 and its associated numéraire the money market account in Section 14.4.

We will assume in the following sections that changes of numéraire with the numéraires presented are possible.

14.3 RISK-NEUTRAL MEASURE

One of the most common changes in numéraire is the introduction of the risk-neutral measure, and it is linked to TVM as introduced in Section 12.2.5.

In the real world, investors might show differentiated preferences toward certain outcomes, which can be translated into systematic drift. These perceived probabilities of outcomes are the real-world measure $\mathbb{P}$, which we used implicitly when introducing discounting. When such drifts are observed, prices are not random, which introduces many complications to pricing assets with a stochastic process, and most notably the inability to invoke the absence of arbitrage. We therefore introduce the concept of a risk-neutral measure, a purely theoretical concept that greatly simplifies computations with random processes.

Remark 14.4: The detailed mathematical underpinnings are outside the scope of this introductory book, so we will focus on the main results and implications of the risk-neutral measure. Key results from measure and martingale theory used as foundations are Girsanov's theorem and the Radon-Nikodym derivative. While several excellent books have been written on these topics, we recommend in particular Shreve [329], Hull [330], and Privault [324]. A notable publication is Geman, El Karoui, and Rochet's proof on changes of numéraire [324, 325].

Definition 14.4 ***(Risk-neutral Measure)*:** A risk-neutral measure $\mathbb{Q}$ is a probability measure under which investors are indifferent to risk.

Risk indifference in Definition 14.4 is a theoretical concept, under which investors have no preference or aversion to risk and will focus on expected returns.

Remark 14.5 ***($\mathbb{P}$ and $\mathbb{Q}$ Quants)*:** We often refer in the industry to quantitative analysts who price derivatives as the $\mathbb{Q}$-quants, as opposed to the $\mathbb{P}$-quants who focus on risk management and asset allocation.

Corollary 14.3: *Under risk-neutral measure $\mathbb{Q}$, all assets' expected returns are equal to the risk-free rate.*

Proof. Assume assets A and B with the same future payoff $P(T)$ at time T. We will assume that A earns the risk-free rate $R_A = R_f$, while B is another risky asset with expected return R_B. For continuous compounding over period T we have the following:

$$PV(A) = P(T) \cdot e^{-R_f T}$$
$$PV(B) = P(T) \cdot e^{-R_B T}$$

Under the risk-neutral measure $\mathbb{Q}$, given Definition 14.4, investors are indifferent to risk and therefore the expected present value of both assets is equal. Assuming R_f, R_B deterministic, we have the following:

$$\mathbf{E}_{\mathbb{Q}}[PV(A)] = \mathbf{E}_{\mathbb{Q}}[PV(B)]$$
$$P(T) \cdot e^{-R_f T} = P(T) \cdot e^{-\mathbf{E}_{\mathbb{Q}}[R_B] T}$$
$$R_f = \mathbf{E}_{\mathbb{Q}}[R_B]$$

This aligns with the general result that discounted prices are martingales under $\mathbb{Q}$. ■

Remark 14.6 ***(Absence of Risk Premia)*****:** Corollary 14.3 implies that there is no risk premium when pricing under measure $\mathbb{Q}$.

One of the strongest results is Corollary 14.4.

Corollary 14.4 ***(No-arbitrage Under Risk-neutral Measure)*****:** *Under risk-neutral measure $\mathbb{Q}$, there is no arbitrage.*

Proof. Assume portfolio Π with initial value zero and terminal value $V(T) \geq 0$ with $\mathbb{Q}[V(T) > 0] > 0$, which is an arbitrage opportunity.

Under risk-neutral measure $\mathbb{Q}$, by Corollary 14.3, the expected discounted value must equal the initial value:

$$\mathbf{E}_{\mathbb{Q}}[e^{-r_f T} V(T)] = 0$$

Since $V(T) \geq 0$ and $e^{-r_f T} > 0$, we have $e^{-r_f T} V(T) \geq 0$.

For the expectation to be zero while the random variable is nonnegative, we must have $V(T) = 0$ almost surely under $\mathbb{Q}$.

This is impossible since $\mathbb{Q}[V(T) > 0] > 0$. ■

Using the risk-neutral measure, we retrieve important results discussed in Section 12.2.5, such as discounting from Definition 12.7.

Proposition 14.1 ***(Discounting with Risk-free Rate)*****:** Under the risk-neutral measure, the present value of future payoffs is obtained by discounting at the risk-free rate.

Proof. Direct application of Corollary 14.3. ■

We present the direct corollary of Proposition 14.1 for blockchains as Proposition 14.5.

Risk-neutral pricing is most commonly used for complex derivatives, since many results for simpler products can be found by relying only on no-arbitrage arguments, as we did earlier in Section 12.2.5. Specifically, it is essential in options pricing theory.

Reusing the notations of Corollary 14.1 and Definition 14.2, we can express the numéraire under the equivalent martingale measure from Definition 14.3 as follows.

For any numéraire n, the equivalent martingale measure $\mathbb{Q}$ ensures that the following holds for any price process S:

$$\forall 0 \leq t \leq T, \quad \mathbf{E}_{\mathbb{Q}}\left[S^n(T) \mid \mathcal{F}_t\right] = S^n(t) \tag{14.1}$$

with S^n a martingale.

Remark 14.7: A more intuitive interpretation of Equation 14.1 is that the expected value of the relative value of an asset at a future time T is equal to its observed value at time t, under the risk-neutral measure $\mathbb{Q}$.

We will see in Section 14.4 that the numéraire n in Equation 14.1 is the money market account.

The introduction of the risk-neutral measure allows us to discount using the instantaneous (forward) rate curve, which we used in Chapter 12 and discussed in Chapter 13.

Proposition 14.2 ***(Discounting with Forward Rate Curve Under Risk-neutral Measure)*****:** Under the risk-neutral measure $\mathbb{Q}$, given instantaneous forward rates $f(0;t)$ at time 0 for maturity t and the short rate r observed at time t with information $\mathcal{F}_t$, we have the following for discounting:

$$\exp\left(-\int_0^t f(0;u)du\right) = \mathbf{E}_{\mathbb{Q}}\left[\exp\left(-\int_0^t r(u)du\right)\middle|\ \mathcal{F}_0\right]$$

Remark 14.8: Note in Proposition 14.2 that we cannot flip the expectation and the integral signs, since the integral is stochastic in nature. We can only do this when r is deterministic.

Proof. Application of Corollary 14.3 with the ZCB, which we discuss in Section 13.2. ∎

Another way to interpret Proposition 14.2 is that, while we discount in Section 12.2.5 by integrating over time, it is consistent with risk-neutral pricing to use the current forward rate curve to discount for future maturities. The latter is expected to capture all the information available as of now, in line with Equation 14.1.

Remark 14.9: We have implied $r(t) \approx f(0;t)$ in this material so far. This is not completely correct because in practice there is an error term corresponding to the convexity adjustment for Jensen's inequality and notations of Proposition 14.2. We flip the inequality because of the negative sign in the exponential term in the following:

$$\begin{aligned}
\mathbf{E}_{\mathbb{Q}}\left[\exp\left(-\int_0^t r(u)\,du\right)\right] &\geq \exp\left(-\int_0^t \mathbf{E}_{\mathbb{Q}}\left[r(u)\right]du\right)\\
\exp\left(-\int_0^t f(0;u)du\right) &\geq \exp\left(-\int_0^t \mathbf{E}_{\mathbb{Q}}\left[r(u)\right]du\right)\\
\int_0^t f(0;u)du &\leq \int_0^t \mathbf{E}_{\mathbb{Q}}\left[r(u)\right]du
\end{aligned}$$

Note that the inequality holds for the averaged rates; stronger assumptions would be required to establish it for the instantaneous rates being integrated.

Most importantly, the result of Proposition 14.2 implies that under no-arbitrage we can substitute $r(t)$ with $f(0;t)$ for discounting. We cannot predict, today t_{now}, the future rates with certainty $r(t > t_{\text{now}})$, but we can use all the information available as of today $f(t_{\text{now}};t)$.

14.4 MONEY MARKET ACCOUNT

One of the most common numéraires is the money market account[3] [324, 331, 332].

Definition 14.5 ***(Money Market Account)*****:** The money market account is an investment account where interest is paid at a very short-term rate, corresponding to the risk-free rate.

[3]The Black-Scholes model, which we introduced in Section 3.2.5, uses an analogous concept [91] while not labeling it as money market account.

Remark 14.10: In practice, the money market account assumes continuous reinvestment at the short rate.

The money market account from Definition 14.5 is a theoretical concept. We can introduce the corresponding numéraire Π_M with the instantaneous risk-free interest rate r, with t the time:

$$d\Pi_M(t) := \Pi_M(t) \cdot r(t)dt$$

When we assume the risk-free instantaneous interest rate is a function of time, we obtain the following:

$$\Pi_M(t) = \exp\left(\int_0^t r(u)du\right)$$

When we apply Corollary 14.1 to the numéraire $\Pi_M(t)$, we obtain the following:

$$S^{\Pi_M}(t) = S(t) \cdot \exp\left(-\int_0^t r(u)du\right)$$

Remark 14.11 ***(Numéraire for the Risk-neutral Measure)*****:** We know from the FTAP, Theorem 14.1, that there exists a unique equivalent martingale measure, for which the money market account is the numéraire. Using Proposition 14.1 and the definition of the money market account, we can conclude that Π_M is the numéraire under the risk-neutral measure $\mathbb{Q}$.

A point to note is that conversely, we don't need to price under the risk-neutral measure $\mathbb{Q}$ to discount using the money market account.

Remark 14.12 ***(Money Market Account Under Real-world Measure)*****:** The money market account is still commonly used under the real-world measure $\mathbb{P}$, as discussed in Section 12.2.5. However, we need to clarify that this stems from two different rationales:

- Under $\mathbb{P}$, the money market account is used as a proxy of wealth accumulation, without invoking the no-arbitrage condition. Based on our estimation of investors' expectations, it is one of many reasonable discounting numéraires we can choose from. Because there is possibility for arbitrage, we cannot prove one numéraire is more adequate than another. Other possible numéraires are a basket of assets, or historical rates of returns of an index.
- Under $\mathbb{Q}$, the money market account is the only adequate numéraire because of the no-arbitrage argument.

14.5 VALIDATOR ACCOUNT

We argue the staking process is an equivalent to money market account under certain conditions.

In reference to Theorems 12.2 and 12.3, we introduce a numéraire Π_B on that blockchain. We call this numéraire the validator account, as it represents one investor's share of the stake on a validator node in a PoS blockchain.

Definition 14.6 *(Validator Account)*: A validator account is an account on a blockchain that allows the holder to stake their native coin and receive staking rewards at the corresponding instantaneous staking rate r:

$$d\Pi_B(t) := \Pi_B(t) \cdot r(t)dt$$

We use the notation Π_B since the validator account is defined for a given blockchain. Without loss of generality, we set $\Pi_B(0) = 1$ throughout the book.

Remark 14.13 *(Is MEV Part of the Staking Rate?)*: We note that on a PoS blockchain, validators typically hold the privilege of ordering transactions. This leads to potential additional returns, called maximum extractable value (MEV). However, we argue that these returns are opportunistic and thus cannot qualify as a rate.

We can obtain for the validator account an expression similar to the money market account:

$$\Pi_B(t) = \exp\left(\int_0^t r(u)du\right)$$

Remark 14.14: It is possible, while assuming continuous compounding, to define accordingly the staking rate as the sum of staking rewards $(r_b)_{b\in\mathbb{N}}$ for each block b. This is technically more accurate given that staking is a process that happens block-by-block. We would therefore write, with $M \in \mathbb{N}$ the coordinate of the last block in network time such that $M = \max\{k \in \mathbb{N} \mid k < t\}$, the following:

$$\begin{aligned}\Pi_B(t) &= \exp\left(\int_0^t r(u)du\right)\\ &= \exp\left(\sum_{b=0}^{M-1} r_b\right)\end{aligned}$$

where $r_b = \ln(1 + R_b)$ and R_b is the discrete staking reward rate for block b. Equivalently, r_b represents the continuously compounded rate equivalent to the discrete block reward.

To reuse Hull's analogy [319], changing between such notations is just a change of unit, as are kilometers and miles. We present more results linked to such change in Proposition 17.6.

Remark 14.15 *(Novel Framework)*: This is a formal treatment of staking as a bank-like deposit account and formalization of the validator account as an appropriate discounting numéraire [333].

Theorem 14.2 *(Staking as Validator Account)*: *If a given blockchain has a staking mechanism, then staking provides a tradable implementation of the theoretical validator account.*

Proof. We price on a blockchain with staking so that Theorem 12.3 applies. The staking reward payoff is deterministic. Using network time t_B, the payoff time is certain, corresponding exactly to $t_B + 1$ for a notional amount staked at time t_B.

Therefore, the validators get paid the short-term risk-free rate for each time increment of network time, which matches the required behavior $d\Pi_B(t) = r(t)dt$ from Definition 14.6.

Since staking positions are tradable through liquid staking derivatives that can be transferred between parties, and these derivatives maintain strictly positive value proportional to the underlying stake, staking provides a concrete realization of the theoretical validator account. ∎

Remark 14.16: Theorem 14.2 is a direct consequence of Theorem 12.3 and Definition 14.6. This is a strong result, which is usually not seen in TradFi.

Proposition 14.3: The validator account provides a risk-free rate of return on the blockchain with staking.

Proof. Direct application of Theorem 12.3 and Definition 14.6. ∎

Remark 14.17 ***(Wrapped Tokens as Numéraire)*****:** While, as mentioned earlier, the existence of a risk-free rate is optional in the context of pricing theory, we provided in Section 12.2.3, and more specifically in Remark 12.15, arguments to construct one on blockchains without staking. However, if we were to not admit its existence, an alternative solution is to choose as numéraire an asset that is not native to the blockchain but which can be traded on it, such as a wrapped token.

This numéraire becomes a benchmark asset for pricing and can be used to derive the value of other assets on the blockchain. It will not be perfectly risk-free, as per Corollary 12.7, and would only be an approximation.

We can therefore apply the results of Corollary 14.1 to the numéraire described in Section 14.4.

Corollary 14.5: *Under the conditions of Theorem 14.2, the numéraire* Π_B *is a numéraire for the blockchain.*

Proof. We can verify that Π_B as defined in Definition 14.6 is a numéraire as per Definition 14.1:

1. By construction, $\Pi_B > 0$.
2. Π_B can be replicated and such contract is tradable as per Theorem 14.2.

We note that we only need to have a blockchain with a staking mechanism to satisfy the second point. ∎

Remark 14.18 ***(Technical Conditions for Validator Account)*****:** For completeness, and following Remark 14.4, we present additional mathematical conditions satisfied by the validator account Π_B, meaning it can be a valid numéraire in the change of measure framework. Beyond Corollary 14.5 [333], the following properties ensure the existence of the Radon-Nikodym derivative:

Continuity. Π_B is continuous by composition, given r is piecewise continuous.

Adaptedness is verified since the rate $r(t)$ is $\mathcal{F}_t$-measurable.

Integrability. For all $T < \infty$, we have $\mathbf{E}_{\mathbb{P}}\left[\exp\left(\int_0^T r(u)du\right)\right] < \infty$ with $\mathbb{P}$ the real-world probability measure. In practice, staking rates are bounded, ensuring this condition holds even when $r(t)$ is modeled stochastically.

These conditions ensure admissible Radon-Nikodym derivatives, allowing us to apply Girsanov's theorem as with any standard numéraire in mathematical finance.

We can also construct a probability measure for the validator account, analogous to the risk-neutral measure associated with the money market account.

Proposition 14.4 ***(Blockchain Measure)*:** There exists a unique equivalent martingale measure $\mathbb{B}$ such that all asset prices expressed as units of Π_B are martingales.

We chose to call the validator account measure $\mathbb{B}$ the blockchain measure, since it is the measure specific to that given blockchain, under which all assets can be priced on that blockchain without a risk premium, as per Remark 14.6.

Proof. By direct application of Theorem 14.1, the FTAP. ■

The introduction of the blockchain measure $\mathbb{B}$ allows us to extend the results related to discounting to that blockchain.

Corollary 14.6: *Under blockchain measure $\mathbb{B}$, any asset's expected return is equal to the staking rate.*

Proof. Similar reasoning as for Corollary 14.3, but with the staking rate instead of the risk-free rate. ■

Remark 14.19 ***(Benchmark Staking Rates)*:** In practice, the observation of the risk-free rate in DeFi is done via rate benchmarks. On Ethereum for example, the reference benchmark rate is the Ether Staking Offered Rate [334].

Proposition 14.5 ***(Discounting with Staking Rate)*:** Under the blockchain measure $\mathbb{B}$, the present value of future payoffs is obtained by discounting at the staking rate.

Proof. Direct application of Corollary 14.6. ■

We can therefore extend the definition of the discount factor $\mathcal{D}(R;T)$ for the blockchain, in a way similar to Definition 12.7.

Definition 14.7 ***(Blockchain Discount Factor)*:** The discount factor for the blockchain $\mathcal{D}(R; T)$ is defined as

$$\mathcal{D}(R;T) = e^{-RT}$$

with R the staking reward rate and T the discounting horizon.

As a result of Proposition 14.4, given the collection of information $\mathcal{F}_t$ available at time t, we can write the following for any asset with price S:

$$\forall 0 \leq t \leq T, \quad S^{\Pi_B}(t) = \mathbf{E}_{\mathbb{B}}\left[S^{\Pi_B}(T) \mid \mathcal{F}_t\right]$$
$$\frac{S(t)}{\Pi_B(t)} = \mathbf{E}_{\mathbb{B}}\left[\frac{S(T)}{\Pi_B(T)} \mid \mathcal{F}_t\right]$$

Proposition 14.4 states that all prices expressed in units of the validator account are martingales under the associated probability measure $\mathbb{B}$. We can therefore apply pricing results analogous to TradFi on DeFi products, as per Table 14.1.

Remark 14.20: For convenience, we often denote S^{Π_B} as $S^{\mathbb{B}}$ given that Π_B is the unique numéraire under $\mathbb{B}$.

Remark 14.21 ***(Flash Loans and Atomic Arbitrage)*:** We will discuss the concept of martingale from Definition 14.2 in DeFi only at the scale of block-to-block. Within the same transaction block, arbitrages are possible, in particular in the form of so-called flash loans.

Flash loans allow borrowing without collateral, as long as the loan is repaid with the same block. Atomic arbitrages are therefore possible between two lenders within the same block.

We still need to extend such results to blockchains without staking. The existence of a money market account equivalent without staking has been disputed[4] [335], but we suggest two options to extend the results of this section to such blockchains:

1. We can construct a theoretical validator account that uses a pool of most reputable lenders, as described in Remark 12.15. It would, however, not be tradable.
2. We can approximate a validator account by using a wrapped token that can be traded on the blockchain, as discussed in Remark 14.17.

TABLE 14.1 Analogies in Arbitrage Pricing Theory

Numéraire	Measure	Usage
None	$\mathbb{P}$ physical/real-world	Observed in prices
Money market account	$\mathbb{Q}$ risk-neutral	Off-chain asset pricing
Validator account	$\mathbb{B}$ blockchain	On-chain asset pricing

[4]Brody et al. [335] still constructed an alternative framework for interest rates in cryptocurrencies. Given no assumption of staking, they did so in the absence of money market account.

The main issue with the first option is that the FTAP cannot be used with an asset that is not tradable.

14.6 STABLECOINS

We provide an introduction to stablecoins in Section 7.2. In this section, we will discuss their pricing in the context of discounting.

In the context of pricing, because we use the validator account as numéraire from Section 14.5, the stablecoin issued on a blockchain is discounted as per Proposition 14.6.

Proposition 14.6: From the perspective of on-chain participants using Π_B as numéraire, the discounting rate for a stablecoin issued on a given blockchain is that chain's risk-free rate.

Proof. The stablecoin is akin to a wrapped token; Corollary 12.7 applies. Thus, when valuing future stablecoin cash flows from the on-chain perspective with numéraire Π_B, the appropriate discount rate is the blockchain's risk-free rate, not the fiat currency risk-free rate. ∎

Remark 14.22 ***(Stablecoins as Zero-coupon Instruments)*:** Payment stablecoins are perpetual zero-coupon instruments: they pay no interest to holders while issuers capture yields on reserves. Like ZCBs, they pay no coupon, but unlike bonds, they have no maturity. For holders, the opportunity cost of holding stablecoins equals the blockchain's risk-free rate that they forgo.

The result of Proposition 14.6 might be surprising. An initial intuition would be that stablecoins are pegged to fiat currency and should therefore earn the same yield as fiat currency assets, with an adjustment for the risk premium of depegging. However, the stablecoin's utility derives from its payment functionality and liquidity services, not from yield generation. This still holds if the stablecoin pays interest, although as discussed in Section 7.2, this is often not the case and is now prohibited under the United States' GENIUS Act [178].

Remark 14.23: There exists an inherent exchange risk linked to the peg for stablecoins. Only the reward of the stablecoin, if it exists, denominated in the native blockchain coin, may be deemed risk-free.

Another implication of Proposition 14.6 is that the same stablecoin, even if it produces cash flows tied to the fiat currency risk-free rate, will be discounted differently on different blockchains.

Remark 14.24: Note that in the chapter, we define risk-free in the context of arbitrage pricing. There are risks associated with the high concentration of stablecoins [336]. Despite not bearing interest, they serve as critical collateral in DeFi, and there are also risks that the stablecoin might lose its peg.

CHAPTER 15

Cross-chain Asset Pricing

Cross-chain asset pricing in DeFi requires frameworks that accommodate heterogeneous blockchain architectures, varying block times, and bridge settlement delays. This chapter adapts traditional FX methodologies to multi-chain ecosystems while addressing unique challenges of decentralized finance.

- Develop pricing models for assets bridging on-chain and off-chain environments, extending arbitrage pricing theory concepts.
- Analyze the Siegel paradox in cross-chain carry trade contexts.
- Derive interchain valuation frameworks accounting for network time misalignments.

Building on forward rate frameworks and arbitrage pricing theory, we extend these concepts to cross-chain environments, beginning with on-off-chain pricing relationships.

15.1 ON-OFF-CHAIN PRICING

Discounting for digital assets linked to off-chain payoffs, and vice versa, is a direct application of change of numéraire. It shares methodological and conceptual similarities with FX products in TradFi [324, 325], and in particular the carry trade, which we discuss in Section 6.2.

The idea of the carry trade is to take advantage of an interest rate differential. In TradFi, this is done by borrowing in a currency with a low interest rate and lending in another with a higher interest rate. In DeFi, this can be done by borrowing off-chain and lending on-chain, or vice versa.

Several stochastic processes are involved:

- The off-chain discounting (short) rate r_f
- The on-chain discounting (short) rate r
- The spot price $S(t)$ of the on-chain asset at time t, expressed in units of the off-chain asset

Remark 15.1 *(Risks of the Carry Trade)*: The carry trade relies on relatively stable assumptions about two interest rates and one spot price. Any significant change in these variables can turn the trade unprofitable.

We need to make two assumptions about t_1, the time when the contract ends:

1. The time t_1 is known in advance.
2. At t_1, it is possible to receive a payoff on-chain.

If the contract were specified with t_1 as the end of a staking period, t_1 would become a stochastic variable when observed in physical time, as discussed in Section 12.1.1.

The main idea behind on-off-chain pricing is illustrated in Figure 15.1. We assume the contract buyer is off-chain, and therefore we must represent off-chain an asset that has the same payoff as the on-chain asset. This means that we discount off-chain. We use the convention whereby the spot price S is the price of one unit of the on-chain asset expressed in off-chain units.

15.1.1 Ex Post Valuation

We build our intuition with deterministic rates, or as if we had already observed them; this is called an ex post assumption.

The sequence of actions in Figure 15.1 is as follows:

1. The contract buyer purchases an on-chain asset at time t_0 at spot price $S(t_0)$.
2. The contract buyer holds the on-chain asset until time t_1, earning the on-chain risk-free rate r.
3. At time t_1, the contract buyer sells the on-chain asset using the prevailing spot price $S(t_1)$.

This means the payoff on-chain can be expressed as follows. We write the principal P, but it is understood that it is expressed off-chain:

$$\text{Payoff}^{\text{on-chain}} = P \cdot S(t_0) \exp\left(\int_{t_0}^{t_1} r(u)du\right)$$

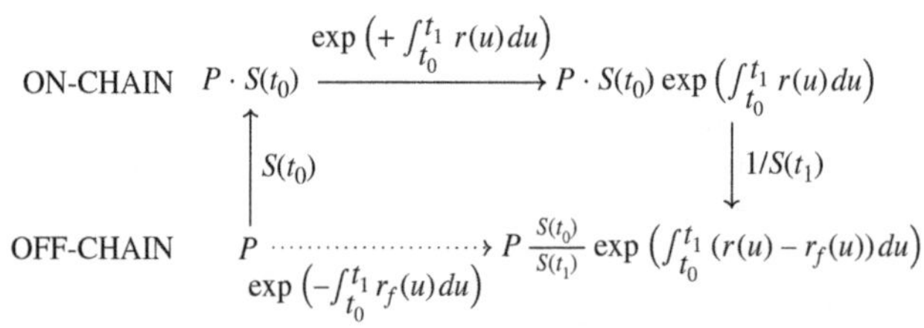

FIGURE 15.1 **On-off-chain Discounting.** An investment of principal P off-chain is discounted at the risk-free short rate r_f. It can be used to purchase an on-chain asset at spot price S, earning the risk-free short rate r of the blockchain.

We need to express it back after conversion off-chain:

$$\text{Payoff} = P\frac{S(t_0)}{S(t_1)} \exp\left(\int_{t_0}^{t_1} r(u)du\right)$$

Using Definition 12.7, we can now discount off-chain from the perspective of the buyer under the risk-neutral measure $\mathbb{Q}$. We assume the rates are known, so we do not use an expectation:

$$\begin{aligned} PV &= \mathcal{D}(r_f; t_1) \cdot \text{Payoff} \\ &= P\frac{S(t_0)}{S(t_1)} \exp\left(-\int_{t_0}^{t_1} r_f(u)du\right) \exp\left(\int_{t_0}^{t_1} r(u)du\right) \\ &= P\frac{S(t_0)}{S(t_1)} \exp\left(\int_{t_0}^{t_1} \left(r(u) - r_f(u)\right) du\right) \end{aligned} \tag{15.1}$$

15.1.2 Ex Ante Valuation

We now assume that both r_f and r are stochastic processes. This assumption reflects a more realistic scenario where we price the contract before the rates are known, which is called ex ante. We recall the concepts introduced previously:

- $\mathbb{Q}$ is the risk-neutral measure associated with the off-chain asset (Definition 14.4), and its associated numéraire is the money market account Π_M (Definition 14.5).
- $\mathbb{B}$ is the blockchain measure associated with the on-chain asset (Corollary 14.6), and its associated numéraire is the validator account Π_B (Definition 14.6).

We will compute the price in expectation from the buyer's perspective, so we assume no-arbitrage for the spot process S under the risk-neutral measure $\mathbb{Q}$.

This no-arbitrage condition means that the expected discounted price of the on-chain asset under $\mathbb{B}$ must equal the expected discounted price of the off-chain asset under $\mathbb{Q}$, and that the double-discounted spot price is a martingale. Given all information available at time t_0, written $\mathcal{F}_{t_0}$, we can write what follows:

$$\mathbf{E}_{\mathbb{Q}}\left[\frac{1}{S(t_1)}\frac{\Pi_B(t_1)}{\Pi_M(t_1)} \,\middle|\, \mathcal{F}_{t_0}\right] = \frac{1}{S(t_0)}\frac{\Pi_B(t_0)}{\Pi_M(t_0)} \tag{15.2}$$

Equation 15.2 expresses the martingale property of $\frac{1}{S(t)}\frac{\Pi_B(t)}{\Pi_M(t)}$ under the risk-neutral measure $\mathbb{Q}$.

Remark 15.2 *(Choice of Numéraire)*: There are two numéraires one is likely to choose in this case. In our example, we are from the perspective of the buyer off-chain, so it makes sense to pick measure $\mathbb{Q}$ and its corresponding numéraire. An alternative solution would have been to place ourselves on-chain, with risk measure $\mathbb{B}$. Under that measure, Equation 15.2 would have been written as follows:

$$\mathbf{E}_{\mathbb{B}}\left[S(t_1)\frac{\Pi_M(t_1)}{\Pi_B(t_1)} \,\middle|\, \mathcal{F}_{t_0}\right] = S(t_0)\frac{\Pi_M(t_0)}{\Pi_B(t_0)}$$

We can now recompute the present value in the risk-neutral measure $\mathbb{Q}$, using the numéraire Π_M. We reuse the steps described previously to compute the payoff, using this time the numéraires:

$$\text{Payoff}^{\text{on-chain}} = P \cdot S(t_0)\frac{\Pi_B(t_1)}{\Pi_B(t_0)}$$

The off-chain term that corresponds to an equivalent compounding is $\frac{\Pi_M(t_1)}{\Pi_M(t_0)}$:

$$\begin{aligned} PV &= \mathbf{E}_{\mathbb{Q}}\left[\frac{1}{S(t_1)}\left(\frac{\Pi_M(t_1)}{\Pi_M(t_0)}\right)^{-1} P \cdot S(t_0)\frac{\Pi_B(t_1)}{\Pi_B(t_0)} \,\middle|\, \mathcal{F}_{t_0}\right] \\ &= P \cdot \mathbf{E}_{\mathbb{Q}}\left[\frac{1}{S(t_1)}\frac{\Pi_B(t_1)}{\Pi_M(t_1)}\left(\frac{1}{S(t_0)}\frac{\Pi_B(t_0)}{\Pi_M(t_0)}\right)^{-1} \,\middle|\, \mathcal{F}_{t_0}\right] \end{aligned}$$

We can then use Equation 15.2 to obtain the following:

$$\begin{aligned} PV &= P\left(\frac{1}{S(t_0)}\frac{\Pi_B(t_0)}{\Pi_M(t_0)}\right)\left(\frac{1}{S(t_0)}\frac{\Pi_B(t_0)}{\Pi_M(t_0)}\right)^{-1} \\ &= P \end{aligned}$$

This result expresses the net PV equal to zero property, described in Remark 12.18. This is expected because we assumed no arbitrage under $\mathbb{Q}$. This same reasoning can help us to price more complex derivatives, such as option contracts.

Remark 15.3 *(S as Numéraire)*: Another possible numéraire is the spot price S. This can be a convenient choice for pricing specific option contracts. One would then introduce a measure $\mathbb{B}/\mathbb{Q}$ (the sequence corresponds to the quoting convention).

To express the martingale property we introduce $P^{\mathbb{B}}$ as the principal expressed on the blockchain (equivalent to P used earlier). The equivalent of Equation 15.2 becomes the following:

$$\mathbf{E}_{\mathbb{B}/\mathbb{Q}}\left[\frac{1}{S(t_1)}\frac{P^{\mathbb{B}}(t_1)}{\Pi_M(t_1)} \,\middle|\, \mathcal{F}_{t_0}\right] = \frac{1}{S(t_0)}\frac{P^{\mathbb{B}}(t_0)}{\Pi_M(t_0)}$$

In Section 11.2.1, we introduced the Geometric Brownian Motion (GBM), which is a widely used model for price processes such as the spot price S.

15.2 SIEGEL PARADOX

Under measure $\mathbb{Q}$, the choice of whether we position ourselves off-chain or on-chain is actually not strictly equivalent. We have the following equalities that hold. Recall the martingale conditions:

$$\begin{aligned} \mathbf{E}_{\mathbb{Q}}\left[\frac{1}{S(t_1)}\frac{\Pi_B(t_1)}{\Pi_M(t_1)} \,\middle|\, \mathcal{F}_{t_0}\right] &= \frac{1}{S(t_0)}\frac{\Pi_B(t_0)}{\Pi_M(t_0)} \\ \mathbf{E}_{\mathbb{Q}}\left[\frac{1}{S(t_1)} \,\middle|\, \mathcal{F}_{t_0}\right] &= \frac{1}{S(t_0)}\frac{\Pi_M(t_1)}{\Pi_M(t_0)}\left(\frac{\Pi_B(t_0)}{\Pi_B(t_1)}\right)^{-1} \end{aligned} \qquad (15.3)$$

Now consider the reciprocal. By Jensen's inequality, which is strict when $\mathrm{Var}_{\mathbb{Q}}(S(t_1) \mid \mathcal{F}_{t_0}) > 0$:

$$\mathbf{E}_{\mathbb{Q}}\left[\frac{1}{S(t_1)} \,\middle|\, \mathcal{F}_{t_0}\right] > \frac{1}{\mathbf{E}_{\mathbb{Q}}[S(t_1) \mid \mathcal{F}_{t_0}]} \tag{15.4}$$

We note that the right-hand side term is the following:

$$\frac{1}{\mathbf{E}_{\mathbb{Q}}[S(t_1) \mid \mathcal{F}_{t_0}]} = \frac{1}{S(t_0)} \frac{\Pi_B(t_1)}{\Pi_B(t_0)} \left(\frac{\Pi_M(t_1)}{\Pi_M(t_0)}\right)^{-1}$$

Multiplying both sides of inequality Equation 15.4 by $\mathbf{E}_{\mathbb{Q}}[S(t_1) \mid \mathcal{F}_{t_0}]$ from Equation 15.3, we obtain the following:

$$\mathbf{E}_{\mathbb{Q}}[S(t_1) \mid \mathcal{F}_{t_0}] \cdot \mathbf{E}_{\mathbb{Q}}\left[\frac{1}{S(t_1)} \,\middle|\, \mathcal{F}_{t_0}\right] > 1 \tag{15.5}$$

Equation 15.5 is the Siegel paradox, first identified by Siegel for FX rates [337] and often associated with the Nalebuff puzzle [338, 339]. It shows that even under a single risk-neutral measure, the product of the expected exchange rate and its expected reciprocal exceeds unity.

Remark 15.4 ***(Siegel Paradox and Convexity Risk)*****:** We can develop intuition for this result as follows. Consider symmetric price moves:

- Holding S: If S doubles to $2S$, we gain $+100\%$. If S halves to $S/2$, we lose -50%.
- Holding $1/S$: If S doubles to $2S$, then $1/S \to 1/(2S)$, we lose -50%. If S halves to $S/2$, then $1/S \to 2/S$, we gain $+100\%$.

The positions appear symmetric. But using expectations under $\mathbb{Q}$, we obtain different values:

$$\mathbf{E}_{\mathbb{Q}}[S] = \frac{1}{2}(2S) + \frac{1}{2}\left(\frac{S}{2}\right) = \frac{5S}{4}$$

$$\mathbf{E}_{\mathbb{Q}}\left[\frac{1}{S}\right] = \frac{1}{2}\left(\frac{1}{2S}\right) + \frac{1}{2}\left(\frac{2}{S}\right) = \frac{5}{4S}$$

Thus we obtain the same result as Equation 15.5:

$$\mathbf{E}_{\mathbb{Q}}[S] \cdot \mathbf{E}_{\mathbb{Q}}[1/S] = \frac{5S}{4} \cdot \frac{5}{4S} = \frac{25}{16} > 1$$

The Siegel paradox in FX means that the expected return from holding foreign currency differs depending on which currency serves as the numéraire [340]. This is paradoxical because one might assume that the expected return should be invariant across currencies, corresponding to an equality in Equation 15.5. Instead, each investor observes a different expected return depending on the currency in which it is measured. The Siegel paradox is about perspective and the choice of numéraire.

Applied to on-off-chain pricing discussed in Section 15.1, a fiat currency holder may perceive a different expected return whether they measure their returns in fiat currency or in cryptocurrency. The same logic applies to cross-chain investors.

The paradox becomes relevant in carry trade contexts, which we discuss in Section 6.2, because higher yields create an asymmetry in the expected future exchange rates.

15.3 INTERCHAIN VALUATION

The mathematical framework derived in Section 15.1 extends easily to interchain discounting.

We will assume that the contract end time t_1 is known in advance. We must also assume that both t_0 and t_1 are valid times when operations can be settled on all blockchains involved.

Physical time can no longer serve as the common reference, and we need to construct an interchain time that reflects the different network times of the blockchains involved. The precise formulation is naturally discrete, following the approach outlined in Section 12.1.1. At physical time t, let $t_{B_A}(t)$ and $t_{B_B}(t)$ denote the network times, more precisely block heights, on chains A and B. The joint block progression is defined as follows:

$$t_{B_{A\cap B}}(t) = \min(t_{B_A}(t), t_{B_B}(t)) \tag{15.6}$$

This ensures both chains have processed at least $\lfloor t_{B_{A\cap B}}(t) \rfloor$ blocks. In practice, this is equivalent to taking the time from the slower-ticking blockchain.

Remark 15.5 ***(Continuous-time Notation)*****:** For intuition, we might write $dt_{B_{A\cap B}} = \max(dt_{B_A}, dt_{B_B})$ to indicate that the joint time advances at the pace of the slower chain when expressed in continuous form. This is a notational shorthand; the discrete definition is what we use in practice.

In practice, this means that we approximate the join time by taking the slower chain's time.

Once this adjustment is made, we can use this interchain time as the common reference for pricing. Note that this does not mean that chains tick synchronously. For simplicity, we assume $t_{B_{A\cap B}} = t_{B_A}$, which we call the slow blockchain, and we take the perspective of a contract buyer on that slow chain.

We assume the contract starts at $t_{B_{A\cap B},0} = t_{B_A,0}$ and ends at $t_{B_{A\cap B},1} = t_{B_A,1}$. We write the first tick immediately after $t_{B_A,0}$ on blockchain B as $t_{B_B,0+}$. Symmetrically, the last tick on blockchain B immediately before $t_{B_A,1}$ is $t_{B_B,1-}$. We call the interval between $t_{B_B,0+}$ and $t_{B_B,1-}$ the carry period when the notional is invested in the validator account of the fast chain B, as shown in Figure 15.2.

Remark 15.6 ***(Synchronized Observations)*****:** We note that we are making the assumption that both chains can observe each other's state, in particular exchange rates $S(t_{BB,1-})$ and $S(t_{BA,0})$ across chains.

In practice, chains operate asynchronously, which can create a lag for these observations. For precise modeling, we could introduce separate filtrations $\mathcal{F}_t^A$ and $\mathcal{F}_t^B$ which capture the information lag. We would then price under expectation, conditioned on the information available on the corresponding chain. For the first exchange rate, that would be inbound chain B at time $t_{B_B,0}$ under $\mathcal{F}_t^B$.

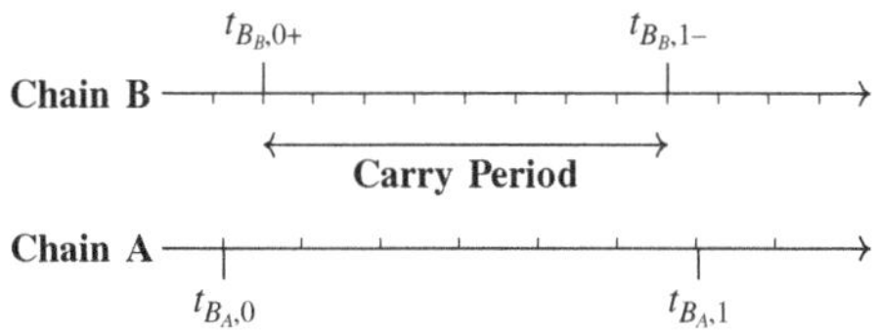

FIGURE 15.2 **Illustration of the Interchain Carry Period.** The diagram shows the alignment of network times between the slow chain A and the fast chain B, with the carry period highlighted between $t_{B_B,0+}$ and $t_{B_B,1-}$.

We argue that this implicit assumption of synchronized observations is reasonable, in particular for liquid pairs with short time horizons.

We assume deterministic staking rates, with instantaneous rates r_A and r_B. This is in essence an ex post valuation.

1. The contract buyer on chain A exchanges their principal at $t_{B_A,0}$ at the prevailing spot rate $S(t_{B_A,0})$.
2. The principal is bridged and enters chain B at the next available slot $t_{B_B,0+}$.
3. The principal earns interest on chain B at rate r_B until it is exited.
4. The principal is exchanged from chain B at $t_{B_B,1-}$ at the prevailing spot rate $S(t_{B_B,1-})$.
5. Settlement on chain A takes place at $t_{B_A,1}$.

The spot rate S represents the price of buying an asset on chain B in units of chain A.

This creates gaps where the principal earns no interest as it is not recorded yet on either chain, while being discounted.

In our example, we compute the payoff on blockchain B as follows, with P the principal denominated on chain A:

$$\text{Payoff}_B = P \cdot S(t_{B_A,0}) \frac{\Pi_{B_B}(t_{B_B,1-})}{\Pi_{B_B}(t_{B_B,0+})}$$

At the same time, the equivalent compounding interest on chain A would be the following. This corresponds to our discounting term under the blockchain measure on chain A:

$$\mathcal{D}(t_{B_A,0}, t_{B_A,1}) = \frac{\Pi_{B_A}(t_{B_A,0})}{\Pi_{B_A}(t_{B_A,1})}$$

Note that the spot exchange S are timestamped when they are agreed on the outbound chain, $S(t_{B_A,0})$ and $S(t_{B_B,1-})$.

We obtain the following:

$$\begin{aligned} PV &= \mathcal{D}(t_{B_A,0}, t_{B_A,1}) \cdot P \frac{S(t_{B_A,0})}{S(t_{B_B,1-})} \frac{\Pi_{B_B}(t_{B_B,1-})}{\Pi_{B_B}(t_{B_B,0+})} \\ &= P \frac{S(t_{B_A,0})}{S(t_{B_B,1-})} \frac{\Pi_{B_A}(t_{B_A,0})}{\Pi_{B_A}(t_{B_A,1})} \frac{\Pi_{B_B}(t_{B_B,1-})}{\Pi_{B_B}(t_{B_B,0+})} \\ &= P \frac{S(t_{B_A,0})}{S(t_{B_B,1-})} \exp\left(-\int_{t_{B_A,0}}^{t_{B_A,1}} r_A(u)du\right) \exp\left(\int_{t_{B_B,0+}}^{t_{B_B,1-}} r_B(u)du\right) \end{aligned} \tag{15.7}$$

We now rearrange the terms in Equation 15.7 to obtain the following:

$$PV = P\frac{S(t_{B_A,0})}{S(t_{B_B,1-})}\exp\left(\int_{t_{B_B,0+}}^{t_{B_B,1-}} r_B(u) - r_A(u)du\right) \\ \cdot \exp\left(-\left(\int_{t_{B_A,0}}^{t_{B_B,0+}} r_A(u)du + \int_{t_{B_B,1-}}^{t_{B_A,1}} r_A(u)du\right)\right) \tag{15.8}$$

We recognize two terms in Equation 15.8. One is the differential of rates, similar to Equation 15.1 in Section 15.1; it corresponds to the period of pure carry on the fast blockchain B:

$$\int_{t_{B_B,0+}}^{t_{B_B,1-}} r_B(u) - r_A(u)du$$

However, there is another term which is pure discounting from the clock misalignment between both chains; this term is new:

$$-\left(\int_{t_{B_A,0}}^{t_{B_B,0+}} r_A(u)du + \int_{t_{B_B,1-}}^{t_{B_A,1}} r_A(u)du\right)$$

We can easily see that if the latter is too large, it will cancel out the pure carry term and can even lead to depreciation. This is the key result of interchain pricing, where there is a minimum duration $\Delta t_B := t_{B_B,1-} - t_{B_B,0+}$ below which a seemingly attractive carry trade is unprofitable:

$$\Delta^* := \min\left\{\Delta t_B := t_{B_B,1-} - t_{B_B,0+} \mid PV(\Delta t_B) \geq P\right\}$$

Δ^* is the minimum holding time on the fast blockchain. Computing Δ^* is easy when staking rates are constant $\bar{r}_A$ and $\bar{r}_B$. We rewrite Equation 15.8, assuming $\bar{r}_B > \bar{r}_A > 0$ and stable exchange rate $S(t_{B_B,1-}) = S(t_{B_A,0})$:

$$\begin{aligned} PV &= P\exp\left(\Delta^*(\bar{r}_B - \bar{r}_A)\right) \\ &\quad \cdot \exp\left(-\left((t_{B_B,0+} - t_{B_A,0})\bar{r}_A + (t_{B_A,1} - t_{B_B,1-})\bar{r}_A\right)\right) \\ 1 &= \exp\left(\Delta^*(\bar{r}_B - \bar{r}_A)\right) \cdot \exp\left(-\left((t_{B_A,1} - t_{B_A,0} - \Delta^*)\bar{r}_A\right)\right) \end{aligned}$$

Taking logarithms and solving for Δ^*:

$$\begin{aligned} 0 &= \Delta^*(\bar{r}_B - \bar{r}_A) - (t_{B_A,1} - t_{B_A,0} - \Delta^*)\bar{r}_A \\ 0 &= \Delta^*\bar{r}_B - (t_{B_A,1} - t_{B_A,0})\bar{r}_A \\ \Delta^* &= (t_{B_A,1} - t_{B_A,0})\frac{\bar{r}_A}{\bar{r}_B} \end{aligned}$$

Remark 15.7 ***(Interpretation of Δ^*):*** The break-even holding time on the fast blockchain Δ^* increases as carry opportunities $\bar{r}_B/\bar{r}_A$ shrink. This creates a natural barrier to high-frequency interchain arbitrage. When $\bar{r}_B = \bar{r}_A$, the minimum holding time equals the total contract duration, meaning no carry profit is possible.

We can extend this framework to stochastic rates in the same way as in Section 15.1 by reintroducing the blockchain measures.

CHAPTER 16

Overview of Interest Rate Models

Interest rate models provide essential frameworks for pricing rate-dependent products and modeling staking rewards in DeFi. This chapter surveys key models and their applications to digital asset valuation.

- Present the Cox-Ingersoll-Ross (CIR) model and its square-root process for mean-reverting rates.
- Examine the SABR model and its applications to cryptocurrency markets.
- Provide an overview of jump-diffusion models for capturing rate discontinuities.

We begin with foundational frameworks, starting with the CIR model. Table 16.1 provides a comparative overview of the models discussed.

16.1 CIR MODEL

The Cox-Ingersoll-Ross (CIR) model [300] was introduced in 1985 to model interest rates. It is a one-factor model, which means that there is only one stochastic process. It is commonly used for short-term rates, alongside the Hull-White model, as discussed in Remark 11.6.

Definition 16.1 *(Cox-Ingersoll-Ross [CIR] Model)*: The Cox-Ingersoll-Ross (CIR) model is a stochastic process defined as

$$dR_t = \theta\left(\mu - R_t\right) dt + \sigma\sqrt{R_t} dW_t$$

with θ the rate of mean-reversion, μ the long-term mean, σ the volatility, and W_t a Wiener process.

Remark 16.1: The drift term of the CIR model in Definition 16.1 is identical to the OUP and Vasicek model in Definition 11.7.

It has been effective for short-term interest rates and is a predecessor to the Heston model [296, 301], which we introduced in Section 11.3.2. The variance in the Heston model is introduced as a square-root process, in reference to the CIR model.

While the CIR model itself has decreased in popularity, it is still a foundational model and remains extensively referenced in mathematical finance. One notable iteration is the CIR++ model introduced by Brigo and Mercurio [341, 342] in 2001.

TABLE 16.1 Comparison of Interest Rate Models Presented in This Chapter for Rate Modeling and Pricing

	CIR	SABR	SVJC	HJM
Mean reversion	Yes	No	Yes	Flexible
Stochastic volatility	No	Yes	Yes	Yes
Jump processes	No	No	Yes	No
Closed-form solution	Yes	Approximate	No	No
Complexity	Low	Medium	High	Very high

The application of the CIR model in its original form in the context of digital assets has been relatively limited, although there has been recent research on fitting it to fees [343] on Ethereum. Jump models have become more popular instead, which we discuss in Section 16.3.

16.2 SABR MODEL

The Stochastic Alpha, Beta, Rho (SABR)[1] model is a stochastic volatility model introduced by Hagan et al. [344] in 2002. One of its objectives was to capture the correlation between price and volatility,[2] while remaining fairly simple to use.

Definition 16.2 ***(SABR Model)*:** The SABR model is a stochastic process for the price P_t defined as

$$dP_t = \sigma(t)(P_t)^{\beta} dW_t^P$$

$$d\sigma(t) = \alpha\sigma(t)dW_t^{\sigma}$$

with $\alpha \in \mathbb{R}_+$ the volatility of volatility, $\beta \in [0; 1]$ the skewness, W_t^P and W_t^{σ} two correlated Wiener processes such that

$$dW_t^P dW_t^{\sigma} = \rho dt$$

with $\rho \in (-1; 1)$.

As for the Heston model, there is an alternative to Definition 16.2 that uses independent Wiener processes, which is more common.

The CIR model, while ensuring nonnegative interest rates, a desirable feature before the Great Financial Crisis (GFC), became less appealing as negative rates emerged in TradFi after the GFC. In contrast, the Hull-White model, which permits negative rates and serves as a predecessor to the Heath-Jarrow-Morton (HJM) model framework introduced in Section 16.4, became more popular as a result.

---

[1]Alpha, Beta, and Rho are parameters in Definition 16.2. The model is also sometimes known as the Hagan, Kumar, Lesniewski, and Woodward (HKLW) model.

[2]This is also a feature of the Heston model [345], which we discussed in Section 11.3.2.

Definition 16.3 *(SABR Model [Alternative])*: The SABR model is a stochastic process for the price P_t defined as

$$dP_t = \sigma(t)(P_t)^{\beta}\left(\rho dW_t^{\sigma} + \sqrt{1-\rho^2}dZ_t\right)$$

$$d\sigma(t) = \alpha\sigma(t)dW_t^{\sigma}$$

with $\alpha \in \mathbb{R}_+$ the volatility of the volatility, $\beta \in [0; 1]$ the skewness, $\rho \in (-1; 1)$ the correlation, W_t^{σ} and Z_t two independent Wiener processes.

The SABR model is one of the most commonly used models in the field of interest rate derivatives because of its simplicity and good fit with observed market data [346]. While this model has only had limited applications in the field of cryptocurrencies [347], we expect it to be gradually adopted by practitioners in DeFi, as it was in TradFi.

16.3 SVJC MODEL

As mentioned in Sections 16.1 and 11.3.3, jump processes have become increasingly popular both in TradFi and in DeFi. There were notable works in the 1990s [348, 349] in option pricing, alongside the development of rough volatility models from 1998 [303] onward.

There is a growing body of research on jump processes for digital asset pricing, in particular around Bitcoin [289, 350–353]. While we drew the reader's attention to rough volatility models in Section 11.3.3, we want to mention another jump process model in particular, developed specifically for cryptocurrencies.

Hou et al. [219] introduced in 2020 a Stochastic Volatility with a Correlated Jump (SVJC) model, which bears similarities with the CIR model introduced in Section 16.1. It is an extension of an earlier jump model developed by Bates [348] for FX options and is used for pricing cryptocurrency options [98, 219, 354].

Definition 16.4 *(Stochastic Volatility Jump-correction [SVJC] Model)*: The SVJC model is a stochastic process defined as

$$d \log P_t = \mu dt + \sqrt{\sigma^2(t)}dW_t^P + Z_t^P dN_t$$

with $\sigma^2(t)$ the variance process, which follows a mean-reverting process

$$d\sigma^2(t) = \kappa\left(\theta - \sigma^2(t)\right)dt + \xi\sqrt{\sigma^2(t)}dW_t^{\sigma} + Z_t^{\sigma}dN_t$$

with κ the mean-reversion rate, θ the long-term variance, μ the drift, ξ the volatility of variance. We also introduced two distinct Wiener processes W_t^P and W_t^{σ} respectively, with correlation ρ:

$$dW_t^P dW_t^{\sigma} = \rho dt$$

Z_t^{σ} and Z_t^P are the random jump sizes and N_t is a Poisson process with constant intensity λ:

$$\mathrm{P}\left(dN_t = 1\right) = \lambda dt$$

We note the similarity of the variance process in Definition 16.4 with the variance of the CIR model in Definition 16.1 and the Heston model in Definition 11.10. The case where $\lambda = 0$ in Definition 16.4 is actually equivalent to the Heston model.

Remark 16.2: The process modeled in Definition 16.4 is for $\log P_t$, which represents the log-price process. By Itô's lemma, $d \log P_t$ gives the instantaneous return with a corrective term.

A notable result of this model, linked to the leverage effect (SF5), is that the SVJC model captures positive correlation between returns and volatility [219]. This is referred to as the inverse leverage effect [219, 220, 355].

16.4 HJM MODEL

In this section, we present the HJM model, which is one of the most popular modeling frameworks for interest rate curves. In the late 1980s, Heath, Jarrow, and Morton introduced a framework for modeling the evolution of interest rates [356, 357]. The eponymous model, called the HJM model [357–359], describes the dynamics of the forward interest rate curve under no-arbitrage conditions. It relies on the instantaneous forward rates, which are represented on the interest rate curve we presented in Section 13.3.

The broad appeal of the HJM model is its versatility. Its parameters are highly flexible and can be recalibrated for different volatility conditions. The model has become a classic in quantitative finance and is still relevant,[3] with many extensions [359].

The underlying mathematics of the HJM model are out of scope for this introductory book,[4] but given its significance, we want to highlight some of the key model features.

- The HJM model also assumes pricing in the risk-neutral measure, which was discussed in Section 14.3.
- The HJM model aims to model the full forward rate curve. It is a continuous-time model, which means that the forward rate curve is modeled as a stochastic process.
- The entire forward rate forecast must be simulated to compute the expectation [359], which we discussed in Remark 10.2.

As for most Monte Carlo simulations, which we present in Section 10.1, pricing with the HJM model is a two-step process.

[3] A notable application of the HJM model is the pricing of CDS, which we introduced in Section 5.7.1.

[4] For more advanced readers, we recommend the following references in particular, beyond the original paper [357]:

- Gorokhov's MIT lecture [360] on the topic, which provides a broader context and is available as part of the institution's OpenCourseWare program
- Van Deventer et al.'s [358] introduction to the HJM model, which relies on several examples

1. Several realizations of the stochastic process are simulated, using the model's differential equation for the payoffs. Typically, the outcome of each step is represented as a binomial tree.[5] HJM model trees are non-recombining,[6] meaning that each branch will lead to a different outcome than other branches.
2. The outcomes are averaged, which corresponds to taking the expectation, and the result is appropriately discounted, as per Definition 12.7.

Finite difference methods, also mentioned in Section 10.1, can be applied to solve the HJM model for simpler problems with additional assumptions.

While the HJM model represents the full forward curve, there exist simpler short rate models, which are used only for short-term rates. We discussed these models in Remark 11.6.

[5]This is because in many representations, the stochastic variation dW is assumed to be either an increment ("up" outcome) or a decrement ("down" outcome).

[6]These types of simulation-tree shapes are also called bushy trees.

Open Problems

These thought experiments are guided explorations into the concepts discussed in this part of the book.
Hints are available at www.tomespel.com/books/mfin25.

Problem V.1: The validator account is a continuously compounding numéraire. Assume we use it without any reinvestment, meaning the rewards are not continuously reinvested. What is the implication on pricing under that numéraire?

Problem V.2: Assume that we use the mining rewards as numéraire. What would such numéraire look like?

Problem V.3: Maximum extractable value (MEV) allows validators to reorder transactions for profit. How does this additional revenue stream affect the risk-free rate?

Problem V.4: Assume we define a bullish probability measure on the blockchain, where investors expect the value of the underlying assets to increase over time. Can this numéraire support arbitrage-free pricing?

Problem V.5: Assume that one user of blockchain A user identifies a carry opportunity on blockchain B. A uses PoW and B PoS. How does that impact Siegel's paradox?

Problem V.6: During high congestion, gas fees can exceed staking rewards. Can the effective risk-free rate become negative?

PART Six

Staking Contract

"If your model is so smart, why don't you bet on it?"

Nate Silver, On the Edge

CHAPTER 17

Direct Staking Contracts

Staking mechanisms in digital assets differ fundamentally from dividend-paying instruments in TradFi. This chapter develops mathematical frameworks for direct staking contracts, treating staking rewards as interest-rate-like payments rather than dividends due to their payment structure in native tokens.

- Develop mathematical models for direct staking contracts and reward mechanisms.
- Present ex ante and ex post valuation approaches under different accrual assumptions.
- Examine activation queues, cool-down periods, and queue overrun risk impacts on staking valuations.

We begin by analyzing the financial structure of staking contracts, representing agreements between stakers and PoS blockchain protocols.

17.1 DIRECT STAKING

In this chapter, we are solely in network time t_B, from Definition 12.1. Each increment of one unit $t_B \in \mathbb{Z}$ corresponds to a new block on the blockchain. However, because staking is a network-driven process, all other operations happen precisely at the end of each block, which are the settlement times as per Remark 12.4.

Remark 17.1: The reason why we stick to network time is that we cannot make the assumption from Section 15.1 when the end of the contract is known in physical time. The issuance of new blocks, and the corresponding staking reward, is only certain in network time, while it can be viewed as a random process in physical time.

There is usually a minimum number of coins required to stake directly, as pointed out in Section 2.5.1, although staking pools allow investors to participate with smaller amounts by pooling their coins together.

Definition 17.1 ***(Staker)*****:** The (long) holder of a staking contract is called a staker.

Remark 17.2 ***(Validators and Stakers)*****:** Validators are, by definition, direct stakers. They face the blockchain protocol directly. Conversely, not all stakers are validators, which is why we define the staking contract based on cash flows.

A staked coin cannot be traded because the protocol itself is locking the coin away. A staked coin in isolation will not be used for other applications by the protocol either, as only the staker can redeem it.

Remark 17.3 ***(Market Completeness)*****:** While the coin is staked, it itself cannot be traded, and only the staker has a claim on the coin. This may seem a serious challenge to market completeness[1] assumptions for pricing of coins on PoS blockchains. We argue that it is still adequate to represent it as a future claim, and therefore as a bond contract in pricing, with the borrower being the network protocol itself.

The protocol also controls when the coin is released after staking: at the end of the staking period, the staker will collect both the principal and the staking reward. We will refer to the staking arrangement as the staking contract, as Definition 17.2.

Definition 17.2 ***(Staking Contract)*****:** A staking contract is an agreement between a staker and a blockchain protocol, where the staker agrees to lock a coin for a fixed period, or maturity, M in exchange for a staking reward $R \cdot M$.

We note that the only monetary injection on most blockchains is the staking reward, as discussed in Section 2.1.1.1. There is a vague resemblance with inflation-adjusted ZCBs described in Remark 13.4, where the variability of the staking reward could be seen as some form of inflation. However, we will prefer a more generic definition of the staking reward.

Remark 17.4: In Definition 17.2, we define the staking reward R as a continuously compounded rate of return. For discrete staking periods, we will denote simple rates as r.

We note from Definition 17.2 that the staking contract only exists with the native coin of a blockchain, which we defined as coin.

We can now identify the main differences between staking and a ZCB in Table 17.1.

TABLE 17.1 Comparison Between Direct Staking and Zero-coupon Bond (ZCB)

	Direct Staking	Zero-coupon Bond (ZCB)
Entry Payment	Principal paid in full at initiation (usually at par)	Typically purchased at a discount to par
Accrual	Typically non-accrual (not reinvested)	No accrual; interest is implicit in the discount
Payoff at Maturity	Principal repaid plus staking reward	Principal repaid only (no coupon; discount reflects interest)
Rate	Typically unknown at initiation	Known at initiation
Maturity and Rate Certainty	Maturity/reward often uncertain (network-time maturity fixed)	Maturity and rate (discount) are known at contract initiation

[1] A market is deemed complete if transaction costs are negligible and every asset has a price at all times.

Remark 17.5: Most native coins will not have a fixed staking reward. When such a staking reward is known in advance, it is often because a third party will endorse the risk of the variability of the staking reward, similar to the holder of the variable rate of a fixed-or-floating IRS.

On a pricing theory perspective, we can resolve the problem arising from the unknown maturity by observing the following:

- Each staking period corresponds to a block of transactions. There cannot be any transaction recorded outside a staking period.
- If instead of pricing in terms of physical time, we use the network time, then the release of staked coin is predictable and is the end of a staking interval.

This is one of the reasons why we introduced the concept of network time in Section 12.1.1, which will allow us to price correctly these tokens, leading to Proposition 17.1.

Proposition 17.1 ***(Maturity of Staking Contract)*:** In network time, the maturity of a staking contract is fixed and equal to multiples of one staking period.

Proposition 17.1 is important because it allows us to price the staked coin in a way similar to a ZCB with a fixed maturity, closer to what we know for the ZCB. It is also an illustration of Theorem 14.2, with the staking contract being the representation of time value of money under network time.

Corollary 17.1 ***(Stability of Staking Contract)*:** *The price of a staking contract, when expressed in a network's native coin, is fixed between two blocks.*

The practical result of Corollary 17.1 is that while one can only enter the staking agreement at fixed times, it will not have any initial discounting while pricing on-chain. We always assume that we will enter the next immediately available staking contract. Under no-arbitrage, which we discussed in Section 12.2.1.1, the net PV of a staking contract is zero.[2]

There are two practical characteristics of staking, which depend on the protocol:

- Most blockchains will not natively allow staking for only one block, a practice also referred to as micro-staking.
- The staking process locks the coins for a predetermined period and distributes the reward in a separate transaction. The rewards from one block do not accrue to the initial stake. In financial terms, this means that the staking contract does not allow reinvestment, and therefore the staking reward is not compounded from block to block. Lock-up periods, also called cool-downs, were introduced in part to reduce the incentive for early withdrawal.

Remark 17.6 ***(Zero-curve with Staking Contracts)*:** Because direct staking contracts do not pay coupons, they are functionally analogous to the ZCBs described in Section 17.1.

---

[2]The exchange of principal is not relevant under no-arbitrage pricing.

There are differences in contract structure as highlighted in Table 17.1, but on a pricing perspective, they can be treated similarly. This can allow for a construction of a staking-curve in DeFi, with the same methodology as the zero-curve in TradFi described in Section 13.2.

17.2 WITH ACCRUAL

We first discuss a simple model for staking with accrual, where rewards are reinvested into the stake. The staking contract is initiated at any time between two blocks, and we illustrate such a contract in Figure 17.1.

Remark 17.7 *(Stochastic Nature of Staking Rewards)*: The sequence of staking rewards $(R_b)_{b \geq 0}$ is inherently uncertain, as each R_b is a random variable. This uncertainty leads to two distinct perspectives in valuation:

Ex ante valuation before future rates are known, relying on expectation

Ex post valuation after the actual rates have been realized, using observed outcomes

The ex post case is the easiest one to introduce the main concepts, and we will then move to the ex ante valuation.

17.2.1 Ex Post Valuation

Proposition 17.2 *(Payoff of Staking Contract [Ex Post, with Restaking])*: Let P_{face} be the face value of the staked coins, and $(R_b)_{b=0}^{M-1}$ the realized sequence of continuously compounded staking rewards for blocks $[0, M-1]$ and $M \in \mathbb{N}^*$ the maturity of the contract. The payoff V at maturity is the following:

$$V(M) = P_{\text{face}} \exp\left(\sum_{b=0}^{M-1} R_b\right)$$

Remark 17.8 *(Choice of Measure)*: In this section, we are implicitly using the real measure $\mathbb{P}$. By definition, if we use the blockchain measure $\mathbb{B}$, which we introduced in Section 14.5 as Proposition 14.4, the price of the contract would simply be P_{face}.

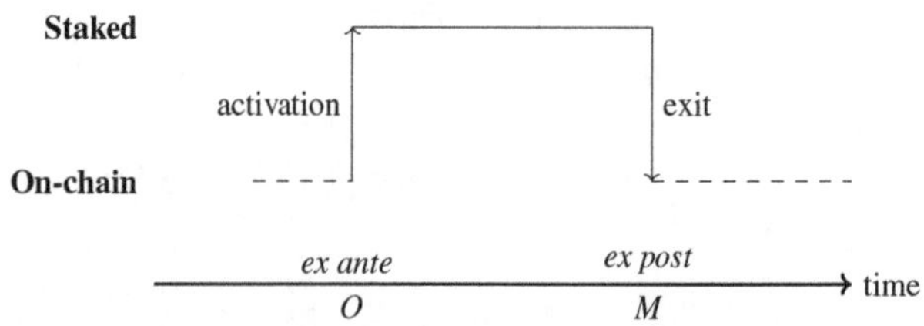

FIGURE 17.1 **Staking Contract Cash Flow Diagram.** The staking period is shown between O (start) and M (maturity), with activation and exit transitions.

Proof. We know from Theorem 12.3 that the risk-free rate in the network's native coin is given by the sequence of staking rewards $(R_b)_{b \geq 0}$. This means that the expected payoff at maturity can be expressed in terms of these rewards. For each block, the discounting is defined as follows:

$$\mathcal{D}(R_b) = e^{-R_b} \quad \forall b \geq 0$$

Between the beginning of the next block, which we set as 0 for convenience, and maturity M, this means locking the staked assets for blocks $[0, M-1]$.

At maturity, the corresponding payoff is as follows:

$$\begin{aligned} V(M) &= P_{\text{face}} e^{R_0} \cdot e^{R_1} \cdot \dots \cdot e^{R_{M-1}} \\ &= P_{\text{face}} \exp\left(R_0 + R_1 + \dots + R_{M-1}\right) \\ &= P_{\text{face}} \exp\left(\sum_{b=0}^{M-1} R_b\right) \end{aligned} \tag{17.1}$$

■

Proposition 17.3 ***(PV of Staking Contract)*:** The net PV of a staking contract in its native coin is zero.

Proof. We know from Theorem 12.3 that the risk-free rate in the network's native coin is given by the sequence of staking rewards $(R_b)_{b \geq 0}$. As a result, discounting for each block with the blockchain discounting $\mathcal{D}$, we have

$$\begin{aligned} PV &= V(M) \cdot \mathcal{D}(R_0) \cdot \dots \cdot \mathcal{D}(R_{M-1}) \\ &= P_{\text{face}} \end{aligned}$$

which corresponds to a net PV of zero (see Remark 12.18). ■

Ex post valuation describes payoffs after rates are realized, but decisions are made beforehand. Hence, we now discuss ex ante valuation, which treats $(R_b)_{b \geq 0}$ as a stochastic process and prices the contract using expectations of future staking rates.

17.2.2 Ex Ante Valuation

The main issue we face is that for the staking contract, the series of rewards $(R_b)_{b \geq 0}$ is not known in advance, as pointed out in Table 17.1. When future staking rates are unknown, we work with expectations under the real-world measure $\mathbb{P}$.

Proposition 17.4 ***(Expected Payoff of Staking Contract)*:** Under the real-world measure $\mathbb{P}$, the expected payoff at maturity is the following:

$$\mathbf{E}_{\mathbb{P}}[V(M)] = P_{\text{face}} \cdot \mathbf{E}_{\mathbb{P}}\left[\exp\left(\sum_{b=0}^{M-1} R_b\right)\right]$$

By Jensen's inequality for the convex exponential function, we have the following:

$$\mathbf{E}_{\mathbb{P}}\left[\exp\left(\sum_{b=0}^{M-1} R_b\right)\right] \geq \exp\left(\mathbf{E}_{\mathbb{P}}\left[\sum_{b=0}^{M-1} R_b\right]\right)$$

with equality if and only if $\sum_{b=0}^{M-1} R_b$ is deterministic. In that scenario, the ex ante valuation equals the ex post valuation because future staking rates are known with certainty. When staking rates $(R_b)_{b=0}^{M-1}$ are also independent, we can simplify:

$$\mathbf{E}_{\mathbb{P}}[V(M)] = P_{\text{face}} \cdot \prod_{b=0}^{M-1} \mathbf{E}_{\mathbb{P}}\left[\exp\left(R_b\right)\right]$$

Under the blockchain measure $\mathbb{B}$, this uncertainty does not affect the PV, which remains P_{face}. That is because the staking contract and the validator account, the numéraire under $\mathbb{B}$, have the same payoff.

Remark 17.9: This does not mean that $\mathbb{B}$ is assuming ex post information; it means that $\mathbb{B}$ treats all future staking rewards as known and certain.

The key difference between the real-world measure $\mathbb{P}$ and the blockchain measure $\mathbb{B}$ is how they treat uncertainty. $\mathbb{P}$ incorporates the uncertainty of future staking rates into its expectations, but $\mathbb{B}$ assumes that all information is known and that the PV can be calculated without this uncertainty, as described in Section 14.5.

In practice, market participants will likely assume for very short maturities M that the staking rate is near-constant. For longer horizons, proper staking rate models are needed, and stochastic processes are described in Chapter 16.

17.3 NON-ACCRUAL

Most blockchains do not follow an accrual model, meaning that the staking rewards are only made available at the end of the staking period, and do not compound from block to block. The cash flows are unchanged from Figure 17.1.

We can reuse most of the existing framework but adjust the staking rate used instead. This is similar to converting quoted yields from the compounding convention to the noncompounding convention.

17.3.1 Ex Posts Valuation

Proposition 17.5 ***(Payoff of Staking Contract [Ex Post, Without Restaking])*:** Let P_{face} be the face value of the staked coins, and $(r_b)_{b=0}^{M-1}$ the realized sequence of simple staking rewards for blocks $[0, M-1]$ and $M \in \mathbb{N}^*$ the maturity of the contract. The payoff V at maturity is as follows:

$$V(M) = P_{\text{face}}\left(1 + \sum_{b=0}^{M-1} r_b\right)$$

Proof. We use the notation of Proposition 17.5.

For each period b, we have the following reward with staking rate r_b under the discrete compounding assumption:

$$\text{Reward}_b = P_{\text{face}} r_b$$

Because there is no reinvestment, the total reward is the sum of all the rewards:

$$\begin{aligned}\text{Reward} &= \sum_{b=0}^{M-1} \text{Reward}_b \\ &= \sum_{b=0}^{M-1} P_{\text{face}} r_b\end{aligned}$$

Recall the total payoff at the end of the staking period is the sum of all rewards, plus the principal:

$$V(M) = P_{\text{face}} + \text{Reward}$$

■

We note that the PV is not necessarily equal to the face value when we apply discounting under $\mathbb{B}$.

The validator account grows as $\exp\left(\sum_{b=0}^{M-1} R_b\right)$ while the non-accrual staking contract only grows as $\left(1 + \sum_{b=0}^{M-1} r_b\right)$. Even with the rate equivalence $r_b = e^{R_b} - 1$ and $r_b > 0$, we have the following inequality:

$$\exp\left(\sum_{b=0}^{M-1} R_b\right) = \prod_{b=0}^{M-1}(1 + r_b) > \left(1 + \sum_{b=0}^{M-1} r_b\right)$$

Under $\mathbb{B}$ we obtain Equation 17.2 for the PV:

$$\begin{aligned}PV^{\mathbb{B}}(t_B = 0) &= \frac{P_{\text{face}}\left(1 + \sum_{b=0}^{M-1} r_b\right)}{\exp\left(\sum_{b=0}^{M-1} R_b\right)} \\ &< P_{\text{face}}\end{aligned} \tag{17.2}$$

Remark 17.10: The discount in Equation 17.2 reflects the opportunity cost of not being able to compound rewards.

It is important to note the distinction between the present value results in this section versus those in Section 17.2. The result of Equation 17.2 is also well known in TradFi, in particular for ZCB, which are noncompounding by construction. This is not a flaw, but a feature of choosing numéraires with compounding; these are fundamentally different contract structures. The difference in present values captures the economic cost of not being able to compound rewards.

An alternative view for Equation 17.2 is that, while our choice of numéraire creates a valuation discount for noncompounding direct staking, this discount captures the economic cost of capital lock-up. This is a real economic consideration in DeFi, which we discuss more in Remark 17.15.

Corollary 17.2: *Using the notation of Proposition 17.5, for constant rate $\bar{r}$, this simplifies to the following:*

$$V(M) = P_{\text{face}}(1 + \bar{r}M)$$

Following up on Remark 14.14, we can now draw the equivalence between the nonaccrual model with immediate reinvestment and the accrual model from Section 17.2.

Proposition 17.6 ***(Indifference to Accrual Under Immediate Reinvestment):*** Using the same notations as before, when staking rewards can be immediately restaked without cost or delay, both accrual models converge when the following holds:

$$r_b = e^{R_b} - 1$$

with r_b the effective staking rate for staking period b and R_b the continuously compounded return over the same period.

Proof. We write the payoff in Proposition 17.5 assuming reinvestment at the end of each staking period b:

$$P_{\text{face}} \prod_{b=0}^{M-1} (1 + r_b)$$

We now equate it with the payoff in Proposition 17.2:

$$P_{\text{face}} \prod_{b=0}^{M-1} (1 + r_b) = P_{\text{face}} \exp\left(\sum_{b=0}^{M-1} R_b\right)$$

This holds when each staking period b satisfies $1 + r_b = e^{R_b}$. ■

17.3.2 Ex Ante Valuation

When rates are unknown ex ante, we work with expectations under the real-world measure $\mathbb{P}$.

Proposition 17.7 ***(Expected Payoff Without Accrual):*** Under the real-world measure $\mathbb{P}$, the expected payoff at maturity without accrual is given by the following:

$$\mathbf{E}_{\mathbb{P}}[V(M)] = P_{\text{face}}\left(1 + \mathbf{E}_{\mathbb{P}}\left[\sum_{b=0}^{M-1} r_b\right]\right)$$

If rates are independent and identically distributed such that $\forall b,\ \mathbf{E}_{\mathbb{P}}[r_b] = \bar{r}_b$, Proposition 17.7 simplifies to the following:

$$\mathbf{E}_{\mathbb{P}}[V(M)] = P_{\text{face}}\left(1 + \bar{r}_b M\right)$$

As noted in Remark 17.8, under the blockchain measure $\mathbb{B}$, the numéraire is the validator account. If Proposition 17.6 does not hold, then the equivalence between accrual and non-accrual models breaks down.

Remark 17.11 *(Compounding Period)*: One will note that on networks where the protocol allows for fast withdrawal and deposit of staked coins, there is actually no difference between the accrued and non-accrued models, provided the compounding rate is computed as the one over the staking period. Cardano is an example of such a blockchain where the staking rewards are paid at the end of each epoch, and these can be immediately added back to the staking pool.

There are, however, a couple of constraints to have such simplification:

- The protocol must allow for fast withdrawal and deposit of staked coins.
- The staking period must be fixed in number of blocks.
- The rewards must be paid immediately at the end of the staking period.

Note that there is no constraint that the staking period is aligned for all validators; they just need to be the same in length. This is because while the overall staking period rewards will differ (since not the same blocks are included), this does not mean that the implied risk-free rate is different. It is simply measured over different periods, and no-arbitrage holds.

17.4 NON-ACCRUAL WITH QUEUE MECHANISMS

We now present the most realistic model for the staking contract, in line with what most protocols use. Because there is no reinvestment in most staking protocols, it is theoretically more profitable to stake and unstake as often as possible, so as to reinvest the staking rewards. This is actually difficult to do in practice, due to protocol queues. The terminology we use in this section is the one for the Ethereum blockchain, albeit the concepts exist on other chains.

There are two possible queues, depending on the protocol:

Activation queue where new stakers wait to start earning rewards. The coins are neither at stake, nor are earning rewards yet. The process of entering the queue is called the request, or initiation.

Exit queue where stakers wait to withdraw their coins after unstaking, which is also referred to as the voluntary exit. This process is also called the cool-down period. The coins are still at stake, but they stopped earning rewards. The process of leaving the queue is often called the withdrawal.

The coins are unavailable from the moment the activation queue is joined, until the exit queue is left. The time spent in each queue can be deterministic, as a number of blocks, or can be stochastic too. We illustrate these concepts in Figure 17.2.

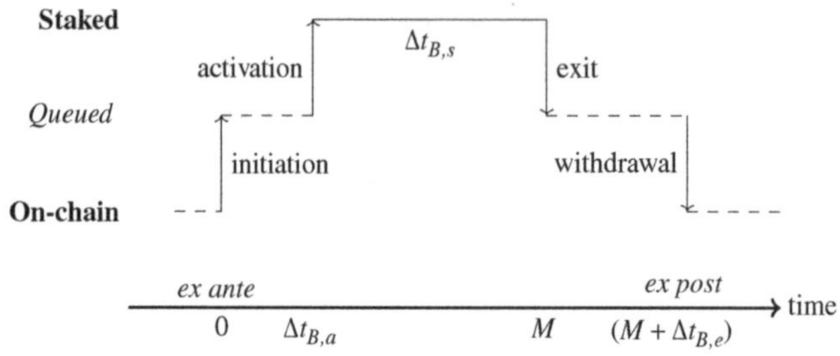

FIGURE 17.2 **Staking Contract Cash Flow Diagram with Activation and Exit Queues.** The staking period includes activation and exit queues, with transitions for initiation, activation, exit, and withdrawal.

Remark 17.12 ***(Are Queues Akin to Settlement?)*:** When pricing in quantitative finance, the settlement parameters are usually ignored. This is even more true for blockchains where it is instantaneous and all transactions in network time have immediate delivery versus payment. If so is the case, then the logic of Section 17.3 holds.

However, for many protocols, the time spent in queues is not negligible and is not akin to TradFi settlement, as pointed out in Remark 17.11. We therefore argue that queues need to be discounted for in pricing direct staking contracts.

We set the following conventions:

- The activation queue duration $\Delta t_{B,a}$ is the time spent in the activation queue before earning rewards.
- The time spent while staking is $\Delta t_{B,s}$.
- The maturity M of the staking contract corresponds to until the exit instruction of staking:

$$M := \Delta t_{B,a} + \Delta t_{B,s}$$

- The exit queue duration $\Delta t_{B,e}$ is the time spent in the exit queue after unstaking. It is also commonly called the cool-down period.

We illustrate these timestamps in Figure 17.2.

Remark 17.13 ***(About the Choice of M)*:** One might wonder why the maturity M should not also account for the time spent in the exit queue $\Delta t_{B,e}$. We propose to exclude it for two reasons:

1. Only the initiation and the exit instructions are sent by the staker. The activation and the withdrawal are determined by the protocol. It makes little practical sense to denominate such an essential contract characteristic with a parameter unknown to either party at initiation.
2. The exit instruction M is actually almost deterministic at contract initiation. This is because for M large enough, it is almost certain that $\Delta t_{B,s} > 0$, regardless of the effective $\Delta t_{B,a}$.

We note that this also better aligns our pricing with the TradFi conventions discussed in Remark 17.11. In practice, computing the PV with the cool-down period simply means there is a final discounting to be applied between M and $M + \Delta t_{B,e}$.

We will assume in the sections below that $M > \Delta t_{B,a}$ for simplicity.

17.4.1 Ex Post Valuation

Under the conditions when the staking contract has an activation queue, and the rate r is known in advance, it aligns closely with the structure of the forward-forward agreement (FFA), which we introduced in Section 13.3. The differences between both contracts are presented in Table 17.2.

Recall that in network time, $\left(\Delta t_{B,a}, \Delta t_{B,s}, \Delta t_{B,e}, M\right) \in \mathbb{N}^4$.

Proposition 17.8 *(Payoff of Staking Contract [Ex Post, Without Restaking, with Queues]):* Let P_{face} be the face value of the staked coins, and $(r_b)_{b=\Delta t_{B,a}}^{M-1}$ the realized sequence of simple staking rewards during the staking period $\Delta t_{B,s}$. The payoff V at the exit instruction is as follows:

$$V(M) = P_{\text{face}}\left(1 + \sum_{b=\Delta t_{B,a}}^{M-1} r_b\right)$$

Note in Proposition 17.8 that rewards are only earned during the staking period, not during the activation queue.

Proof. Following the structure of Proposition 17.5 during the staking period $[\Delta t_{B,a}, M)$, rewards accumulate as follows:

$$\begin{aligned}\text{Reward} &= P_{\text{face}} \sum_{b=0}^{\Delta t_{B,s}-1} r_{b+\Delta t_{B,a}} \\ &= P_{\text{face}} \sum_{b=\Delta t_{B,a}}^{M-1} r_b\end{aligned}$$

TABLE 17.2 Comparison Between Staking and Forward-forward Agreement (FFA)

	Staking with Queues	Forward-forward Agreement (FFA)
Entry Payment	Principal locked at initiation (earning after activation)	No upfront payment
Earning Period	Only during $\Delta t_{B,s}$, from $\Delta t_{B,a}$ to M	From 0 to M
Settlement	Activation and exit queues	Times for settlement are ignored for pricing
Rate	Staking rates may vary	Forward rate fixed at inception

There is no reward earned during the activation queue, for times $t_B \in [0, \Delta t_{B,a})$. Therefore, payoff at exit instruction is simply the principal and the reward earned during the staking period $\Delta t_{B,s}$:

$$V(M) = P_{\text{face}} + \text{Reward} = P_{\text{face}} \left(1 + \sum_{b=\Delta t_{B,a}}^{M-1} r_b \right)$$

■

Proposition 17.9 *(PV of Staking Contract [Ex Post, Without Restaking, with Queues])*: Under the blockchain measure $\mathbb{B}$, the PV at initiation is as follows:

$$PV^{\mathbb{B}}(t_B = 0) = P_{\text{face}} \cdot \frac{1 + \sum_{b=\Delta t_{B,a}}^{M-1} r_b}{\exp\left(\sum_{b=0}^{M-1} R_b\right)}$$

with $(R_b)_{b\geq 0}$ the continuously compounded risk-free rate sequence and $(r_b)_{b\geq 0}$ the simple staking rates.

Proof. The contract has two periods for pricing:

1. Activation queue $[0, \Delta t_{B,a})$ where no rewards are earned
2. Staking period $[\Delta t_{B,a}, M)$, where rewards are earned at simple rate r_b

Note that we exclude the exit queue from pricing per Remark 17.13.

The payoff at maturity M is given by Proposition 17.8 as follows:

$$V(M) = P_{\text{face}} \left(1 + \sum_{b=\Delta t_{B,a}}^{M-1} r_b \right)$$

Under $\mathbb{B}$, the numéraire validator account compounds continuously over the entire period $[0, M)$ as follows:

$$\Pi_B(M) = \Pi_B(0) \cdot \exp\left(\sum_{b=0}^{M-1} R_b \right)$$

We can now compute the PV:

$$PV^{\mathbb{B}}(t_B = 0) = \frac{V(M)}{\exp\left(\sum_{b=0}^{M-1} R_b\right)}$$

$$= P_{\text{face}} \cdot \frac{1 + \sum_{b=\Delta t_{B,a}}^{M-1} r_b}{\exp\left(\sum_{b=0}^{M-1} R_b\right)}$$

■

Remark 17.14 ***(Impact of Queues and Noncompounding on Valuation)*****:** The present value discount arises from two sources:

Activation queue which gives no reward during $t_B \in [0, \Delta t_{B,a})$

Staking period without reinvestment when simple rewards cannot match the continuously compounding numéraire

Even with rate equivalence $r_b = e^{R_b} - 1$, we have the following:

$$1 + \sum_{b=\Delta t_{B,a}}^{M-1} r_b \leq \exp\left(\sum_{b=\Delta t_{B,a}}^{M-1} R_b\right) \leq \exp\left(\sum_{b=0}^{M-1} R_b\right)$$

Therefore $PV^{\mathbb{B}}(t_B = 0) \leq P_{\text{face}}$. This discount represents both the opportunity cost of not being able to compound rewards and the TVM during the activation queue.

A direct observation from Proposition 17.9 is that there are two ways to increase the PV:

1. To operate on a blockchain with a very small entry queue $\Delta t_{B,a}$ to reduce the time without earning the reward
2. To create the contract such that $\Delta t_{B,s}$ is minimized, as close as possible as one staking period, to reduce the discount linked to compounding

Remark 17.15 ***(Why Not Define the VA Without Compounding?)*****:** It seems that a simpler solution would have been to define the validator account in Section 14.5 assuming no compounding. This is a valid consideration, and we can construct a corresponding blockchain measure without restaking.

However, while this would have simplified computations in this section, it does not capture the purpose of the validator account, which as a numéraire was constructed to represent wealth accumulation, in the spirit of the money market account. Continuous compounding proves highly advantageous when analyzing the most prevalent staking mechanism, LSTs, in Section 18.1.

17.4.2 Ex Ante Valuation

In this section, we will assume that the activation queue duration $\Delta t_{B,a}$ is known at contract initiation.

Proposition 17.10 ***(Expected Payoff with Known Queues)*****:** Under the real-world measure $\mathbb{P}$, when queue duration $\Delta t_{B,a}$ is known but rates $(r_b)_{b\geq 0}$ are stochastic, we can write the expected payoff as follows:

$$\mathbf{E}_{\mathbb{P}}[V(M)] = P_{\text{face}}\left(1 + \sum_{b=\Delta t_{B,a}}^{M-1} \mathbf{E}_{\mathbb{P}}[r_b]\right)$$

In Proposition 17.10, when rates are identically distributed with $\mathbf{E}_{\mathbb{P}}[r_b] = \bar{r}$, we obtain the following result:

$$\mathbf{E}_{\mathbb{P}}[V(M)] = P_{\text{face}}\left(1 + \Delta t_{B,s} \cdot \bar{r}\right)$$

The present value under $\mathbb{B}$ follows from Proposition 17.9, with expectations taken over the rate distributions. In practice, protocols often provide reliable estimates for queue durations based on current network conditions, making this assumption reasonable.

17.4.3 Queue Overrun Risk

By construction of the staking contract, a given agreed price will imply both an expected staking reward and an expected time in the activation queue. If the activation queue is long, which we refer to as an overrun, then the effective staking reward will be lower than expected. We now consider the case where the activation queue duration $\Delta t_{B,a}$ is stochastic while assuming the staking rate r is known.

Definition 17.3 *(Queue Overrun)*: A queue overrun occurs when the realized activation queue duration exceeds its expected value:

$$\Delta t_{B,a} > \mathbf{E}_{\mathbb{P}}[\Delta t_{B,a}]$$

Definition 17.3 can be rephrased in terms of staking period, given $M := \Delta t_{B,a} + \Delta t_{B,s}$:

$$\Delta t_{B,s} < \mathbf{E}_{\mathbb{P}}[\Delta t_{B,s}]$$

The contract buyer effectively receives protection against validator queue congestion, on top of the expected staking reward. Note that this protection is not an option; this is akin to a forward contract with binding obligations for both parties. This creates a dynamic where sellers have an incentive to collectively limit the number of such staking contracts to prevent congestion, so they can replicate the payoffs through direct staking.

Proposition 17.11 *(Payoff with Stochastic Queue Duration)*: Under the real-world measure $\mathbb{P}$, when activation queue duration $\Delta t_{B,a}$ is stochastic but the per-block rate $\bar{r}$ is constant, we can write the following:

$$\mathbf{E}_{\mathbb{P}}[V(M)] = P_{\text{face}}\left(1 + \bar{r} \cdot \mathbf{E}_{\mathbb{P}}\left[\left(M - \Delta t_{B,a}\right)^{+}\right]\right)$$

with $(x)^{+} := \max(x, 0)$ that accounts for the possibility that $\Delta t_{B,a} \geq M$.

Remark 17.16 *(Queue Duration Distribution)*: The previous framework is a simplification, given that queue durations are stochastic.

In Proposition 17.11, the condition $\Delta t_{B,a} \geq M$ corresponds to a complete queue overrun as per Definition 17.3. In practice, such a contract would have a minimum staking period, and the exit process would begin as soon as possible, which is usually $\Delta t_{B,s} = 1$. This would correspond to a new overrun maturity $M' = \Delta t_{B,a} + 1 > M$.

If we no longer make the assumption in Proposition 17.11 that rates are constant, we can rewrite the expected payoff with the blockchain measure $\mathbb{B}$. However, we now have two stochastic processes $\Delta t_{B,a}$ and r_b. The valuation becomes significantly more complex as we must model the joint distribution of $(\Delta t_{B,a}, (r_b)_{b\geq 0})$.

Remark 17.17 *(Alternative Numéraire for Queue Risk)*: Just as we constructed the blockchain measure $\mathbb{B}$ where prices divided by the validator account form a martingale, one could theoretically construct a measure where queue durations are martingales. This would facilitate pricing queue-contingent claims, though such numéraire would be difficult to interpret economically.

CHAPTER 18

Other Staking Contracts

Direct staking presents significant barriers, including illiquidity during staking periods and queue risks. The DeFi ecosystem has developed alternative mechanisms that address these limitations. This chapter extends our staking framework to analyze these innovations and their pricing implications.

- Analyze liquid staking and liquid restaking mechanisms and their valuation models.
- Examine protocol value concepts and exchange rate dynamics in pricing frameworks.
- Discuss yield farming and its distinction from traditional staking contracts.

We begin with liquid staking tokens (LSTs), which have emerged as preferred alternatives to direct staking for many investors.

18.1 LIQUID STAKING

Historically, the staking contract did not allow exit once tokens were staked, although recent updates have gradually allowed for withdrawals. LST emerged as a solution by providing transferable tokens that represent staked assets.

Liquid staking remains relevant given the illiquidity[1] of staked tokens, as discussed in Section 17.4. LST effectively transform the nontradable staking contracts analyzed in Chapter 17 into tradable tokens. We compare liquid staking with direct staking in Table 18.1.

18.1.1 Liquid Staking Rewards

LSTs typically pay a staking reward at regular intervals, either as the underlying coin or as additional LST as a form of payment-in-kind (PIK). When rewards are paid as LSTs, there is automatic compounding, since the newly issued LSTs will also accrue rewards over time. We focus on this type of LST, which are the most common. Because of their greater convenience compared with direct staking, LSTs have become increasingly popular.

[1]The illiquidity comes in many forms. The two most important are the existence of entry and exit queues and the minimum amount required to stake.

TABLE 18.1 Comparison Between Direct Staking and Liquid Staking

	Direct Staking	Liquid Staking
Entry Payment	Principal paid in full at initiation	Principal exchanged for LST at protocol value X
Settlement	Activation and exit queues	Instant via secondary market
Liquidity	Locked away until exit	Fully liquid, tradeable
Accrual	Staking rewards not reinvested	Rewards automatically compound in LST
Payoff at Maturity	Principal plus staking rewards	LST tokens convertible at spot rate, close to protocol value $X(M)$
Rate	Variable, risk-free under $\mathbb{B}$	Variable, risk-free under $\mathbb{B}$ if no peg risk

Remark 18.1: Ethereum initially did not offer destaking, resulting in the most popular LSTs being built on top of its blockchain. Lido and RocketPool are two prominent examples [361, 362] and are layer 3 platforms. The corresponding LSTs are also on that same application layer but might rely on scaling layer 2 solutions.

In this section we define r_{LST} as the LST staking rate, distinct from the risk-free rate r of the native coin. We will construct a simple liquid staking contract, a carry trade of simply holding an LST, with maturity M, to illustrate the main concepts related to LSTs, similar to the simple staking contract in Section 17.1 and presented in Figure 17.1. To maintain consistency with Chapter 17, we work in network time with continuous compounding approximation.

18.1.2 Pricing in LST Units

The most intuitive way to price LSTs is to use them directly as the unit of account. We use the same concepts and notations as those introduced in Section 14.1.

Proposition 18.1 *(Payoff of Liquid Staking Contract [LST Numéraire])*: Let $P_{\text{face}}^{\text{LST}}$ be the face value in LST units, and r_{LST} the realized LST staking rate. The payoff $V_{\text{LST}}^{\text{LST}}$ at maturity M is as follows:

$$V_{\text{LST}}^{\text{LST}}(M) = P_{\text{face}}^{\text{LST}} \exp\left(\int_0^M r_{\text{LST}}(u)du\right)$$

A common misconception is to price LSTs directly by discounting with the risk-free rate of the mainnet. This is often incorrect when the LST payoff is denominated in LSTs. Because these are effectively wrapped tokens, we must account for exchange rate risk, or make the assumption of no peg risk with the native coin as numéraire, which we discuss in Remark 18.4. We explore the peg risk implications in Section 18.1.5.

Remark 18.2 ***(LSTs Payoffs in Native Coin)*:** When the LST pays interest in the native coin, it then makes sense to price using the native coin's risk-free rate as the discount factor. The PV of the LST is given by the following, ex post:

$$
\begin{aligned}
PV_{\mathrm{LST}}^{\mathrm{LST}} &= V_{\mathrm{LST}}^{\mathrm{LST}}(M)\exp\left(-\int_0^M r(u)du\right) \\
&= P_{\mathrm{face}}^{\mathrm{LST}}\exp\left(\int_0^M (r_{\mathrm{LST}}(u)-r(u))du\right)
\end{aligned}
$$

However, this type of arrangement is not common.

It is possible to construct, as we did in Section 14.1, a measure where LSTs serve as numéraire. Under appropriate assumptions, we would find that the PV equals $P_{\mathrm{face}}^{\mathrm{LST}}$, which is the canonical result for forward contracts as per Remark 12.18.

18.1.3 Protocol Value

LSTs are IOUs that represent claims on underlying staked assets. From a pricing perspective, they are similar to wrapped tokens. The ratio of underlying assets to LSTs issued is called the protocol value [64], which is in essence a peg reserve ratio.

Definition 18.1 ***(Protocol Value)*:** Let N_{LST} be the total supply of LSTs and N_c be the underlying staked coins plus accumulated rewards. The protocol value is defined as follows:

$$
X(t) = \frac{N_c(t)}{N_{\mathrm{LST}}(t)}
$$

The protocol value represents a fair value of the LST based on its underlying, when expressed in the native coin. In practice, most LSTs are managed such that there is an emission or burning mechanism to keep the protocol value from deviating significantly [361], often maintaining $X(t) \approx 1$ at issuance.

Remark 18.3 ***(Accumulative LSTs)*:** When staking rewards accrue, N_c increases while N_{LST} remains constant. Thus X increases, giving each LST a claim on more underlying assets, effectively auto-compounding without issuing new tokens. These are called accumulative or non-redistributive tokens. This mechanism enhances the value proposition of LSTs for holders without a need for emission of new LSTs.

We can provide more results under the ex post assumption, assuming no significant inflow or outflow of LSTs, and no emission or burning of LSTs.

Proposition 18.2 ***(Protocol Value Dynamics)*:** In the case where there is no significant outflow or inflow and no emission or burning of LSTs, the protocol value evolves deterministically as follows:

$$
X(T) = X(0)\cdot\exp\left(\int_0^T r_{\mathrm{LST}}(u)du\right)
$$

Proof. Since N_{LST} remains constant while N_c grows at the staking rate, we have the following:

$$X(T) = \frac{N_c(T)}{N_{\mathrm{LST}}(T)}$$

$$= \frac{N_c(0) \cdot \exp\left(\int_0^T r_{\mathrm{LST}}(u)du\right)}{N_{\mathrm{LST}}(0)}$$

$$= X(0) \cdot \exp\left(\int_0^T r_{\mathrm{LST}}(u)du\right)$$

■

In practice, protocols may not hold a constant LST supply, violating the assumption in Proposition 18.2. The protocol value dynamics then become as follows:

$$X(T) = X(0) \cdot \frac{N_c(T)/N_c(0)}{N_{\mathrm{LST}}(T)/N_{\mathrm{LST}}(0)}$$

Proposition 18.2 resembles an FX forward rate where the LST supply has zero interest rate, while the staked coins grow at r_{LST}.

Corollary 18.1 *(Liquid Staking Contract Fair Value Under Perfect Tracking)*: *Under the assumptions of Proposition 18.2, if $r_{\mathrm{LST}} = r$, then under the blockchain measure $\mathbb{B}$, one LST is worth exactly $X(t)$ native coins at time t.*

Proof. From Proposition 18.2 with $r_{\mathrm{LST}} = r$, the protocol value grows at the risk-free rate. Under $\mathbb{B}$, this makes X/Π_B a martingale; hence, the fair value equals the spot protocol value. ■

18.1.4 Pricing Under Blockchain Measure

We can price LSTs under blockchain measure $\mathbb{B}$ from the perspective of the native coin. In this section, we assume no peg risk such that $\forall(t_1, t_2), X(t_1) = X(t_2) = X$. We now are ex ante, introducing expectations given the stochastic process r_{LST}.

Remark 18.4 *(No Peg Risk Assumption)*: The no peg risk assumption is critical for pricing under $\mathbb{B}$. Without an explicit model for X, the validator account Π_B under $\mathbb{B}$ is an inadequate numéraire to capture the exchange rate dynamics between LSTs and native coins.

Note that for convenience we now use P_{face} in coins units, which is equivalent to P_{face}/X in LST units.

Proposition 18.3 *(Liquid Staking Contract Value Under Blockchain Measure [No Peg Risk])*: We assume no peg risk, such that X is constant. Under $\mathbb{B}$ with native coin as numéraire, consider a liquid staking contract with face value P_{face} in native coin units, with maturity M. The value at time 0 given all the information available $\mathcal{F}_0$ at that time is the following:

$$PV_{\text{LST}}^{\mathbb{B}} = P_{\text{face}} \cdot \mathbf{E}_{\mathbb{B}}\left[\exp\left(\int_0^M (r_{\text{LST}}(u) - r(u))du\right) \Bigg| \mathcal{F}_0\right]$$

Proof. The face value P_{face} in native coins corresponds to P_{face}/X in LST units at constant exchange rate X. From Proposition 18.1, the terminal payoff in LST units is as follows:

$$V_{\text{LST}}^{\text{LST}}(M) = \frac{P_{\text{face}}}{X} \cdot \exp\left(\int_0^M r_{\text{LST}}(u)du\right)$$

We now convert back to native coins using protocol value X from Definition 18.1:

$$\begin{aligned} \text{Payoff} &= V_{\text{LST}}^{\text{LST}}(M) \cdot X \\ &= \frac{P_{\text{face}}}{X} \cdot \exp\left(\int_0^M r_{\text{LST}}(u)du\right) \cdot X \\ &= P_{\text{face}} \cdot \exp\left(\int_0^M r_{\text{LST}}(u)du\right) \end{aligned}$$

As per Corollary 12.7, we discount by the validator account Π_B under $\mathbb{B}$:

$$\begin{aligned} PV_{\text{LST}}^{\mathbb{B}} &= \mathbf{E}_{\mathbb{B}}\left[\frac{P_{\text{face}} \cdot \exp\left(\int_0^M r_{\text{LST}}(u)du\right) \cdot \Pi_B(0)}{\Pi_B(M)} \Bigg| \mathcal{F}_0\right] \\ &= P_{\text{face}} \cdot \mathbf{E}_{\mathbb{B}}\left[\exp\left(\int_0^M (r_{\text{LST}}(u) - r(u))du\right) \Bigg| \mathcal{F}_0\right] \end{aligned}$$

■

Corollary 18.2 ***(Perfect Tracking Under $\mathbb{B}$ Without Peg Risk):*** *When $r_{\text{LST}} = r$ almost surely, $PV_{\text{LST}}^{\mathbb{B}} = P_{\text{face}}$.*

Proof. Direct application of Proposition 18.3 with $r_{\text{LST}} = r$. ■

Remark 18.5: Echoing Remark 17.15, LSTs are a case where our definition of the validator account with compounding interest simplifies our computation.

18.1.5 Pricing Only with Peg Risk

The pricing involves exchange rate risk between the LST and native coin, similar to FX derivatives. Despite Remark 18.4, in reality, the exchange rate X should reflect the cumulative difference between staking rewards and the native coin's risk-free rate. Empirical evidence shows this liquid staking basis varies with staking rewards, market volatility, and other factors [363]. In this section we will assume that r_{LST} and r are deterministic and focus on X being stochastic.

Reusing the same methodology as in Chapters 14 and 15, we define the protocol value X as numéraire and associate the measure $\mathbb{X}$. This relates to Remark 15.3 in Chapter 15.

Remark 18.6: Using $\mathbb{X}$ allows us to price derivatives that depend on the protocol value dynamics. Under this measure, assets discounted by X become martingales after appropriate adjustments. Note that here, we are not explicitly modeling the exchange rate X.

Under measure $\mathbb{X}$, the adjusted native coin value becomes a martingale, assuming appropriate technical conditions hold:

$$\begin{aligned}\mathbf{E}_{\mathbb{X}}\left[\frac{\Pi_B(M)}{X(M)}\,\middle|\,\mathcal{F}_0\right] &= \frac{\Pi_B(0)}{X(0)}\\ &= \frac{1}{X(0)}\end{aligned} \tag{18.1}$$

A popular stochastic model for such price processes X is the GBM introduced in Section 11.2.1.

Proposition 18.4 ***(Liquid Staking Contract Value Under Measure*** $\mathbb{X}$***):*** Under measure $\mathbb{X}$ with protocol value as numéraire, assuming deterministic rates, the value at time 0 of an LST position with face value P_{face} in native coin held until maturity M is the following:

$$PV_{\text{LST}}^{\mathbb{X}} = P_{\text{face}} \cdot \exp\left(\int_0^M (r_{\text{LST}}(u) - r(u))du\right)$$

In Proposition 18.4, the face value P_{face} is already in native coin.

Proof. The sequence of reproducing the cash flows is the following:

1. The contract buyer purchases the LST at time 0 at spot price $X(0)$:

$$\text{LSTunits} = \frac{P_{\text{face}}}{X(0)}$$

2. The contract buyer holds the LST until maturity M.
3. At maturity M, the contract buyer sells the LST using the prevailing spot price $X(M)$.

From Proposition 18.1, the LST position grows as follows:

$$V_{\text{LST}}(M) = \frac{P_{\text{face}}}{X(0)} \cdot \exp\left(\int_0^M r_{\text{LST}}(u)du\right)$$

We need to convert back to the native coin at maturity M:

$$\begin{aligned}\text{Payoff} &= V_{\text{LST}}(M) \cdot X(M)\\ &= \frac{P_{\text{face}}}{X(0)} \cdot \exp\left(\int_0^M r_{\text{LST}}(u)du\right) \cdot X(M)\end{aligned}$$

Under $\mathbb{X}$, we discount by the protocol value X:

$$PV_{\text{LST}}^{\mathbb{X}} = X(0) \cdot \mathbf{E}_{\mathbb{X}}\left[\frac{\text{Payoff}}{X(M)} \,\middle|\, \mathcal{F}_0\right]$$

$$= X(0) \cdot \mathbf{E}_{\mathbb{X}}\left[\frac{P_{\text{face}}}{X(M)} \cdot \exp\left(\int_0^M r_{\text{LST}}(u)du\right) \,\middle|\, \mathcal{F}_0\right]$$

Since rates are deterministic and X follows a process independent of the rate path under measure $\mathbb{X}$, we can separate the expectation:

$$PV_{\text{LST}}^{\mathbb{X}} = P_{\text{face}} \cdot \exp\left(\int_0^M r_{\text{LST}}(u)du\right)$$

With deterministic r and r_{LST}, the change of numéraire ensures equivalence with pricing under $\mathbb{B}$, as per Corollary 12.7; hence the following:

$$PV_{\text{LST}}^{\mathbb{X}} = P_{\text{face}} \cdot \exp\left(\int_0^M (r_{\text{LST}}(u) - r(u))du\right)$$

■

As expected, we find the same result under $\mathbb{X}$ as for Proposition 18.3 under $\mathbb{B}$ with the absence of peg risk assumption. However, recall we have made the assumption that the rates r_{LST} and r are deterministic. We now though properly account for X being stochastic, with the martingale property in Equation 18.1 ensuring no arbitrage.

The equivalence between pricing under $\mathbb{X}$ and $\mathbb{B}$ without peg risk reflects the fact that when rates are deterministic, the choice of numéraire does not affect the final valuation, only the mathematical approach.

18.1.6 Pricing with Both LST Rate and Peg Risk

There are two main approaches, which we briefly outline here:

- **Joint modeling** with r_{LST} and X as two separate but correlated stochastic processes. This would require us to model their joint probability distribution, a more general but more computationally intensive approach.
- **Derived exchange rate** where X is modeled as a function of the accumulated rate differential. As described in Proposition 18.2, accumulative LSTs operate with no burn and no new issuance, which constrains the exchange rate dynamics according to the rate differential. This means that the exchange rate adjusts to reflect staking rewards, similar to covered interest rate parity in FX markets. We present some of these models in Chapter 11. This approach is more common.

In the context of the second approach, OUPs introduced in Section 11.2.2 as the Vasicek model are appropriate, albeit simple, for modeling interest rates in TradFi. Early research in DeFi seems to suggest that even simpler models, such as moving averages, provide satisfactory performance [364].

18.2 LIQUID RESTAKING

Liquid restaking tokens (LRTs) allow users to use the same staked coins to earn rewards from several applications, which was introduced in Section 2.5.2. A Liquid Restaking Token (LRT) is a type of LST where

- the underlying principal P_{face} is staked in the base protocol, earning staking rewards at rate r_{LST};
- an LST is issued, which is immediately used via a middleware protocol sitting between layer 1 and layer 2 to stake microservices called Actively Validated Services (AVSs); and
- the investor receives an LRT in return.

The reward arises both from the original staking and the restaking of assets [67, 64], sometimes referred to as double-dipping. A comparison between liquid staking and liquid restaking is presented in Table 18.2.

The slashing risk is compounded because it can arise from validating on the mainnet or from the Actively Validated Services (AVSs). In practice, LRTs command higher rewards than LSTs. There are two ways to represent LRTs in the context of pricing:

Single conversion is the simplest methodology, where we essentially do the same as for the LST, adjusting for a different reward rate $r_{\text{LRT}}^{\text{total}}$.

Double conversion is more accurate to the technology but compounds complexity.

Since we have already covered the single conversion case, let us provide an outline for the double conversion case. Here too, we define a benchmark liquid restaking contract as we did in Sections 17.1 and 18.1. We reuse the same notations as for the LST, except for the protocol value, which we rewrite as X_{LST}, and introduce the protocol value for the LRT.

TABLE 18.2 Comparison Between Liquid Staking and Liquid Restaking

	Liquid Staking	Liquid Restaking
Entry Payment	Principal exchanged for LST at protocol value X	Principal exchanged for LRT via double conversion
Settlement	Instant via secondary market	Instant via secondary market
Liquidity	Fully liquid, tradeable	Fully liquid, tradeable
Accrual	Rewards automatically compound in LST	Rewards automatically compound from both layers
Payoff at Maturity	LST tokens convertible at spot rate, close to protocol value $X_{\text{LST}}(M)$	LRT convertible at $X_{\text{LST}}(M) \cdot X_{\text{LRT}}(M)$
Rate	Variable, risk-free under $\mathbb{B}$ if no peg risk	Variable; accretion $\approx (r_{\text{LST}} + r_{\text{LRT}})$ under $\mathbb{B}$ (no peg risk)

Definition 18.2 ***(Protocol Value for LRTs)*****:** Let N_{LRT} be the total supply of LRTs and N_{LST} be the underlying LSTs plus accumulated rewards. The protocol value for the LRT is defined as follows:

$$X_{\text{LRT}}(t) = \frac{N_{\text{LST}}(t)}{N_{\text{LRT}}(t)}$$

We note that by construction, Definition 18.2 can be combined with Definition 18.1 to obtain the combined exchange rate from coins to LRTs:

$$\begin{aligned} X_{\text{combined}}(t) &= \frac{N_c(t)}{N_{\text{LRT}}(t)} \\ &= \frac{N_c(t)}{N_{\text{LST}}(t)} \cdot \frac{N_{\text{LST}}(t)}{N_{\text{LRT}}(t)} \\ &= X_{\text{LST}}(t) \cdot X_{\text{LRT}}(t) \end{aligned} \tag{18.2}$$

When modeling the stochastic dynamics of X_{combined}, we often assume independence between X_{LST} and X_{LRT}. In practice, these may be correlated, in which case the joint distribution must be modeled, potentially using copulas or factor models.

Definition 18.2 fits the technical construction of the liquid restaking contract closely, since the restaking layer is usually managed by an entity other than the LST provider.

We first write the payoff in LRT units.

Proposition 18.5 ***(Payoff of Liquid Restaking Contract [LRT Numéraire])*****:** Let $P_{\text{face}}^{\text{LRT}}$ be the face value in LRT units, and r_{LRT} the realized LRT restaking rate relative to LST. The payoff V_{LRT} at maturity M is the following:

$$V_{\text{LRT}}(M) = P_{\text{face}}^{\text{LRT}} \exp\left(\int_0^M r_{\text{LRT}}(u)du\right)$$

Remark 18.7: We define r_{LRT} as the rate at which LRT compounds relative to LST. If we were to use a rate that compounds relative to coins, we would need to adjust the conversion using X_{LST}.

Proof. Using Proposition 18.5, we can now write the payoff in different units, using the same methodology as in Section 18.1.4 with the assumption of no peg risk on X_{LRT}. When we express $P_{\text{face}}^{\text{LST}}$ in LST units, converting from LRT units requires division by X_{LRT}:

$$\begin{aligned} V_{\text{LRT}}(M) &= \frac{P_{\text{face}}^{\text{LST}}}{X_{\text{LRT}}} \exp\left(\int_0^M r_{\text{LRT}}(u)du\right) \cdot X_{\text{LRT}} \\ &= P_{\text{face}}^{\text{LST}} \exp\left(\int_0^M r_{\text{LRT}}(u)du\right) \end{aligned}$$

■

We can now also express the payoff in coin units, starting with P_{face} in coin units. We need to account for both conversion layers in the following, assuming no peg risk:

$$
\begin{aligned}
V_{\text{LRT}}(M) = \frac{P_{\text{face}}}{X_{\text{LRT}} \cdot X_{\text{LST}}} \\
&\cdot X_{\text{LRT}} \cdot \exp\left(\int_0^M r_{\text{LRT}}(u)du\right) \\
&\cdot X_{\text{LST}} \cdot \exp\left(\int_0^M r_{\text{LST}}(u)du\right) \\
&= P_{\text{face}} \exp\left(\int_0^M (r_{\text{LST}}(u) + r_{\text{LRT}}(u))du\right)
\end{aligned}
\tag{18.3}
$$

Equation 18.3 shows the payoff in coin units with a clear breakdown of the contributions from both the LST and LRT accruals.

Proposition 18.6 ***(Liquid Restaking Contract Value Under Blockchain Measure [No Peg Risk]):*** We assume no peg risk, such that X_{LST} and X_{LRT} are constant. Under $\mathbb{B}$ with native coin as numéraire, consider a liquid restaking contract with face value P_{face} in coin units, with maturity M. The value at time 0 given all the information available $\mathcal{F}_0$ at that time is the following:

$$PV^{\mathbb{B}}_{\text{LRT}} = P_{\text{face}} \cdot \mathbf{E}_{\mathbb{B}}\left[\exp\left(\int_0^M (r_{\text{LST}}(u) + r_{\text{LRT}}(u) - r(u))du\right) \middle| \mathcal{F}_0\right]$$

Proof. Following the approach of Proposition 18.3, accounting for both conversion layers and reward rates as shown in Equation 18.3. ∎

The rate $(r_{\text{LST}} + r_{\text{LRT}} - r)$ represents the excess return from both staking and restaking over the native coin's risk-free rate, where r_{LRT} is the additional rate earned from restaking relative to the LST rate.

It is also possible to extend the framework to consider peg risk, but in that case, the single conversion approach is easier to manage.

18.3 YIELD FARMING

We introduced yield farming in Section 2.5.3. Yield farming contracts are agreements between liquidity providers, here investors who deposit crypto assets, and protocols. The latter are most often DEXs and their AMMs.

Remark 18.8 ***(Impermanent Loss in AMMs):*** In practice, during the process of yield farming, the underlying assets are continuously risk-managed by the AMMs, leading to periodic rebalancing through arbitrage.

When the assets in a liquidity pool diverge in value, this creates an opportunity cost known as impermanent loss in the context of DeFi. This loss represents the difference between the value of assets in the pool, versus simply holding them. The loss only becomes permanent when the liquidity provider withdraws their assets from the pool at the new price ratio.

For simplicity, we will assume no impermanent loss in this section, but we could represent it in the form of P_{face} being stochastic.

The tokens that represent yield farming are called yield tokens. There is a common confusion that it is a form of staking, often attached to a layer 2 or layer 3 solution. It however does not meet our definition of staking, since it is not native to the protocol. We illustrate some of the key differences in Table 18.3.

From a pricing perspective, yield farming is essentially a bond with variable rate. We present two modeling approaches, based on how the reward is paid. We assume that the default risk of the solution is priced in the yield.

18.3.1 Reward Paid in Native Coin

When the reward is paid in the native coin, we can model it as a bond with variable rate, similar to a floating rate note.

Proposition 18.7 *(Yield Farming Value with Native Coin Rewards)*: Under $\mathbb{B}$ with native coin as numéraire, consider a yield farming contract with principal P_{face} in coin units, maturity M, and yield rate y. The value at time 0 is the following:

$$PV_{\text{YF}}^{\mathbb{B}} = P_{\text{face}} \cdot \mathbf{E}_{\mathbb{B}}\left[\exp\left(\int_0^M (y(u) - r(u))du\right) \middle| \mathcal{F}_0\right]$$

Proof. Application of Corollary 12.7 to the floating rate payoff. ∎

18.3.2 Reward Paid-in-kind

When the reward is earned as a PIK, we must account for the exchange rate risk between the coin and the reward token. This payment method is the most common and is conceptually similar to how we priced LSTs in Section 18.1.

TABLE 18.3 Comparison Between Staking and Yield Farming

	Direct Staking	Yield Farming
Entry Payment	Principal paid at initiation	Liquidity provided to a pool (may involve LP tokens)
Settlement	Activation and exit queues	Typically instantaneous
Rate	Variable, risk-free under $\mathbb{B}$	Variable, not risk-free under $\mathbb{B}$
Reward Token	Native coin	Usually PIK

Proposition 18.8 *(Yield Farming Value with Token Rewards)*: Under $\mathbb{B}$, consider a yield farming contract paying rewards in tokens with exchange rate X from the reward token to the native coin. Assuming independence between X and y, the value at time 0 is the following:

$$PV^{\mathbb{B}}_{\text{YF,tok}} = P_{\text{face}} \cdot \mathbf{E}_{\mathbb{B}}\left[X(M) \cdot \exp\left(\int_0^M (y(u) - r(u))du \right) \middle| \mathcal{F}_0 \right]$$

The key insight is that yield farming introduces market risk through X. This explains why yield farming typically offers higher nominal rates: they must compensate for this additional exchange rate risk.

Open Problems

These thought experiments are guided explorations into the concepts discussed in this part of the book.
Hints are available at www.tomespel.com/books/mfin25.

Problem VI.1: Assume a blockchain with PoS stops operating for an extended period. What is the implication for the TVM on that chain?

Problem VI.2: On a PoS blockchain, the activation queues have lengthened considerably. However, forwards on the direct staking contract show contango. Why could this be the case?

Problem VI.3: An LST trades persistently at a premium to its protocol value. Under which circumstances would a corresponding LRT, which earns strictly more yield, trade at a discount?

Problem VI.4: Assume that there are two identical European call options exist on staking contracts with identical fixed maturities. Contract A has no queues; Contract B has variable activation queues. Contract B trades at lower Implied Volatility (IV) than Contract A. Why is that the case?

Afterword

Digital assets are such a fascinating field. I hope this book helps you explore it further. In this work, we presented several key contributions to DeFi pricing theory. We have made the explicit distinction between the value of a blockchain and the value of its assets. We have highlighted three essential constructs for pricing in DeFi: the network time, the validator account, and the wrapped token. Network time reflects the blockchain-specific temporal framework that affects all pricing models. The validator account serves as a numéraire for DeFi pricing theory under a $\mathbb{B}$ measure for blockchain assets. Wrapped tokens enable cross-chain pricing and require new mathematical frameworks for proper valuation.

Together, these concepts allow us to bridge the current body of TradFi knowledge, in particular arbitrage pricing theory, to DeFi. However, in developing these tools, we must remember a fundamental truth about our discipline. Too often, quantitative analysts obsess and debate over what could be a perfect model. Such a pursuit is an illusion. Although the object of our field is scientific rigor, our subject remains the study of apparent chaos. This book also faces the challenge of serving three audiences at once: practitioners want tools, traders want insights, and academics want rigor. As a practitioner, not an academic, I am acutely aware of the limitations of models, as much as I am convinced of the soundness of scholarly research.

Quantitative finance is a science that provides a framework, not absolute truths. We might find a perfect model, but in the presence of randomness, we would need an infinite amount of time to observe its outcome accurately. And, even if a "true" model were indeed to be found, with an accurate fair price, there is no guarantee that markets will eventually trade at such value. Consequently, pragmatic approaches will continue to prove more valuable than abstract theory. This is even more critical in the fast-changing world of DeFi.

In this spirit, I wrote this book for those who have the humility to learn and grow, those who understand that curiosity drives us to better understand how markets really work. In finance, the stakes are high, and the impact of our industry on society is significant. Too often, we are scared to challenge established norms and explore new ideas. When there is doubt and misunderstanding, the fear of being wrong prevents us from asking the right questions. I wish many books follow, that new theories will emerge, and that the scientific conversation will follow its course.

I hope future works will deepen areas this volume could only introduce. The breadth attempted here provides a map and I encourage others to chart specific territories in greater detail.

Thank you for the time you invested in reading my book. Gathering theories and formulating new frameworks in this emerging field has been an exciting challenge.

We are at the dawn of a new era in quantitative finance and your actions, not just your ideas, will shape the future of our industry. With DeFi growing, a new breed of quants, the $\mathbb{B}$-quants, emerge alongside the $\mathbb{P}$- and $\mathbb{Q}$-quants. I am excited about the contributions you will make, and I look forward to seeing what you will bring to this field.

Your feedback and comments are welcome at `research@tomespel.com`.

Glossary

A

Actively validated service, AVS microservices on a blockchain, associated with LRTs.

Altchain blockchains that are neither Bitcoin nor Ethereum.

Altcoin coins that are associated with altchains.

B

Bank for International Settlements, BIS an international financial institution that serves as a bank for central banks and fosters international monetary and financial cooperation.

Basis point one hundredth of one percent.

Basis risk the financial risk that arises when the price of a derivative instrument does not move in line with the price of its underlying.

Block time the time it takes to mine a new block on a blockchain.

Blockchain a technology that consists of a shared database distributed across a network.

C

Capital asset pricing model, CAPM an economic model that describes the relationship between the return of an investment and the market as a whole.

Central bank digital currency, CBDC digital forms of fiat money issued by a country's central bank.

Centralized exchange, CEX a digital asset trading platform operated by a central authority, responsible for custody and trading operations.

Coin the native asset on a blockchain, used to compensate for the processing of transactions.

Consensus mechanism the protocol that allows the nodes on a network to agree on the state of the blockchain.

Credit default swap, CDS financial derivatives that allow investors to manage their exposure to a credit event, such as a default.

Custodian an entity responsible for holding and safeguarding assets on behalf of clients.

D

Decentralized application, dApp applications that run on a blockchain network, and are not controlled by a single entity; typically operate on top of a layer 2 protocol and sometimes referred to as layer 3.

Decentralized autonomous organization, DAO a collection of smart contracts that manage a community or organization.

Decentralized exchange, DEX dApps used to trade digital assets that run on layer 3, without the need for a centralized management of the exchange.

Decentralized finance, DeFi a financial ecosystem that relies on Web3 technologies, such as Blockchain, to reduce intermediation and facilitate the exchange of value between its participants.

Delegated proof of stake, DPoS a consensus mechanism where token holders vote for which validator nodes will process a new block of transactions.

Delivery versus payment, DvP a settlement mechanism where the transfer of securities occurs if and only if the corresponding payment is made, reducing settlement risk.
Digital asset classification standard, DACS a classification system for digital assets based on seven sectors.
Discounted cash flow, DCF a method to value a business based on future cash flows.
Dividend discount valuation, DDV a method to value a business based on future dividend payments.
Double-spending a risk that a digital asset can be spent more than once if transactions are improperly recorded on the blockchain; the consensus mechanism aims at managing that risk.

E

Efficient market hypothesis, EMH a theory that states that asset prices reflect all available information to participants.
Ethereum request for comments, ERC a standard for smart contracts on the Ethereum blockchain.
Ethereum virtual machine, EVM the computational environment for the smart contracts on the Ethereum blockchain.

F

Fiat currency government-issued currency that is not backed by a commodity, such as gold; most major currencies are fiat currencies.
Foreign exchange, FX the market where currencies are traded.

G

Generally accepted accounting principles, GAAP a set of accounting standards used primarily in the United States, developed by the Financial Accounting Standards Board (FASB), and distinct from the International Financial Reporting Standards (IFRS).
GENIUS Act a 2025 United States piece of legislation that was the first of its kind to regulate stablecoins.
Global Industry Classification Standard, GICS a standardized classification system for categorizing companies into sectors and industries, developed by MSCI and Standard & Poor's in 1999.
Great financial crisis, GFC a global financial crisis that began in 2008 and is widely considered to be the most severe since the 1929 crash that led to the Great Depression. It led to an overhaul of the financial system and was a source of inspiration for the creation of Bitcoin, and by extension the broader digital asset ecosystem.
Greek computed measures of sensitivity of an option price.

H

Härdle-Harvey-Reule (HHR) Classification a broad classification methodology for digital assets.
Hash rate the measure of computational power used to mine a new block. It is exclusive to proof-of-work blockchains.
Hashed time lock contract, HTLC a smart contract used to escrow tokens.

I

I owe you, IOU a promissory note that is typically less formalized than a formal loan.
Implied volatility, IV given an observed market option price, the corresponding volatility in the BSM model.
International financial reporting standards, IFRS a set of accounting standards developed by the International Accounting Standards Board (IASB) and used in most countries, except in the United States, where GAAP are used.
International Swaps and Derivatives Association, ISDA the main trade organization for over-the-counter derivatives.

L

Layer 0 technology infrastructure platforms that allow for the construction of interoperable blockchains, typically layer 1 protocols.

Layer 1 the foundational layer of a blockchain network, usually with the original coin to manage the network.

Layer 2 applications built on top of layer 1 protocols. They typically are faster and are more efficient than layer 1 but still rely on it for consensus and security.

Layer 3 applications built on top of layer 2 protocols. They differ from layer 2 in that they do not interact directly with layer 1. They are also referred to as decentralized applications (dApps).

Ledger the context of blockchains is the shared record of transactions that is distributed across nodes in the network.

Liquid staking token a token that represents the staked funds on a blockchain network.

M

Mainnet the main network of a blockchain.

Market maker participants in a financial market that provide quotes to buy and sell at the same time. They are a type of liquidity provider.

Maximum extractable value, MEV the profit that validators can obtain by ordering transactions within a block.

Meme coin cryptocurrencies that are created with the purpose to be humorous.

Mixer a service that allows digital asset users to transact with higher levels of anonymity by mixing different transactions to obfuscate the origin of each transaction.

Money market account a commonly used numéraire in pricing theory.

N

Non-fungible token, NFT the blockchain representation of virtual or physical assets that are unique and indivisible.

Numéraire a standardized unit of measure for value.

O

Oracle an entity that provides external data to a blockchain network, for use in smart contracts.

Ordinary least squares, OLS a linear regression method, where parameters are estimated by minimizing the sum of squared residuals.

P

Proof of authority, PoA a consensus mechanism that relies on the reputation of validators to process a new block of transactions.

Proof of history, PoH a consensus mechanism that relies on the timestamp of transactions to process a new block of transactions.

Proof of stake, PoS a consensus mechanism that relies on the amount of tokens held by a validator to process a new block of transactions.

Proof of work, PoW a consensus mechanism that relies on computational power held by miners to process a new block of transactions.

S

Sidechain blockchains that operate independently but are connected to a parent chain.

Smart contract on-chain, pre-coded, and self-executing instructions commonly found on layer 2 protocols.

Stablecoin a type of cryptocurrency that are backed by another asset. Most are pegged to a fiat currency.

Staking the process of committing digital assets to support the validation of new blocks on a blockchain network. It usually results in compensation for the staker.

T

Term structure refers to the prices, or yields, of a derivative as a function of maturity. The only variable is the maturity with all other parameters fixed, including its underlying.

Traditional finance, TradFi the conventional financial ecosystem that relies on regulated and centralized institutions to establish trust.

U

United States Strategic Crypto Reserve the strategic reserve of digital assets established in 2025 for the US economy.

V

Validator account a pricing concept in DeFi analogous to the money market account in TradFi.

W

Wallet a software concept that allows users to store digital assets. It is often compared to a bank account.

Wash trade deceitful trades that give the appearance of activity and volume.

Wrapped token a token that is issued on one blockchain to represent an asset on another blockchain.

Wu-Wheatley-Sornette (WWS) Characterization a methodology that assigns coefficients to a digital asset based on the growth dynamics of its market capitalization.

Y

Yieldcoin a type of stablecoin that generate interest for holders.

Z

Zipf-Briscoe-Odlyzko-Tilly (ZBOT) Law an empirical valuation method for networks based on the number of its users.

References

1 French Hill. Digital Asset Market Clarity Act, 2025. https://www.congress.gov/bill/119th-congress/house-bill/3633.

2 Antony Lewis. *The Basics of Bitcoins and Blockchains: An Introduction to Cryptocurrencies and the Technology that Powers Them*. Mango Media Inc., 2018.

3 David Chaum. Blind signatures for untraceable payments. In David Chaum, Ronald L. Rivest, and Alan T. Sherman, editors, *Advances in Cryptology*, pages 199–203, Springer, Boston, MA, 1983. https://doi.org/10.1007/978-1-4757-0602-4_18.

4 Wei Dai. B-Money, 1998. http://www.weidai.com/bmoney.txt.

5 Satoshi Nakamoto. Bitcoin: A Peer-to-Peer Electronic Cash System. pages 1–9. White Paper, 2008.

6 Ray Dalio. The mechanics in words and concepts. In *How Countries Go Broke: The Big Cycle*, Principles Series, pages 35–64. Simon & Schuster, New York, 1st edition, 2025.

7 Don Tapscott and Alex Tapscott. *Blockchain Revolution: How the Technology Behind Bitcoin Is Changing Money, Business, and the World*. Portfolio/Penguin, New York, 2016.

8 BBC. Bitcoin: El Salvador Makes Cryptocurrency Legal Tender. *BBC Online*, 2021. https://www.bbc.com/news/world-latin-america-57398274.

9 Yuval Noah Harari. BIS Innovation Summit 2024: AI and the Evolution of Financial Systems: Harmonising Innovation with Societal Welfare, 2024. https://youtu.be/HArRwLwc-bA?si=2HCGUhU0suHIVjOE.

10 Sebastian Sinclair. From Novelty to Nostalgia: New Liberty Standard's Crypto Legacy. *Blockworks*, 2023. https://blockworks.co/news/new-liberty-standard-crypto-legacy. Section: Markets.

11 New Liberty Standard. Exchange Rate – New Liberty Standard, 2009. https://web.archive.org/web/20091229132610/http://newlibertystandard.wetpaint.com/page/Exchange+Rate.

12 CoinDesk. CoinDesk Turns 10: The Legacy of Mt. Gox – Why Bitcoin's Greatest Hack Still Matters. *Consensus Magazine*, 2023. https://www.coindesk.com/consensus-magazine/2023/05/04/the-legacy-of-mt-gox-why-bitcoins-greatest-hack-still-matters.

13 CoinMarketCap. A Look Back in Time: Bitcoin Price History and Events Timeline. *CoinMarketCap*. https://coinmarketcap.com/academy/article/bitcoin-price-history-and-events-timeline.

14 laszlo. Pizza for Bitcoins?, 2010. https://bitcointalk.org/index.php?topic=137.msg1195%23msg1195.

15 worldly. European Bitcoin Conference 2011, Prague, Nov 25–27, 2011. https://bitcointalk.org/index.php?topic=40272.0.

16 Vitalik Buterin. Ethereum: A Next-Generation Smart Contract and Decentralized Application Platform. White Paper, 2014.

17 Nick Szabo. The Idea of Smart Contracts, 1997. https://nakamotoinstitute.org/library/the-idea-of-smart-contracts/.

18 Uniswap Foundation. About – Uniswap Foundation, 2018. https://www.uniswapfoundation.org/about.

19 Kaidong Wu, Yun Ma, Gang Huang, and Xuanzhe Liu. A First Look at Blockchain-based Decentralized Applications. *arXiv*, 2019. http://arxiv.org/abs/1909.00939.

20 Sotheby's. Quantum – Natively Digital: A Curated NFT Sale, 2021. https://www.sothebys.com/buy/1122db9b-f3bd-45d5-b299-412bf9d846b5/lots/32fc8f27-fca0-49e4-b1d0-20856bbf118d.

21 Bored Ape Yacht Club. Welcome to the BAYC Clubhouse. https://boredapeyachtclub.com/collections/bayc.
22 Decentraland. Welcome to Decentraland. https://decentraland.org/.
23 Gucci. SUPERPLASTIC and Gucci, 2022. https://www.gucci.com/us/en/st/stories/article/super gucci.
24 Ethereum Foundation. ERC-721 Non-Fungible Token Standard, 2023. https://ethereum.org/en/developers/docs/standards/tokens/erc-721/.
25 Mars Cat Voyage. Mars Cat Voyage Terms, 2021. https://marscatsvoyage.com/terms.
26 Karamfil Todorov. Launch of the first US Bitcoin ETF: Mechanics, impact, and risks. *BIS Quarterly Review*, 6:11–12, 2021.
27 Mieszko Mazur and Efstathios Polyzos. Spot Bitcoin ETF. *SSRN Electronic Journal*, 2024. https://doi.org/10.2139/ssrn.4810965.
28 Tom J. Espel. Impact of US Bitcoin ETF Introduction on BTC and ETH Intraday Regime Seasonality. In *Proceedings of the Future Technologies Conference (FTC)* 2024, Volume 2, volume 1155 of *Lecture Notes in Networks and Systems*, pages 30–46, London, 2024. Springer Nature, Switzerland. https://doi.org/10.1007/978-3-031-73122-8_3.
29 Pooja Singh. Is the financial market ready for cryptocurrency ETFs? – A critical evaluation. *The Journal of Risk Finance*, 23(4):456–460, 2022. https://doi.org/10.1108/JRF-08-2022-241.
30 Marijn Janssen, Vishanth Weerakkody, Elvira Ismagilova, Uthayasankar Sivarajah, and Zahir Irani. A framework for analysing blockchain technology adoption: Integrating institutional, market and technical factors. *International Journal of Information Management*, 50:302–309, 2020. https://doi.org/10.1016/j.ijinfomgt.2019.08.012.
31 Raphael Auer, Marc Farag, Ulf Lewrick, Lovrenc Orazem, and Markus Zoss. *Banking in the Shadow of Bitcoin? The Institutional Adoption of Cryptocurrencies*. Working Paper 10355, CESifo Working Paper, 2023. https://www.econstor.eu/handle/10419/271999.
32 The White House. Fact Sheet: President Donald J. Trump Establishes the Strategic Bitcoin Reserve and U.S. Digital Asset Stockpile, 2025. https://www.whitehouse.gov/fact-sheets/2025/03/fact-sheet-president-donald-j-trump-establishes-the-strategic-bitcoin-reserve-and-u-s-digital-asset-stockpile/.
33 Executive Order. Establishment of the Strategic Bitcoin Reserve and United States Digital Asset Stockpile, 2025. https://www.whitehouse.gov/presidential-actions/2025/03/establishment-of-the-strategic-bitcoin-reserveand-united-states-digital-asset-stockpile/.
34 Eric Lombrozo, Johnson Lau, and Pieter Wuille. BIP 141 Segregated Witness (Consensus layer), 2015. https://github.com/bitcoin/bips/blob/master/bip-0141.mediawiki.
35 Bitcoin Cash. Bitcoin Cash – Peer-to-Peer Electronic Cash. https://bitcoincash.org/.
36 Jaynti Kanani, Sandeep Nailwal, Anurag Arjun, and Mihailo Bjelic. maticnetwork/whitepaper, 2020. https://github.com/maticnetwork/whitepaper. Original date: 2018-06-12, T06: 04:51Z.
37 Mihailo Bjelic, Sandeep Nailwal, Amit Chaudhary, and Wenxuan Deng. POL: One token for all Polygon chains. White Paper, 2024.
38 Sidechains Adam Back, Matt Corallo, Luke Dashjr, Mark Friedenbach, Gregory Maxwell, Andrew K. Miller, Andrew Poelstra, and Jorge Timón. Enabling Blockchain Innovations with Pegged. 2014. https://www.semanticscholar.org/paper/Enabling-Blockchain-Innovations-with-Pegged-Back-Corallo/1b23cd2050d5000c05e1da3c9997b308ad5b7903.
39 Peter Gaži, Aggelos Kiayias, and Dionysis Zindros. Proof-of-Stake Sidechains, 2018. https://eprint.iacr.org/2018/1239.
40 Johnny Dilley, Andrew Poelstra, Jonathan Wilkins, Marta Piekarska, Ben Gorlick, and Mark Friedenbach. Strong Federations: An Interoperable Blockchain Solution to Centralized Third-Party Risks. *arXiv*, 2017. http://arxiv.org/abs/1612.05491.
41 Shinobi. Federated Sidechains Are Bitcoin's Original Upgradeable Sidechain Implementation. *Bitcoin Magazine*, 2022. https://bitcoinmagazine.com/technical/federated-sidechains-bitcoin-original.

42 Fabian Schär. Decentralized finance: On blockchain- and smart contract-based financial markets. *Review*, 103(2), 2021. https://doi.org/10.20955/r.103.153-74.

43 Ethereum Foundation. ERC-20 Token Standard, 2024. https://ethereum.org/en/developers/docs/standards/tokens/erc-20/.

44 Ethereum Foundation. ERC-1155 Multi-Token Standard, 2023. https://ethereum.org/en/developers/docs/standards/tokens/erc-1155/.

45 Christine A. Parlour. Decentralized exchanges. *SSRN Electronic Journal*, 2021. https://doi.org/10.2139/ssrn.3905316.

46 Yuen Lo and Francesca Medda. Uniswap and the rise of the decentralized exchange. *SSRN Electronic Journal*, 2020. https://doi.org/10.2139/ssrn.3715398.

47 Decentraland. Decentraland: White Paper 2.0. White Paper 2, Decentraland. White Paper, 2024.

48 The Sandbox Game. The Sandbox Game – Own the Future. Play, Create, Earn. https://www.sandbox.game/en.

49 The Sandbox. The Sandbox Whitepaper v3. White Paper 3, 2024. www.sandbox.game.

50 Simone Casale-Brunet, Leonardo Chiariglione, and Marco Mattavelli. Exploring the Data of Blockchain-based Metaverses. *arXiv*, 2023. http://arxiv.org/abs/2308.16787.

51 Barbara Guidi and Andrea Michienzi. Social games and Blockchain: Exploring the Metaverse of Decentraland. In *2022 IEEE 42nd International Conference on Distributed Computing Systems Workshops (ICDCSW)*, pages 199–204, Bologna, Italy, 2022. IEEE. https://doi.org/10.1109/ICDCSW56584.2022.00045.

52 Dipika Jha, Ankit K. Bhagat, Raju Halder, Rajendra N. Paramanik, and Chandra M. Kumar. Exploring the Decentraland Economy: Multifaceted Parcel Attributes, Key Insights, and Benchmarking. *arXiv*, 2025. http://arxiv.org/abs/2404.07533.

53 Gavin Wood. Polkadot: Vision for a Heterogeneous Multi-Chain Framework. White Paper, 2016. https://github.com/polkadot-io/polkadot-white-paper.

54 Jae Kwon and Ethan Buchman. Cosmos: A Network of Distributed Ledgers. White Paper, Polkadot, 2019. https://github.com/cosmos/cosmos/blob/master/WHITEPAPER.md.

55 Joseph Abadi and Markus Brunnermeier. Blockchain Economics. Technical Report w25407, National Bureau of Economic Research, Cambridge, MA, 2018. http://www.nber.org/papers/w25407.pdf.

56 Adam Back. Hashcash – A Denial of Service Counter-Measure. White Paper, 2002.

57 Fahad Saleh. Blockchain without waste: Proof-of-Stake. *The Review of Financial Studies*, 34(3): 1156–1190, 2021. https://doi.org/10.1093/rfs/hhaa075.

58 Ethereum Foundation. Proof-of-Stake (PoS), 2024. https://ethereum.org/en/developers/docs/consensus-mechanisms/pos/.

59 ZCash. What are zk-SNARKs? 2023. https://z.cash/learn/what-are-zk-snarks/.

60 Thomas Chen, Hui Lu, Teeramet Kunpittaya, and Alan Luo. A Review of zk-SNARKs. *arXiv*, 2023. http://arxiv.org/abs/2202.06877.

61 Thomas Espel, Laurent Katz, and Guillaume Robin. Proposal for Protocol on a Quorum Blockchain with Zero Knowledge, 2017. https://eprint.iacr.org/2017/1093.

62 Fran Casino, Thomas K. Dasaklis, and Constantinos Patsakis. A systematic literature review of blockchain-based applications: Current status, classification and open issues. *Telematics and Informatics*, 36:55–81, 2019. https://doi.org/10.1016/j.tele.2018.11.006.

63 Sylvain Carre and Franck Gabriel. Security and credit in proof-of-stake DeFi protocols. *SSRN Electronic Journal*, 2022. https://doi.org/10.2139/ssrn.4307207.

64 Krzysztof Gogol, Yaron Velner, Benjamin Kraner, and Claudio Tessone. SoK: Liquid Staking Tokens (LSTs) and Emerging Trends in Restaking (Version Number: 3). *arXiv*, 2024. https://arxiv.org/abs/2404.00644.

65 Lin William Cong, Zhiheng He, and Ke Tang. *The Tokenomics of Staking*. Technical Report w33640, National Bureau of Economic Research, Cambridge, MA, 2025. http://www.nber.org/papers/w33640.pdf.

66 Ethereum Foundation. Ethereum Staking: How Does It Work? 2025. https://ethereum.org/en/staking/.
67 EigenLayer. Eigenlayer: The Restaking Collective. White Paper v1.0. White Paper, 2024.
68 Babylon. Bitcoin Staking: Unlocking 21M Bitcoins to Secure the Proof-of-Stake Economy. White Paper, 2023.
69 IFRS. Financial Instruments, 2025. https://www.ifrs.org/issued-standards/list-of-standards/ifrs-9-financial-instruments/.
70 IFRS Interpretations Committee. Holdings of Cryptocurrencies. Interpretations AP12, International Financial Reporting Standards, London, 2019. https://www.ifrs.org/content/dam/ifrs/supporting-implementation/agenda-decisions/2019/holdings-of-cryptocurrencies-june-2019.pdf.
71 Financial Accounting Standards Board. Accounting Standards Update 2023-08—Intangibles—Goodwill and Other—Crypto Assets (Subtopic 350-60): Accounting for and Disclosure of Crypto Assets. FASB, 2023.
72 Denise Schmandt-Besserat. The evolution of writing. In *International Encyclopedia of Social and Behavioral Sciences*, pages 1–15. Elsevier, 2014.
73 International Swaps and Derivatives Association. ISDA Launches Standard Definitions for Digital Asset Derivatives. Press Release, International Swaps and Derivatives Association, New York, NY, 2023. https://www.isda.org/2023/01/26/isda-launches-standard-definitions-for-digital-asset-derivatives/.
74 John Maynard Keynes. *Treatise on Money: Pure Theory of Money*. MacMillan, London, 1930.
75 Izabella Kaminska. The Curious Case of "Abnormal" Backwardation. *Financial Times*, 2011. https://www.ft.com/content/f427c212-890c-3374-8093-a61bc8ed4f8d.
76 Robert W. Kolb. Is normal backwardation normal? *Journal of Futures Markets*, 12(1):75–91, 1992. https://doi.org/10.1002/fut.3990120108.
77 Philippe Raimbourg and Paul Zimmermann. Is normal backwardation normal? Valuing financial futures with a stochastic, endogenous index-rate covariance. *SSRN Electronic Journal*, 2018. https://doi.org/10.2139/ssrn.3189847.
78 Yeguang Chi, Wenyan Hao, Jiangdong Hu, and Zhenkai Ran. An empirical investigation on risk factors in cryptocurrency futures. *Journal of Futures Markets*, 43(8):1161–1180, 2023. https://doi.org/10.1002/fut.22425.
79 CF Benchmarks. Exploring Bitcoin Basis Trades: How Price Singularity in ETFs and Futures Is Bolstering Market Activity – CFB, 2024. https://www.cfbenchmarks.com/blog/exploring-bitcoin-basis-trades-how-price-singularity-in-etfs-and-futures-is-bolstering-market-activity.
80 Robert J. Shiller. Perpetual futures. In *Macro Markets: Creating Institutions for Managing Society's Largest Economic Risks*, Clarendon Lectures in Economics, pages 42–46. Oxford University Press, Oxford, Calendron Press edition, 1993.
81 Damien Ackerer, Julien Hugonnier, and Urban Jermann. *Perpetual Futures Pricing*. Technical Report w32936, National Bureau of Economic Research, Cambridge, MA, 2024. http://www.nber.org/papers/w32936.pdf.
82 Qihong Ruan and Artem Streltsov. Perpetual Futures Contracts and Cryptocurrency Market Quality, 2024. https://papers.ssrn.com/abstract=4218907.
83 Adam K. Gehr Jr. Undated futures markets. *The Journal of Futures Markets (1986–1998)*, 8(1):89, 1988.
84 Carol Alexander, Jaehyuk Choi, Heungju Park, and Sungbin Sohn. BitMEX Bitcoin derivatives: Price discovery, informational efficiency, and hedging effectiveness. *Journal of Futures Markets*, 40(1):23–43, 2020. https://doi.org/10.1002/fut.22050.
85 Carol Alexander and Daniel F. Heck. Price discovery in Bitcoin: The impact of unregulated markets. *Journal of Financial Stability*, 50:100776, 2020. https://doi.org/10.1016/j.jfs.2020.100776.
86 Songrun He, Asaf Manela, Omri Ross, and Victor von Wachter. Fundamentals of Perpetual Futures. *arXiv*, 2024. http://arxiv.org/abs/2212.06888.

87 Kraken. Options Contract Specifications, 2025. https://support.kraken.com/hc/en-us/articles/options-contract-specifications-demo.

88 Binance. Binance Options Contract Specifications, 2020. https://www.binance.com/en/support/faq/detail/cdee5d43b70d4d2386980d41786a8533.

89 Quant Arb. Alpha in Reading the Contract Specs, 2025. https://www.algos.org/p/alpha-in-reading-the-contract-specs?publicationid=1392884&utmcampaign=email-post-title&r=40tjz2&utmmedium=email.

90 Securities and Exchange Commission. *Investor Alert: Binary Options and Fraud.* Investor Alert 148 (6/13), SEC Office of Investor Education and Advocacy, Washington, DC, 2013.

91 Fischer Black and Myron Scholes. The pricing of options and corporate liabilities. *Journal of Political Economy*, 81(3):637–654, 1973. https://www.jstor.org/stable/1831029.

92 Robert C. Merton. Option pricing when underlying stock returns are discontinuous. *Journal of Financial Economics*, 3(12):125–144, 1976. https://doi.org/10.1016/0304-405X(76)90022-2.

93 John Hull. The Black–Scholes–Merton model. In *Options, Futures, and Other Derivatives*, pages 338–371. Pearson, Harlow, England, London, New York, Boston, San Francisco, Toronto, Sydney, Dubai, Singapore, Hong Kong, Tokyo, Seoul, Taipei, New Delhi, Cape Town, São Paulo, Mexico City, Madrid, Amsterdam, Munich, Paris, Milan, 11th edition, global edition, 2022.

94 John Hull. Volatility Smiles and Volatility Surfaces. In *Options, Futures, and Other Derivatives*, pages 451–469. Pearson, Harlow, England, London, New York, Boston, San Francisco, Toronto, Sydney, Dubai, Singapore, Hong Kong, Tokyo, Seoul, Taipei, New Delhi, Cape Town, São Paulo, Mexico City, Madrid, Amsterdam, Munich, Paris, Milan, 11th edition, global edition, 2022.

95 Patrick Boyle and Jesse McDougall. Volatility smiles. In *Trading and Pricing Financial Derivatives: A Guide to Futures, Options, and Swaps*, pages 127–136. DelG Press, Boston, MA, 2019.

96 Noshaba Zulfiqar and Saqib Gulzar. Implied volatility estimation of Bitcoin options and the stylized facts of option pricing. *Financial Innovation*, 7(1):67, 2021. https://doi.org/10.1186/s40854-021-00280-y.

97 Carol Alexander and Arben Imeraj. Delta hedging Bitcoin options with a smile. *Quantitative Finance*, 23(5):799–817, 2023. https://doi.org/10.1080/14697688.2023.2181205.

98 Jovanka Lili Matic, Natalie Packham, and Wolfgang Karl Härdle. Hedging cryptocurrency options. *Review of Derivatives Research*, 26(1):91–133, 2023. https://doi.org/10.1007/s11147-023-09194-6.

99 Frank J. Fabozzi, editor. Overview of financial instruments. In *The Handbook of Financial Instruments*, Vol. 3, pages 1–13. John Wiley & Sons, Incorporated, Somerset, 2018.

100 Celestino Girón. A characterisation of financial assets based on their cash-flow structure. *IFC Bulletins Chapters*, pages 779-797. Bank for International Settlements, 2023.

101 Jorrit Zwijnenburg, Allison Derrick, Celestino Girón, and Artak Harutyunyan. F.18 The Recording of Crypto Assets in Macroeconomic Statistics. Guidance Note BPM6/2008, International Monetary Fund, Washington, DC, 2022.

102 Bank for International Settlements. Prudential Treatment of Cryptoasset Exposures, 2022. https://www.bis.org/bcbs/publ/d545.htm.

103 Panayiotis Dionysopoulos, Olivier Miart, Lisa Galletta, Paola Rensi, Stathis Bismpikis, and Maria Zhang. Crypto-asset Risks and Hedging Analysis. Technical Report, International Swaps and Derivatives Association, New York, NY, 2022.

104 Wolfgang K. Härdle, Campbell R. Harvey, and Raphael C. G. Reule. Understanding cryptocurrencies. *SSRN Electronic Journal*, 2019. https://doi.org/10.2139/ssrn.3360304.

105 CoinDesk. CoinDesk Indices Launches the Digital Asset Classification Standard, a Roadmap for Investing, 2021. https://www.coindesk.com/markets/2021/12/14/coindesk-indices-launches-the-digital-asset-classification-standard-a-roadmap-for-investing.

106 CF Benchmarks – CME Group. CF Digital Asset Classification Structure (CF DACS) – CME Group, 2023. https://www.cmegroup.com/articles/2023/cf-digital-asset-classification-structure.html.

107 Ke Wu, Spencer Wheatley, and Didier Sornette. Classification of cryptocurrency coins and tokens by the dynamics of their market capitalizations. *Royal Society Open Science*, 5(9):180381, 2018. https://doi.org/10.1098/rsos.180381.

108 Y. Malevergne, A. Saichev, and D. Sornette. Zipf's law and maximum sustainable growth. *Journal of Economic Dynamics and Control*, 37(6):1195–1212, 2013. https://doi.org/10.1016/j.jedc.2013.02.004.

109 Robert Gibrat. *Les Inégalités Économiques*. Sirey, Paris, 1931.

110 FINMA. Regulatory Framework for Initial Coin Offerings (ICOs), 2018. www.finma.ch.

111 Alex Botte and Jennifer Murphy. Valuing Digital Assets with TradFi Tools: Three Methods, 2022. https://blogs.cfainstitute.org/investor/2022/10/25/valuing-digital-assets-with-tradfi-tools-three-methods/.

112 Bob Metcalfe. Metcalfe's law after 40 years of Ethernet. *Computer*, 46(12):26–31, 2013. https://doi.org/10.1109/MC.2013.374.

113 Edyta Abramek. Value generated by social networks in the context of Metcalfe's law. *Informatyka Ekonomiczna*, 4(46):9–19, 2017. https://doi.org/10.15611/ie.2017.4.01.

114 Xing-Zhou Zhang, Jing-Jie Liu, and Zhi-Wei Xu. Tencent and Facebook data validate Metcalfe's law. *Journal of Computer Science and Technology*, 30(2):246–251, 2015. https://doi.org/10.1007/s11390-015-1518-1.

115 Ken Alabi. Digital blockchain networks appear to be following Metcalfe's law. *Electronic Commerce Research and Applications*, 24:23–29, 2017. https://doi.org/10.1016/j.elerap.2017.06.003.

116 Ken Alabi. A 2020 perspective on "Digital blockchain networks appear to be following Metcalfe's law." *Electronic Commerce Research and Applications*, 40:100939, 2020. https://doi.org/10.1016/j.elerap.2020.100939.

117 Timothy Peterson. Metcalfe's law as a model for Bitcoin's value. *SSRN Electronic Journal*, 2017. https://doi.org/10.2139/ssrn.3078248.

118 Dean Curran and Elizabeth Cameron. Metcalfe's law and its inversion: Digital network expansion and systemic risk. *AI & Society*, 2025. https://doi.org/10.1007/s00146-025-02239-4.

119 Bob Briscoe, Andrew Odlyzko, and Benjamin Till. Metcalfe's Law Is Wrong. *IEEE Spectrum*, 2006. https://spectrum.ieee.org/metcalfes-law-is-wrong.

120 Robin I. M. Dunbar. Neocortex size as a constraint on group size in primates. *Journal of Human Evolution*, 22(6):469–493, 1992. https://doi.org/10.1016/0047-2484(92)90081-J.

121 Adam Hayes. What Factors Give Cryptocurrencies Their Value: An Empirical Analysis, 2014. https://papers.ssrn.com/abstract=2579445.

122 Adam Hayes. A Cost of Production Model for Bitcoin, 2015. https://papers.ssrn.com/abstract=2580904.

123 Adam S. Hayes. Cryptocurrency value formation: An empirical study leading to a cost of production model for valuing Bitcoin. *Telematics and Informatics*, 34(7):1308–1321, 2017. https://doi.org/10.1016/j.tele.2016.05.005.

124 Irving Fisher. Purchasing power of money as related to the equation of exchange. In *The Purchasing Power of Money*, pages 8–32. The MacMillan Company, New York, NY, 2nd edition, 1922.

125 Federal Reserve Statistical Release. FRB: H.6 Release–Discontinuance of M3, 2006. https://www.federalreserve.gov/releases/h6/discm3.htm.

126 St Louis Fed. M2. https://fred.stlouisfed.org/series/M2SL.

127 Ingolf Gunnar Anton Pernice, Georg Gentzen, and Hermann Elendner. Cryptocurrencies and the velocity of money. *Cryptoeconomic Systems*, 2020. https://doi.org/10.21428/58320208.f212c00e.

128 Yu Zhang, Mostafa Chegeni, and Claudio Tessone. Velocity, holding time and lifespan of cryptocurrency in transactions. In Stefanos Leonardos, Elise Alfieri, William J. Knottenbelt, and Panos Pardalos, editors, *Mathematical Research for Blockchain Economy*, pages 315–326, Cham, 2024. Springer Nature, Switzerland. https://doi.org/10.1007/978-3-031-68974-115.

129 Carlo Campajola, Marco D'Errico, and Claudio J. Tessone. MicroVelocity: Rethinking the Velocity of Money for Digital Currencies. *arXiv*, 2023. http://arxiv.org/abs/2201.13416.

130 William F. Sharpe. Capital asset prices: A theory of market equilibrium under conditions of risk. *The Journal of Finance*, 19(3):425–442, 1964. https://doi.org/10.1111/j.1540-6261.1964.tb02865.x.

131 John Lintner. The valuation of risk assets and the selection of risky investments in stock portfolios and capital budgets. *The Review of Economics and Statistics*, 47(1):13, 1965. https://doi.org/10.2307/1924119.

132 Jack L Treynor. Toward a theory of market value of risky assets. *Asset Pricing and Portfolio Performance: Models, Strategy and Performance Metrics*, 1961. Unpublished manuscript.

133 Michael Isichenko. Risk. In *Quantitative Portfolio Management: The Art and Science of Statistical Arbitrage*, Wiley Finance Series, pages 155–171. John Wiley & Sons, Hoboken, NJ, 1st edition, 2021.

134 Yukun Liu, Aleh Tsyvinski, and Xi Wu. Common Risk Factors in Cryptocurrency, 2019. https://www.nber.org/papers/w25882.

135 Jiatao Liu, Ian William Marsh, Paolo Mazza, and Mikael Petitjean. Factor structure in cryptocurrency returns and volatility. *SSRN Electronic Journal*, 2019. https://doi.org/10.2139/ssrn.3389152.

136 Jiqian Wang, Feng Ma, Elie Bouri, and Yangli Guo. Which factors drive Bitcoin volatility: Macroeconomic, technical, or both? *Journal of Forecasting*, 42(4):970–988, 2023. https://doi.org/10.1002/for.2930.

137 Eugene F. Fama and James D. MacBeth. Risk, return, and equilibrium: Empirical tests. *Journal of Political Economy*, 81(3):607–636, 1973. https://doi.org/10.1086/260061.

138 Eugene F. Fama and Kenneth R. French. Common risk factors in the returns on stocks and bonds. *Journal of Financial Economics*, 33(1):3–56, 1993. https://doi.org/10.1016/0304-405x(93)90023-5.

139 Robert Tibshirani. Regression shrinkage and selection via the lasso. *Journal of the Royal Statistical Society. Series B (Methodological)*, 58(1):267–288, 1996.

140 Arthur E. Hoerl and Robert W. Kennard. Ridge Regression: Biased estimation for nonorthogonal problems. *Technometrics*, 12(1):55, 1970. https://doi.org/10.2307/1267351.

141 Cetin Ciner, Brian Lucey, and Larisa Yarovaya. Determinants of cryptocurrency returns: A LASSO quantile regression approach. *Finance Research Letters*, 49:102990, 2022. https://doi.org/10.1016/j.frl.2022.102990.

142 Jinchuan Li and Yifeng Zhu. A LASSO Type Factor Model in Cryptocurrency, 2024. https://papers.ssrn.com/abstract=4437594.

143 Linh Hoang Nguyen, Thanaset Chevapatrakul, and Kai Yao. Investigating tail-risk dependence in the cryptocurrency markets: A LASSO quantile regression approach. *Journal of Empirical Finance*, 58:333–355, 2020. https://doi.org/10.1016/j.jempfin.2020.06.006.

144 Karl Pearson. LIII. On lines and planes of closest fit to systems of points in space. *The London, Edinburgh, and Dublin Philosophical Magazine and Journal of Science*, 2(11):559–572, 1901. https://doi.org/10.1080/14786440109462720.

145 Harold Hotelling. Relations between two sets of variates. *Biometrika*, 28(3/4):321, 1936. https://doi.org/10.2307/2333955.

146 Jonathon Shlens. A Tutorial on Principal Component Analysis Version Number: 1. *arXiv*, 2014. https://arxiv.org/abs/1404.1100.

147 Michael Isichenko. Forecast combining. In *Quantitative Portfolio Management: The Art and Science of Statistical Arbitrage*, Wiley Finance Series, pages 129–154. John Wiley & Sons, Hoboken, NJ, 1st edition, 2021.

148 Daniele Bianchi and Mykola Babiak. Mispricing and Risk Compensation in Cryptocurrency Returns, 2021. https://papers.ssrn.com/abstract=3935934.

149 Lee Alan Smales. One cryptocurrency to explain them all? Understanding the importance of Bitcoin in cryptocurrency returns. *Economic Papers: A Journal of Applied Economics and Policy*, 39(2):118–132, 2020. https://doi.org/10.1111/1759-3441.12282.

150 Agam Shah, Yagnesh Chauhan, and Bhaskar Chaudhury. Principal component analysis based construction and evaluation of cryptocurrency index. *Expert Systems with Applications*, 163:113796, 2021. https://doi.org/10.1016/j.eswa.2020.113796.

151 Philip Nadler and Yike Guo. The fair value of a token: How do markets price cryptocurrencies? *Research in International Business and Finance*, 52: 101108, 2020. https://doi.org/10.1016/j.ribaf.2019.101108.

152 Rui Albuquerque, Martin Eichenbaum, Victor Xi Luo, and Sergio Rebelo. Valuation risk and asset pricing. *The Journal of Finance*, 71(6):2861–2904, 2016. https://doi.org/10.1111/jofi.12437.

153 Frank De Jong and Joost Driessen. Liquidity Risk Premia in Corporate Bond Markets, 2006. https://papers.ssrn.com/abstract=686681.

154 Guido Baltussen, Laurens Swinkels, and Pim Van Vliet. Global factor premiums. *Journal of Financial Economics*, 142(3):1128–1154, 2021. https://doi.org/10.1016/j.jfineco.2021.06.030.

155 Austin Adams, Markus Ibert, and Gordon Liao. What Drives Crypto Asset Prices?, 2024. https://papers.ssrn.com/abstract=4910537.

156 Michael Lewis. *The Big Short: Inside the Doomsday Machine*. W.W. Norton, New York, 1st edition, 2010.

157 Patrick Boyle and Jesse McDougall. Credit derivatives. In *Trading and Pricing Financial Derivatives: A Guide to Futures, Options, and Swaps*, pages 191–206. De|G Press, Boston, MA, 2019.

158 John Hull. Swaps. In *Options, Futures, and Other Derivatives*, pages 172–197. Pearson, Harlow, England, London, New York, Boston, San Francisco, Toronto, Sydney, Dubai, Singapore, Hong Kong, Tokyo, Seoul, Taipei, New Delhi, Cape Town, São Paulo, Mexico City, Madrid, Amsterdam, Munich, Paris, Milan, 11th edition, global edition, 2022.

159 John Hull. Credit derivatives. In *Options, Futures, and Other Derivatives*, pages 587–614. Pearson, Harlow, England, London, New York, Boston, San Francisco, Toronto, Sydney, Dubai, Singapore, Hong Kong, Tokyo, Seoul, Taipei, New Delhi, Cape Town, São Paulo, Mexico City, Madrid, Amsterdam, Munich, Paris, Milan, 11th edition, global edition, 2022.

160 Aave Labs. Aave, 2025. https://aave.com/.

161 Compound Labs, Inc. Compound, 2022. https://compound.finance.

162 Hélyette Geman. Equilibrium relationships between spot prices and forward prices. In *Commodities and Commodity Derivatives: Modeling and Pricing for Agriculturals, Metals, and Energy*, pages 23–48. John Wiley & Sons, West Sussex, 2005.

163 John Hull. Determination of forward and futures prices. In *Options, Futures, and Other Derivatives*, pages 124–151. Pearson, Harlow, England, London, New York, Boston, San Francisco, Toronto, Sydney, Dubai, Singapore, Hong Kong, Tokyo, Seoul, Taipei, New Delhi, Cape Town, São Paulo, Mexico City, Madrid, Amsterdam, Munich, Paris, Milan, 11th edition, global edition, 2022.

164 Ralph S. J. Koijen, Tobias J. Moskowitz, Lasse Heje Pedersen, and Evert B. Vrugt. Carry. *Journal of Financial Economics*, 127(2):197–225, 2018. https://doi.org/10.1016/j.jfineco.2017.11.002.

165 Nicholas Kaldor. Speculation and economic stability. *The Review of Economic Studies*, 7(1): 1–27, 1939. https://doi.org/10.2307/2967593.

166 Holbrook Working. The theory of price of storage. *The American Economic Review*, 39(6):1254–1262, 1949.

167 Heylette Geman and Henry Price. In the Vaults: The Features of Cryptocurrency Spot and Future Markets. *The Actuary Magazine*, 2020. https://www.theactuary.com/features/2020/03/2020/03/04/vaults-features-cryptocurrency-spot-and-future-markets.

168 Helyette Geman and Henry Price. Bitcoin spot and derivatives markets: Searching for completeness. *Risk and Decision Analysis*, 8(3–4):113–125, 2021. https://doi.org/10.3233/RDA-202065.

169 Michael Isichenko. Trading costs and market elasticity. In *Quantitative Portfolio Management: The Art and Science of Statistical Arbitrage*, Wiley Finance Series, pages 172–184. John Wiley & Sons, Hoboken, NJ, 1st edition, 2021.

170 Patrick Boyle and Jesse McDougall. Futures & forwards. In *Trading and Pricing Financial Derivatives: A Guide to Futures, Options, and Swaps*, pages 11–26. DeIG Press, Boston, MA, 2019.

171 Kenneth Rogoff. Cryptocurrencies and the future of money. In *Our Dollar, Your Problem: An Insider's View of Seven Turbulent Decades of Global Finance, and the Road Ahead*, The Henry L. Stimson Lectures Series, pages 182–198. Yale University Press, New Haven, 2025 edition, 2025.

172 Anneke Kosse, Marc Glowka, Ilaria Mattei, and Tara N. Rice. *Will the Real Stablecoin Please Stand Up?* Number no 141 in BIS papers. BIS, Bank for International Settlements, Monetary and Economic Department, Basel, 2023.

173 President's Working Group on Financial Markets. Report on Stablecoins. Technical report, US Treasury, 2021. https://home.treasury.gov/system/files/136/StableCoinReport_Nov1_508.pdf.

174 Richard K. Lyons and Ganesh Viswanath-Natraj. What keeps stablecoins stable? *Journal of International Money and Finance*, 131:102777, 2023. https://doi.org/10.1016/j.jimonfin.2022.102777.

175 Jiageng Liu, Igor Makarov, and Antoinette Schoar. Anatomy of a Run: The Terra Luna Crash, 2023. https://www.nber.org/papers/w31160.

176 Matthew Fox. Tether Stablecoin Loses Its Dollar Peg as Contagion from FTX's Collapse Spreads Through the Crypto Market. *Markets Insider*, 2022. https://markets.businessinsider.com/news/currencies/tether-stablecoin-loses-dollar-peg-ftx-collapse-hits-crypto-trust-2022-11.

177 Qihao Chen and Zhuo Huang. Peg instability of USDT: A realized GARCH CoVaR approach. *Applied Economics*, 1–15, 2025. https://doi.org/10.1080/00036846.2025.2473119.

178 Bill Hagerty. Guiding and Establishing National Innovation for U.S. Stablecoins Act, 2025. https://www.congress.gov/119/bills/s1582/BILLS-119s1582es.pdf.

179 Iñaki Aldasoro, Sebastian Doerr, Leonardo Gambacorta, Rodney Garratt, and Priscilla Koo Wilkens. *The Tokenisation Continuum*. Technical Report 72, Bank for International Settlements, Basel, 2023.

180 Gary B. Gorton and Jeffery Y. Zhang. Taming wildcat stablecoins. *University of Chicago Law Review*, 90:909, 2023.

181 Andrew Baum. Tokenisation – The Future of Real Estate Investment? Technical Report, Saïd Business School, University of Oxford, Oxford, 2020.

182 Khalil Alnabulsi. Asset tokenization in real estate: Theoretical perspectives and empirical approaches. In Ammar Jreisat and Mehdi Mili, editors, *Blockchain in Real Estate: Theoretical Advances and New Empirical Applications*, pages 153–168. Springer Nature, Singapore, 2024. https://doi.org/10.1007/978-981-99-8533-3_8.

183 Jo Bronckers. Blockchain in commercial real estate. In Ammar Jreisat and Mehdi Mili, editors, *Blockchain in Real Estate: Theoretical Advances and New Empirical Applications*, pages 53–84. Springer Nature, Singapore, 2024. https://doi.org/10.1007/978-981-99-8533-3_4.

184 Max Zheng and Philipp Sandner. Asset tokenization of real estate in Europe. In Mary C. Lacity and Horst Treiblmaier, editors, *Blockchains and the Token Economy: Theory and Practice*, pages 179–211. Springer International Publishing, Cham, 2022. https://doi.org/10.1007/978-3-030-95108-5_7.

185 Walter Bagehot. The mode in which the value of money is settled in Lombard Street. In *Lombard Street: A Description of the Money Market*, pages 57–61. Project Gutenberg, London, 2003 edition, 1873. https://www.gutenberg.org/ebooks/4359.

186 Laura Levulytė and Alfreda Šapkauskienė. Cryptocurrency in context of fiat money functions. *The Quarterly Review of Economics and Finance*, 82:44–54, 2021. https://doi.org/10.1016/j.qref.2021.07.003.

187 Sang Rae Kim. How the cryptocurrency market is connected to the financial market. *SSRN Electronic Journal*, 2022. https://doi.org/10.2139/ssrn.4106815.

188 Edwin Lefèvre. Chapter 1. In *Reminiscences of a Stock Operator*, Wiley Investment Classics, pages 3–13. Wiley, Hoboken, NJ, 2nd edition, 2006. Originally published: New York: G.H. Doran, 1923.

189 Takatoshi Ito, Eiji Ogawa, and Yuri Nagataki Sasaki. How did the dollar peg fail in Asia? *Journal of the Japanese and International Economies*, 12(4):256–304, 1998. https://doi.org/10.1006/jjie.1998.0415.

190 Colin Ellis and Emilia Gyoerk. Investigating the economic and financial damage around currency peg failures. *Journal of Risk and Financial Management*, 12(2):92, 2019. https://doi.org/10.3390/jrfm12020092.

191 Frederic S. Mishkin. The dangers of exchange-rate pegging in emerging-market countries. *International Finance*, 1(1):81–101, 1998. https://doi.org/10.1111/1468-2362.00005.

192 Austin Adams and Markus Ibert. Runs on Algorithmic Stablecoins: Evidence from Iron, Titan, and Steel. 2022. https://www.federalreserve.gov/econres/notes/feds-notes/runs-on-algorithmic-stablecoins-evidence-from-iron-titan-and-steel-20220602.html.

193 Kanis Saengchote. A DeFi Bank Run: Iron Finance, IRON Stablecoin, and the Fall of TITAN, 2021. https://papers.ssrn.com/abstract=3888089.

194 Antonio Briola, David Vidal-Tomás, Yuanrong Wang, and Tomaso Aste. Anatomy of a stablecoin's failure: The Terra-Luna case. *Finance Research Letters*, 51:103358, 2023. https://doi.org/10.1016/j.frl.2022.103358.

195 Vincent Gramlich, Dennis Jelito, and Johannes Sedlmeir. Maximal extractable value: Current understanding, categorization, and open research questions. *Electronic Markets*, 34(1):49, 2024. https://doi.org/10.1007/s12525-024-00727-x.

196 Raphael Auer, Jon Frost, and Jose María Vidal Pastor. Miners as intermediaries: Extractable value and market manipulation in crypto and DeFi. *BIS Bulletin*, (58):8, 2022.

197 Philip Daian, Steven Goldfeder, Tyler Kell, Yunqi Li, Xueyuan Zhao, Iddo Bentov, Lorenz Breidenbach, and Ari Juels. Flash Boys 2.0: Frontrunning, Transaction Reordering, and Consensus Instability in Decentralized Exchanges. *arXiv*, 2019. http://arxiv.org/abs/1904.05234.

198 Gur Huberman, Jacob D. Leshno, and Ciamac Moallemi. Monopoly without a monopolist: An economic analysis of the Bitcoin payment system. *The Review of Economic Studies*, 88(6): 3011–3040, 2021. https://doi.org/10.1093/restud/rdab014.

199 Daehan Kim, Doojin Ryu, and Robert I. Webb. Determination of equilibrium transaction fees in the Bitcoin network: A rank-order contest. *International Review of Financial Analysis*, 86:102487, 2023. https://doi.org/10.1016/j.irfa.2023.102487.

200 David Easley, Maureen O'Hara, and Soumya Basu. From mining to markets: The evolution of Bitcoin transaction fees. *Journal of Financial Economics*, 134(1):91–109, 2019. https://doi.org/10.1016/j.jfineco.2019.03.004.

201 Archana Jain, Chinmay Jain, and Karolina Krystyniak. Blockchain transaction fee and Ethereum Merge. *Finance Research Letters*, 58:104507, 2023. https://doi.org/10.1016/j.frl.2023.104507.

202 Wim Schoutens. Exotic option pricing. In *Lévy Processes in Finance: pricing Financial Derivatives*, Wiley Series in Probability and Statistics, pages 119–134. J. Wiley, Chichester, West Sussex, New York, 2003. https://doi.org/10.1002/0470870230.

203 Wim Schoutens. Simulation techniques. In *Lévy Processes in Finance: Pricing Financial Derivatives*, Wiley Series in Probability and Statistics, pages 101–118. J. Wiley, Chichester, West Sussex, New York, 2003. https://doi.org/10.1002/0470870230.

204 Michael Isichenko. Market data. In *Quantitative Portfolio Management: The Art and Science of Statistical Arbitrage*, Wiley Finance Series, pages 1–6. John Wiley & Sons, Hoboken, NJ, 1st edition, 2021.

205 Rama Cont. Empirical properties of asset returns: Stylized facts and statistical issues. *Quantitative Finance*, 1(2):223–236, 2001. https://doi.org/10.1080/713665670.

206 Martin Sewell. Characterization of Financial Time Series. *UCL Department of Computer Science, Research Note RN/11/01*, 2011.

207 Ethan Ratliff-Crain, Colin M. Van Oort, James Bagrow, Matthew T. K. Koehler, and Brian F. Tivnan. Revisiting Cont's Stylized Facts for Modern Stock Markets. *arXiv*, 2023. https://arxiv.org/abs/2311.07738v2.

208 Wei-Ru Chen, A. Christian Silva, and Shen-Ning Tung. Stylized facts in Web3. *Frontiers of Mathematical Finance*, 3(4):572–609, 2024. https://doi.org/10.3934/fmf.2024021.

209 Lorenzo Bergomi. Introduction. In *Stochastic Volatility Modeling*, Chapman & Hall/CRC Financial Mathematics Series, pages 1–24. CRC Press Taylor & Francis Group, Boca Raton, FL, London, New York, 2016.

210 Bikramaditya Ghosh, Elie Bouri, Jung Bum Wee, and Noshaba Zulfiqar. Return and volatility properties: Stylized facts from the universe of cryptocurrencies and NFTs. *Research in International Business and Finance*, 65:101945, 2023. https://doi.org/10.1016/j.ribaf.2023.101945.

211 Kennard Fung, Jiin Jeong, and Javier Pereira. More to cryptos than Bitcoin: A GARCH modelling of heterogeneous cryptocurrencies. *Finance Research Letters*, 47:102544, 2022. https://doi.org/10.1016/j.frl.2021.102544.

212 Rasa Bruzge, Jurgita Cerneviciene, Alfreda Sapkauskiene, Aida Macerinskiene, Saulius Masteika, and Kestutis Driaunys. Stylized facts, volatility dynamics and risk measures of cryptocurrencies. *Journal of Business Economics and Management*, 24(3):527–550, 2023. https://doi.org/10.3846/jbem.2023.19118.

213 Kenneth R. French, G. William Schwert, and Robert F. Stambaugh. Expected stock returns and volatility. *Journal of Financial Economics*, 19(1):3–29, 1987. https://doi.org/10.1016/0304-405X(87)90026-2.

214 G. William Schwert. Why does stock market volatility change over time? *The Journal of Finance*, 44(5):1115–1153, 1989. https://doi.org/10.1111/j.1540-6261.1989.tb02647.x.

215 Fisher Black. Studies of stock market volatility changes. *Proceedings of the American Statistical Association, Business and Economic Statistics Section*, 1976:177–181, 1976.

216 Lendie Follett, Steven Kou, Matthew Stuart, and Cindy Yu. Inverse Leverage Effect for Cryptocurrencies and Meme Stocks: A Comprehensive Framework, 2022. https://papers.ssrn.com/abstract=4284817.

217 Yu-Fu Chen and Xiaoyi Mu. Asymmetric Volatility in Commodity Markets, 2020. https://papers.ssrn.com/abstract=3524136.

218 Dirk G. Baur and Thomas Dimpfl. Asymmetric Volatility in Cryptocurrencies, 2018. https://papers.ssrn.com/abstract=3347617.

219 Ai Jun Hou, Weining Wang, Cathy Y. H. Chen, and Wolfgang Karl Härdle. Pricing cryptocurrency options. *Journal of Financial Econometrics*, 18(2):250–279, 2020. https://doi.org/10.1093/jjfinec/nbaa006.

220 Jing-Zhi Huang, Jun Ni, and Li Xu. Leverage effect in cryptocurrency markets. *Pacific-Basin Finance Journal*, 73:101773, 2022. https://doi.org/10.1016/j.pacfin.2022.101773.

221 Alessio Brini and Jimmie Lenz. A Comparison of Cryptocurrency Volatility-benchmarking New and Mature Asset Classes. *arXiv*, 2024. http://arxiv.org/abs/2404.04962.

222 Thanasis Stengos, Theodore Panagiotidis, and Georgios Papapanagiotou. On the volatility of cryptocurrencies. *Research in International Business and Finance*, 62:101724, 2022.

223 Karl Larsson and Marcus Nossman. Jumps and stochastic volatility in oil prices: Time series evidence. *Energy Economics*, 33(3):504–514, 2011. https://doi.org/10.1016/j.eneco.2010.12.016.

224 Albert S. Hu, Christine A. Parlour, and Uday Rajan. Cryptocurrencies: Stylized facts on a new investible instrument. *Financial Management*, 48(4):1049–1068, 2019. https://doi.org/10.1111/fima.12300.

225 H. E. Hurst. Long-term storage capacity of reservoirs. *Transactions of the American Society of Civil Engineers*, 116(1):770–799, 1951. https://doi.org/10.1061/TACEAT.0006518.

226 Timothy Graves, Robert Gramacy, Nicholas Watkins, and Christian Franzke. A brief history of long memory: Hurst, Mandelbrot and the road to ARFIMA, 1951–1980. *Entropy*, 19(9):437, 2017. https://doi.org/10.3390/e19090437.

227 Benoit Mandelbrot. Statistical methodology for nonperiodic cycles: From the covariance to R/S analysis. In *Annals of Economic and Social Measurement*, volume 1, pages 259–290. Nber, 1972.

228 Edgar E. Peters. Fractal time series. In *Chaos and Order in the Capital Markets: A New View of Cycles, Prices, and Market Volatility*, Wiley Finance Editions, pages 61–80. Wiley, New York, 1991.

229 Edgar E. Peters. R/S analysis of the capital markets. In *Chaos and Order in the Capital Markets: A New View of Cycles, Prices, and Market Volatility*, Wiley Finance Editions, pages 81–103. Wiley, New York, 1991.

230 A. Carbone, G. Castelli, and H. E. Stanley. Time-dependent Hurst exponent in financial time series. *Physica A: Statistical Mechanics and Its Applications*, 344(1–2):267–271, 2004. https://doi.org/10.1016/j.physa.2004.06.130.

231 Giuseppe Pernagallo. Random walks, Hurst exponent, and market efficiency. *Quality & Quantity*, 2025. https://doi.org/10.1007/s11135-025-02052-7.

232 Daniel O. Cajueiro and Benjamin M. Tabak. The Hurst exponent over time: Testing the assertion that emerging markets are becoming more efficient. *Physica A: Statistical Mechanics and Its Applications*, 336(3–4):521–537, 2004. https://doi.org/10.1016/j.physa.2003.12.031.

233 Benoit B. Mandelbrot and James R. Wallis. Robustness of the rescaled range R/S in the measurement of noncyclic long run statistical dependence. *Water Resources Research*, 5(5):967–988, 1969. https://doi.org/10.1029/WR005i005p00967.

234 Benoit B. Mandelbrot, and Richard L. Hudson. Noah, Joseph, and Market Bubbles. In *The (Mis)Behaviour of Markets: A Fractal View of Risk, Ruin, and Reward*, pages 197–206. Profile, London, pbk. edition, 2008.

235 Ali Gezer. Chaos in Bitcoin cryptocurrency metrics: Analysis and forecasts. *Arabian Journal for Science and Engineering*, 2024. https://doi.org/10.1007/s13369-024-09357-z.

236 Yuanyuan Zhang, Stephen Chan, Jeffrey Chu, and Saralees Nadarajah. Stylised facts for high frequency cryptocurrency data. *Physica A: Statistical Mechanics and its Applications*, 513: 598–612, 2019. https://doi.org/10.1016/j.physa.2018.09.042.

237 J. Mielniczuk and P. Wojdyłło. Estimation of Hurst exponent revisited. *Computational Statistics & Data Analysis*, 51(9):4510–4525, 2007. https://doi.org/10.1016/j.csda.2006.07.033.

238 Eric Grivel, Bastien Berthelot, Pierrick Legrand, and Audrey Giremus. DFA-based abacuses providing the Hurst exponent estimate for short-memory processes. *Digital Signal Processing*, 116:103102, 2021. https://doi.org/10.1016/j.dsp.2021.103102.

239 R. M. Bryce and K. B. Sprague. Revisiting detrended fluctuation analysis. *Scientific Reports*, 2(1):315, 2012. https://doi.org/10.1038/srep00315.

240 Aaron D. Likens, Madhur Mangalam, Aaron Y. Wong, Anaelle C. Charles, and Caitlin Mills. Better than DFA? A Bayesian Method for Estimating the Hurst Exponent in Behavioral Sciences. *arXiv*, 2023. https://arxiv.org/abs/2301.11262.

241 Bryan D. Jones and Christian Breunig. Noah and Joseph effects in government budgets: Analyzing long-term memory. *Policy Studies Journal*, 35(3): 329–348, 2007. https://doi.org/10.1111/j.1541-0072.2007.00227.x.

242 Ruey S. Tsay. Linear time series analysis and its applications. In *Analysis of Financial Time Series*, Wiley Series in Probability and Statistics, pages 29–108. Wiley, Cambridge, MA, 3rd edition, 2010.

243 James D. Hamilton. Stationary ARMA processes. In *Time Series Analysis*, pages 43–71. Princeton University Press, Princeton, NJ, 1994.

244 George E. P. Box, Gwilym M. Jenkins, Gregory C. Reinsel, and Greta M. Ljung. Linear stationary models. In *Time Series Analysis: Forecasting and Control*, Wiley Series in Probability and Statistics, pages 47–87. Wiley, Hoboken, NJ, 5th edition, 2016.

245 Wayne A. Fuller. Moving average and autoregressive processes. In *Introduction to Statistical Time Series*, Wiley Series in Probability and Statistics, pages 21–111. Wiley, New York, 2nd edition, 1996. https://doi.org/10.1002/9780470316917.

246 Fumio Hayashi. Serial correlation. In *Econometrics*, pages 365–444. Princeton University Press, Princeton, NJ, 2000.

247 Fumio Hayashi. *Econometrics*. Princeton University Press, Princeton, NJ, 2000.

248 James D. Hamilton. Models of nonstationary time series. In *Time Series Analysis*, pages 435–453. Princeton University Press, Princeton, NJ, 1994.

249 George E. P. Box, Gwilym M. Jenkins, Gregory C. Reinsel, and Greta M. Ljung. Linear nonstationary models. In *Time Series Analysis: Forecasting and Control*, Wiley Series in Probability and Statistics, pages 88–128. Wiley, Hoboken, NJ, 5th edition, 2016.

250 Nashirah Abu Bakar and Sofian Rosbi. Autoregressive integrated moving average (ARIMA) model for forecasting cryptocurrency exchange rate in high volatility environment: A new insight of Bitcoin transaction. *International Journal of Advanced Engineering Research and Science*, 4(11):130–137, 2017. https://doi.org/10.22161/ijaers.4.11.20.

251 Amin Azari. Bitcoin Price Prediction: An ARIMA Approach. *arXiv*, 2019. http://arxiv.org/abs/1904.05315.

252 M. Poongodi, V. Vijayakumar, and Naveen Chilamkurti. Bitcoin price prediction using ARIMA model. *International Journal of Internet Technology and Secured Transactions*, 10(4):396, 2020. https://doi.org/10.1504/IJITST.2020.108130.

253 David A. Dickey and Wayne A. Fuller. Distribution of the estimators for autoregressive time series with a unit root. *Journal of the American Statistical Association*, 74(366a):427–431, 1979. https://doi.org/10.1080/01621459.1979.10482531.

254 Wayne A. Fuller. Unit root and explosive time series. In *Introduction to Statistical Time Series*, Wiley Series in Probability and Statistics, pages 545–663. Wiley, New York, 2nd edition, 1996. https://doi.org/10.1002/9780470316917.

255 George E. P. Box, Gwilym M. Jenkins, Gregory C. Reinsel, and Greta M. Ljung. Additional topics and extensions. In *Time Series Analysis: Forecasting and Control*, Wiley Series in Probability and Statistics, pages 352–394. Wiley, Hoboken, NJ, 5th edition, 2016.

256 George E. P. Box, Gwilym M. Jenkins, Gregory C. Reinsel, and Greta M. Ljung. Model identification. In *Time Series Analysis: Forecasting and Control*, Wiley Series in Probability and Statistics, pages 179–208. Wiley, Hoboken, NJ, 5th edition, 2016.

257 George E. P. Box, Gwilym M. Jenkins, Gregory C. Reinsel, and Greta M. Ljung. Parameter estimation. In *Time Series Analysis: Forecasting and Control*, Wiley Series in Probability and Statistics, pages 209–283. Wiley, Hoboken, NJ, 5th edition, 2016.

258 James D. Hamilton. Maximum likelihood estimation. In *Time Series Analysis*, pages 117–151. Princeton University Press, Princeton, NJ, 1994.

259 Wayne A. Fuller. Parameter estimation. In *Introduction to Statistical Time Series*, Wiley Series in Probability and Statistics, pages 404–474. Wiley, New York, 2nd edition, 1996. https://doi.org/10.1002/9780470316917.

260 James D. Hamilton. Forecasting. In *Time Series Analysis*, pages 73–116. Princeton University Press, Princeton, NJ, 1994.

261 Tokuzo Shiga and Shinzo Watanabe. Bessel diffusions as a one-parameter family of diffusion processes. *Zeitschrift für Wahrscheinlichkeitstheorie und verwandte Gebiete*, 27(1):37–46, 1973.

262 Gregory F. Lawler. *Notes on the Bessel process*. Lecture Notes. Available on the webpage of the author, pages 523–531, 2018.

263 Hélyette Geman and Marc Yor. Bessel processes, Asian options, and perpetuities. *Mathematical Finance*, 3(4):349–375, 1993. https://doi.org/10.1111/j.1467-9965.1993.tb00092.x.

264 B. K. Øksendal. The Itô formula and the martingale representation theorem. In *Stochastic Differential Equations: An Introduction with Applications*, Universitext, pages 43–64. Springer, Berlin; New York, 6th edition corr. 4th print edition, 2007.

265 Steven E. Shreve, editor. Ito's formula. In *Continuous-Time Models*, number 2 in Stochastic calculus for finance, pages 167–176. Springer, New York, NY, 2010.

266 Yakov Amihud and Clifford Hurvich. A High-Low Ratio Test for Geometric Brownian Motion, 2025. https://papers.ssrn.com/abstract=5108869.

267 Oldrich Vasicek. An equilibrium characterization of the term structure. *Journal of Financial Economics*, 5(2):177–188, 1977. https://doi.org/10.1016/0304-405X(77)90016-2.

268 John Hull. Equilibrium models of the short rate. In *Options, Futures, and Other Derivatives*, pages 719–731. Pearson, Harlow, England, London, New York, Boston, San Francisco, Toronto, Sydney, Dubai, Singapore, Hong Kong, Tokyo, Seoul, Taipei, New Delhi, Cape Town, São Paulo, Mexico City, Madrid, Amsterdam, Munich, Paris, Milan, 11th edition, global edition, 2022.

269 John Hull and Alan White. Pricing interest-rate-derivative securities. *Review of Financial Studies*, 3(4):573–592, 1990. https://doi.org/10.1093/rfs/3.4.573.

270 John Hull. No-arbitrage models for the short rate. In *Options, Futures, and Other Derivatives*, pages 732–754. Pearson, Harlow, England, London, New York, Boston, San Francisco, Toronto, Sydney, Dubai, Singapore, Hong Kong, Tokyo, Seoul, Taipei, New Delhi, Cape Town, São Paulo, Mexico City, Madrid, Amsterdam, Munich, Paris, Milan, 11th edition, global edition, 2022.

271 Donald R. Van Deventer, Kenji Imai, and Mark Mesler. Special cases of Heath, Jarrow, and Morton interest rate modeling. In *Advanced Financial Risk Management, Second Edition: Tools and Techniques for Integrated Credit Risk and Interest Rate Risk Management*, pages 283–315. Wiley, 1st edition, 2013. https://doi.org/10.1002/9781118597217.

272 Carl Chiarella and Oh Kang Kwon. Classes of interest rate models under the HJM framework. *Asia-Pacific Financial Markets*, 8(1):1–22, 2001.

273 Wim Schoutens. Lévy processes and OU processes. In *Lévy Processes in Finance: Pricing Financial Derivatives*, Wiley Series in Probability and Statistics, pages 43–72. J. Wiley, Chichester, West Sussex, New York, 2003. https://doi.org/10.1002/0470870230.

274 Ken-iti Sato. Basic examples. In *Lévy Processes and Infinitely Divisible Distributions*, number 68 in Cambridge Studies in Advanced Mathematics, pages 1–30. Cambridge University Press, Cambridge, UK; New York, 1999.

275 Ernst Eberlein and Ulrich Keller. Hyperbolic distributions in finance. *Bernoulli*, 1(3):281–299, 1995. https://doi.org/10.2307/3318481.

276 Ole E. Barndorff-Nielsen. Processes of normal inverse Gaussian type. *Finance and Stochastics*, 2(1):41–68, 1997. https://doi.org/10.1007/s007800050032.

277 Hélyette Geman, Dilip B. Madan, and Marc Yor. Time changes for Lévy processes. *Mathematical Finance*, 11(1):79–96, 2001. https://doi.org/10.1111/1467-9965.00108.

278 Peter Carr, Helyette Geman, Dilip B. Madan, and Marc Yor. The fine structure of asset returns: An empirical investigation. *The Journal of Business*, 75(2):305–332, 2002. https://doi.org/10.1086/338705.

279 Wim Schoutens. Imperfections of the Black–Scholes model. In *Lévy Processes in Finance: Pricing Financial Derivatives*, Wiley Series in Probability and Statistics, pages 33–42. J. Wiley, Chichester, West Sussex, New York, 2003. https://doi.org/10.1002/0470870230.

280 Tim Bollerslev. Generalized autoregressive conditional heteroskedasticity. *Journal of Econometrics*, 31(3):307–327, 1986. https://doi.org/10.1016/0304-4076(86)90063-1.

281 Stephen J. Taylor. Forecasting the volatility of currency exchange rates. *International Journal of Forecasting*, 3(1):159–170, 1987. https://doi.org/10.1016/0169-2070(87)90085-9.

282 Chris Brooks. Modelling volatility and correlation. In *Introductory Econometrics for Finance*, pages 415–489. Cambridge University Press, Cambridge, 3rd edition, 2014.

283 Robert F. Engle. Autoregressive conditional heteroscedasticity with estimates of the variance of United Kingdom inflation. *Econometrica*, 50(4):987, 1982. https://doi.org/10.2307/1912773.

284 Stephen J. Taylor. Modeling stochastic volatility: A review and comparative study. *Mathematical Finance*, 4(2):183–204, 1994. https://doi.org/10.1111/j.1467-9965.1994.tb00057.x.

285 Ruey S. Tsay. Conditional heteroscedastic models. In *Analysis of Financial Time Series*, Wiley Series in Probability and Statistics, pages 109–174. Wiley, Cambridge, MA, 3rd edition, 2010.

286 Daniel B. Nelson. Conditional heteroskedasticity in asset returns: A new approach. *Econometrica*, 59(2):347–370, 1991. https://doi.org/10.2307/2938260.

287 Yeguang Chi and Wenyan Hao. Volatility models for cryptocurrencies and applications in the options market. *Journal of International Financial Markets, Institutions and Money*, 75:101421, 2021. https://doi.org/10.1016/j.intfin.2021.101421.

288 Yongrong Huang, Huiqing Wang, Zhide Chen, Chen Feng, Kexin Zhu, Xu Yang, and Wencheng Yang. Evaluating cryptocurrency market risk on the blockchain: An empirical study using the ARMA-GARCH-VaR model. *IEEE Open Journal of the Computer Society*, 5:83–94, 2024. https://doi.org/10.1109/OJCS.2024.3370603.

289 Anne Haubo Dyhrberg. Bitcoin, gold and the dollar – A GARCH volatility analysis. *Finance Research Letters*, 16:85–92, 2016. https://doi.org/10.1016/j.frl.2015.10.008.

290 Harald Kinateder and Vassilios G. Papavassiliou. Calendar effects in Bitcoin returns and volatility. *Finance Research Letters*, 38:101420, 2021. https://doi.org/10.1016/j.frl.2019.101420.

291 Lai T. Hoang and Dirk G. Baur. Forecasting Bitcoin volatility: Evidence from the options market. *Journal of Futures Markets*, 40(10):1584–1602, 2020. https://doi.org/10.1002/fut.22144.

292 Jong-Min Kim, Chulhee Jun, and Junyoup Lee. Forecasting the volatility of the cryptocurrency market by GARCH and stochastic volatility. *Mathematics*, 9(14):1614, 2021. https://doi.org/10.3390/math9141614.

293 Guglielmo Maria Caporale and Timur Zekokh. Modelling volatility of cryptocurrencies using Markov-Switching GARCH models. *Research in International Business and Finance*, 48: 143–155, 2019. https://doi.org/10.1016/j.ribaf.2018.12.009.

294 John Hull and Alan White. The pricing of options on assets with stochastic volatilities. *The Journal of Finance*, 42(2):281–300, 1987. https://doi.org/10.1111/j.1540-6261.1987.tb02568.x.

295 Elias M. Stein and Jeremy C. Stein. Stock price distributions with stochastic volatility: An analytic approach. *Review of Financial Studies*, 4(4):727–752, 1991. https://doi.org/10.1093/rfs/4.4.727.

296 Steven L. Heston. A closed-form solution for options with stochastic volatility with applications to bond and currency options. *Review of Financial Studies*, 6(2):327–343, 1993. https://doi.org/10.1093/rfs/6.2.327.

297 Wim Schoutens. Lévy models with stochastic volatility. In *Lévy Processes in Finance: Pricing Financial Derivatives*, Wiley Series in Probability and Statistics, pages 85–100. J. Wiley, Chichester, West Sussex, New York, 2003. https://doi.org/10.1002/0470870230.

298 Peter Christoffersen, Steven Heston, and Kris Jacobs. The shape and term structure of the index option smirk: Why multifactor stochastic volatility models work so well. *Management Science*, 55(12):1914–1932, 2009. https://doi.org/10.1287/mnsc.1090.1065.

299 Fabrice Douglas Rouah. The double Heston model. In *The Heston Model and Its Extensions in VBA*, pages 287–308. John Wiley & Sons, Ltd, 2015. https://doi.org/10.1002/9781119020523.ch12.

300 John C. Cox, Jonathan E. Ingersoll, and Stephen A. Ross. A theory of the term structure of interest rates. *Econometrica*, 53(2):385, 1985. https://doi.org/10.2307/1911242.

301 Sergei Mikhailov and Ulrich Nogel. Heston's stochastic volatility model: Implementation, calibration and some extensions. In *The Best of Wilmott 1: Incorporating the Quantitative Finance Review*, volume July 2023, pages 401–411. John Wiley & Sons, 2005.

302 Hansjörg Albrecher, Philipp Mayer, Wim Schoutens, and Jurgen Tistaert. The little Heston trap. *Wilmott*, (1):83–92, 2007.

303 Fabienne Comte and Eric Renault. Long memory in continuous-time stochastic volatility models. *Mathematical Finance*, 8(4):291–323, 1998. https://doi.org/10.1111/1467-9965.00057.

304 William Feller. Two singular diffusion problems. *The Annals of Mathematics*, 54(1):173, 1951. https://doi.org/10.2307/1969318.

305 Lorenzo Bergomi and Julien Guyon. The Smile in Stochastic Volatility Models, 2011. https://papers.ssrn.com/abstract=1967470.

306 Ryan McCrickerd and Mikko S. Pakkanen. Turbocharging Monte Carlo pricing for the rough Bergomi model. *Quantitative Finance*, 18(11):1877–1886, 2018. https://doi.org/10.1080/14697688.2018.1459812.

307 Lorenzo Bergomi. Smile Dynamics II, 2005. https://papers.ssrn.com/abstract=1493302.

308 Lorenzo Bergomi. Local volatility. In *Stochastic Volatility Modeling*, Chapman & Hall/CRC Financial Mathematics Series, pages 25–102. CRC Press Taylor & Francis Group, Boca Raton, FL, London, New York, 2016.

309 Christian Bayer, Peter Friz, and Jim Gatheral. Pricing Under Rough Volatility, 2015. https://papers.ssrn.com/abstract=2554754.

310 Jim Gatheral, Thibault Jaisson, and Mathieu Rosenbaum. Volatility Is Rough. *arXiv*, 2014. http://arxiv.org/abs/1410.3394.

311 Rama Cont and Purba Das. Rough volatility: Fact or artefact? *Sankhya B*, 86(1):191–223, 2024. https://doi.org/10.1007/s13571-024-00322-2.

312 Christian Bayer, Peter K. Friz, Masaaki Fukasawa, Jim Gatheral, Antoine Jacquier, and Mathieu Rosenbaum, editors. *Rough Volatility*, Financial Mathematics. SIAM Society for Industrial and Applied Mathematics, Philadelphia, PA, 2024.

313 Christian M. Hafner. Testing for bubbles in cryptocurrencies with time-varying volatility. *Journal of Financial Econometrics*, 2018. https://doi.org/10.1093/jjfinec/nby023.

314 Lukas Krain, Xiaorui Zuo, and Wolfgang Karl Härdle. Cryptos Have Rough Volatility and Correlated Jumps, 2024. https://papers.ssrn.com/abstract=4910607.

315 Siu Hin Tang, Mathieu Rosenbaum, and Chao Zhou. Forecasting volatility with machine learning and rough volatility: Example from the crypto-winter. *Digital Finance*, 6(4):639–655, 2024. https://doi.org/10.1007/s42521-024-00108-1.

316 Tetsuya Takaishi. Rough volatility of Bitcoin. *Finance Research Letters*, 32:101379, 2020. https://doi.org/10.1016/j.frl.2019.101379.

317 Hélyette Geman. Pure jump Lévy processes for asset price modelling. *Journal of Banking & Finance*, 26(7):1297–1316, 2002. https://doi.org/10.1016/S0378-4266(02)00264-9.

318 Leif B. G. Andersen and Vladimir V. Piterbarg. Fundamentals of interest rate modeling. In *Foundations and Vanilla Models*, volume 1 of *Interest Rate Modeling*, pages 165–188. Atlantic Financial Press, London New York, 2010.

319 John Hull. Interest rates. In *Options, Futures, and Other Derivatives*, pages 98–123. Pearson, Harlow, England, London, New York, Boston, San Francisco, Toronto, Sydney, Dubai, Singapore, Hong Kong, Tokyo, Seoul, Taipei, New Delhi, Cape Town, São Paulo, Mexico City, Madrid, Amsterdam, Munich, Paris, Milan, 11th edition, global edition, 2022.

320 Patrick Boyle and Jesse McDougall. Interest rate swaps. In *Trading and Pricing Financial Derivatives: A Guide to Futures, Options, and Swaps*, pages 157–176. DeIG Press, Boston, MA, 2019.

321 James A. Liu. Atomic Swaptions: Cryptocurrency Derivatives. *arXiv*, 2020. http://arxiv.org/abs/1807.08644.

322 Mahdi H. Miraz and David C. Donald. Atomic cross-chain swaps: Development, trajectory and potential of non-Monetary digital token swap facilities. *Annals of Emerging Technologies in Computing*, 3(1):42–50, 2019. https://doi.org/10.33166/AETiC.2019.01.005.

323 Subhra Mazumdar. Towards Faster Settlement in HTLC-based Cross-Chain Atomic Swaps. *arXiv*, 2022. http://arxiv.org/abs/2211.15804.

324 Nicolas Privault. Change of numéraire and forward measures. In *Introduction to Stochastic Finance with Market Examples*, pages 449–478. Chapman and Hall/CRC, 2nd edition, 2022.

325 Hélyette Geman, Nicole El Karoui, and Jean-Charles Rochet. Changes of numéraire, changes of probability measure and option pricing. *Journal of Applied Probability*, 32(2):443–458, 1995. https://doi.org/10.2307/3215299.

326 Steven E. Shreve. Probability theory on coin toss space. In *Stochastic Calculus for Finance. 1: The Binomial Asset Pricing Model*, pages 41–76. Springer, New York, NY, 2004.

327 Steven E. Shreve, editor. Semi-continuous Models. In *Continuous-Time Models*, number 2 in Stochastic calculus for finance, pages 131–138. Springer, New York, NY, 2010.

328 J. Michael Harrison and Stanley R. Pliska. Martingales and stochastic integrals in the theory of continuous trading. *Stochastic Processes and their Applications*, 11(3):215–260, 1981. https://doi.org/10.1016/0304-4149(81)90026-0.

329 Steven E. Shreve. State prices. In *Stochastic Calculus for Finance. 1: The Binomial Asset Pricing Model*, pages 61–88. Springer, New York, NY, 2004.

330 John Hull. Binomial trees. In *Options, Futures, and Other Derivatives*, pages 288–315. Pearson, Harlow, England, London, New York, Boston, San Francisco, Toronto, Sydney, Dubai, Singapore, Hong Kong, Tokyo, Seoul, Taipei, New Delhi, Cape Town, São Paulo, Mexico City, Madrid, Amsterdam, Munich, Paris, Milan, 11th edition, global edition, 2022.

331 Mark Schroder. Changes of numeraire for pricing futures, forwards, and options. *The Review of Financial Studies*, 12(5):1143–1163, 1999.

332 John Hull. Martingales and measures. In *Options, Futures, and Other Derivatives*, pages 670–687. Pearson, Harlow, England, London, New York, Boston, San Francisco, Toronto, Sydney, Dubai, Singapore, Hong Kong, Tokyo, Seoul, Taipei, New Delhi, Cape Town, São Paulo, Mexico City, Madrid, Amsterdam, Munich, Paris, Milan, 11th edition, global edition, 2022.

333 Tom J. Espel. The Validator Account: A New Numéraire for Assets on Blockchains, 2025. https://papers.ssrn.com/abstract=5462475.

334 BeaconChain. ETH.STORE Statistics – Open Source Ethereum Blockchain Explorer. beaconcha.in, 2025. https://beaconcha.in/ethstore.

335 Dorje Brody, Lane Hughston, and Bernhard Meister. Theory of cryptocurrency interest rates. *SIAM Journal on Financial Mathematics*, 11(1):148–168, 2020. https://doi.org/10.1137/19M1263042.

336 Christian Catalini, Alonso de Gortari, and Nihar Shah. Some simple economics of stablecoins. *Annual Review of Financial Economics*, 14:117–135, 2022. https://doi.org/10.1146/annurev-financial-111621-101151.

337 Jeremy J. Siegel. Risk, interest rates and the forward exchange. *The Quarterly Journal of Economics*, 86(2):303–309, 1972.

338 Barry Nalebuff. Puzzles: The other person's envelope is always greener. *Journal of Economic Perspectives*, 3(1):171–181, 1989

339 Keivan Mallahi-Karai and Pedram Safari. Future exchange rates and Siegel's paradox. *Global Finance Journal*, 37:168–172, 2018. https://doi.org/10.1016/j.gfj.2018.04.007.

340 Maurice Obstfeld and Kenneth S. Rogoff. Siegel's paradox. In *Foundations of International Macroeconomics*, pages 586–588. MIT Press, Cambridge, MA, nachdr. edition, 2009.

341 Damiano Brigo and Fabio Mercurio. On deterministic shift extensions of short rate models. *SSRN Electronic Journal*, 2001. https://doi.org/10.2139/ssrn.292060.

342 Damiano Brigo and Fabio Mercurio. One-factor short-rate models. In *Interest Rate Models: Theory and Practice: With Smile, Inflation, and Credit*, Springer Finance, pages 51–136. Springer, Berlin, New York, 2nd edition, 2006.

343 Bumho Son, Seongwan Park, Jaewook Lee, and Huisu Jang. Optimal strategy in blockchain transaction issuances with CIR process. *Computational Economics*, 2025. https://doi.org/10.1007/s10614-024-10839-3.

344 Patrick S. Hagan, Deep Kumar, Andrew S. Lesniewski, and Diana E. Woodward. Managing smile risk. *Wilmott*, 2002 (September 2002), 2002.

345 Patrick S. Hagan, Andrew S. Lesniewski, and Diana E. Woodward. Implied volatility formulas for Heston models. *Wilmott*, 2018(98):44–57, 2018. https://doi.org/10.1002/wilm.10723.

346 Damiano Brigo and Fabio Mercurio. Stochastic volatility models. In *Interest Rate Models: Theory and Practice: With Smile, Inflation, and Credit*, Springer Finance, pages 495–516. Springer, Berlin, New York, 2nd edition, 2006.

347 Elisa Alòs, Eulalia Nualart, and Makar Pravosud. On the Implied Volatility of Inverse Options Under Stochastic Volatility Models (Version Number: 2). *arXiv*, 2024. https://arxiv.org/abs/2401.00539.

348 David Bates. *Jumps and Stochastic Volatility: Exchange Rate Processes Implicit in the PHLX Deutschemark Options*. Technical Report w4596, National Bureau of Economic Research, Cambridge, MA, 1993. http://www.nber.org/papers/w4596.pdf.

349 Darrell Duffie, Jun Pan, and Kenneth Singleton. *Transform Analysis and Asset Pricing for Affine Jump-Diffusions*. Technical Report w7105, National Bureau of Economic Research, Cambridge, MA, 1999. http://www.nber.org/papers/w7105.pdf.

350 Marc Gronwald. Is Bitcoin a commodity? On price jumps, demand shocks, and certainty of supply. *Journal of International Money and Finance*, 97:86–92, 2019. https://doi.org/10.1016/j.jimonfin.2019.06.006.

351 Naeyoung Kang and Jungmu Kim. An empirical analysis of Bitcoin price jump risk. *Sustainability*, 11(7):2012, 2019. https://doi.org/10.3390/su11072012.

352 Jimmy E. Hilliard and Julie T. D. Ngo. Bitcoin: Jumps, convenience yields, and option prices. *Quantitative Finance*, 22(11):2079–2091, 2022. https://doi.org/10.1080/14697688.2022.2109989.

353 Kuo Shing Chen and J. Jimmy Yang. Price dynamics and volatility jumps in Bitcoin options. *Financial Innovation*, 10(1):132, 2024. https://doi.org/10.1186/s40854-024-00653-z.

354 Huei-Wen Teng and Wolfgang K. Härdle. Financial analytics of inverse BTC options in a stochastic volatility world. *SSRN Electronic Journal*, 2022. https://doi.org/10.2139/ssrn.4238213.

355 Anders Trolle and Eduardo Schwartz. *Unspanned Stochastic Volatility and the Pricing of Commodity Derivatives*. Technical Report w12744, National Bureau of Economic Research, Cambridge, MA, 2006. http://www.nber.org/papers/w12744.pdf.

356 David Heath, Robert Jarrow, and Andrew Morton. Bond pricing and the term structure of interest rates: A discrete time approximation. *The Journal of Financial and Quantitative Analysis*, 25(4):419, 1990. https://doi.org/10.2307/2331009.

357 David Heath, Robert Jarrow, and Andrew Morton. Bond pricing and the term structure of interest rates: A new methodology for contingent claims valuation. *Econometrica*, 60(1):77, 1992. https://doi.org/10.2307/2951677.

358 Donald R. Van Deventer, Kenji Imai, and Mark Mesler. Introduction to Heath, Jarrow, and Morton interest rate modeling. In *Advanced Financial Risk Management, Second Edition: Tools and Techniques for Integrated Credit Risk and Interest Rate Risk Management*, pages 123–141. Wiley, 1st edition, 2013. https://doi.org/10.1002/9781118597217.

359 John Hull. Modeling forward rates. In *Options, Futures, and Other Derivatives*, pages 755–772. Pearson, Harlow, England, London, New York, Boston, San Francisco, Toronto, Sydney, Dubai, Singapore, Hong Kong, Tokyo, Seoul, Taipei, New Delhi, Cape Town, São Paulo, Mexico City, Madrid, Amsterdam, Munich, Paris, Milan, 11th edition, global edition, 2022.

360 Denis Gorokhov, Peter Kempthorne, Choongbum Lee, Vasily Strela, and Jake Xia. Topics in Mathematics with Applications in Finance, 2013. https://ocw.mit.edu/courses/18-s096-topics-in-mathematics-with-applications-in-finance-fall-2013.

361 Krzysztof Gogol, Benjamin Kraner, Malte Schlosser, Tao Yan, Claudio Tessone, and Burkhard Stiller. Empirical and Theoretical Analysis of Liquid Staking Protocols. *arXiv*, 2024. http://arxiv.org/abs/2401.16353.

362 David Krause. Exploring Ethereum staking: Mechanics, yields, and future prospects. *International Journal of Cryptocurrency Research (ISSN: 27901386)*, 4(2):164–175, 2024. https://doi.org/10.51483/IJCCR.4.2.2024.164-175.

363 Stefan Scharnowski and Hossein Jahanshahloo. The economics of liquid staking derivatives: Basis determinants and price discovery. *Journal of Futures Markets*, 45(2):91–117, 2025. https://doi.org/10.1002/fut.22556.

364 Sauren Gupta, Apoorva Hathi Katharaki, Yifan Xu, Bhaskar Krishnamachari, and Rajarshi Gupta. Forecasting Cryptocurrency Staking Rewards. *arXiv*, 2024. http://arxiv.org/abs/2401.10931.

Disclaimer

Author's Views The opinions expressed are solely those of the author and do not reflect the views of any institution with which the author is affiliated.

Educational Purpose This textbook is designed to teach financial mathematics concepts using cryptocurrency markets as illustrative examples.

No Financial Advice The content is not intended to serve as financial or investment advice. Nothing contained in this material should be construed as a recommendation, solicitation, or offer to buy or sell any cryptocurrency, security, or any financial instrument. The author is not responsible for any financial loss that may result from the use of the information contained in this material.

Disclosure of Interests The author may or may not hold positions in the cryptocurrencies or related assets mentioned in this material.

AI Usage AI was used in the making of this book for the following tasks: during the research process for general internet and document searches; during the writing phase for generating code snippets in LaTeX; during the editing stage, in particular grammar and style checking. All outcomes were verified and edited by the author.

About the Author

Tom J. Espel is a quantitative strategist with expertise in research and risk management of electronic and illiquid assets. He specializes in applied mathematics, market econometrics, and practical applications of machine learning to emerging financial markets, including digital assets.

He has worked in London, Hong Kong, and Singapore in currencies and commodities, focusing on alpha research, market making, and high-frequency trading. His work centers on frontier assets, markets characterized by scarce data and fragmented liquidity, which has given him deep insight into the challenges of quantitative modeling and risk management in nascent markets and DeFi. His current interests include market microstructure, liquidity and volatility modeling, and machine learning for sparse, noisy data.

Tom has been invited as a guest lecturer in quantitative finance at institutions in London and Hong Kong, sharing his expertise in mathematical finance and risk management. He has also published research in quantitative finance.

He holds an MSc in mathematics and finance from Imperial College London, an MEng in electrical and electronic engineering from CentraleSupélec (Paris-Saclay University), and a BSc in applied economics from Paris Dauphine (PSL University).

In his spare time, Tom is a passionate photographer, a wine enthusiast, and enjoys various sports.

Index